Frontiers in Chinese Linguistics

Volume 11

Editors-in-Chief

Chu-Ren Huang, The Hong Kong Polytechnic University, Hung Hom, Kowloon, Hong Kong

Rui Guo, Peking University, Haidian District, Beijing, China

Frontiers in Chinese Linguistics (FiCL) is a book series jointly published by Springer-Nature and Peking University Press. FiCL aims to publish original and innovative research outcome in the fast expanding and developing discipline of Chinese language sciences. FiCL welcomes submissions of proposals of the following types of books on issues related to Chinese language and linguistics: selection of post-conference papers from leading edge prestigious conferences and workshops; monograph on research with potential to open new frontiers; and outstanding dissertations dealing with new issues and new methodologies. FiCL volumes will be published by Springer with worldwide distribution and by Peking University Press in China. FiCL is the sister series of 语言学前沿, a prestigious book series published in Chinese by Peking University Press introducing new theories and new ideas in Chinese linguistics.

Submission and Peer Review:

The editor welcomes book proposals from experienced scholars as well as young aspiring researchers. Please send a short description of 500 words to the Springer Senior Publishing Editor Rebecca Zhu: Rebecca.zhu@springernature.com. All proposals will undergo peer review to permit an initial evaluation. If accepted, the final manuscript will be peer reviewed internally by the series editor as well as externally (single blind) by Springer ahead of acceptance and publication.

In order to safeguard the quality of its publications, Springer has updated the policy on Publishing Ethics. In line with the philosophy of the Committee on Publishing Ethics (COPE) we follow the principle that we have a prime duty to maintain the integrity of the scientific record. By providing Springer's Guide on Publishing Ethics, we aim to optimally assist Springer Publishing Editors as well as Editors-in-Chief, Editors, Reviewers and Authors with this task. Please refer to the following relative hyperlink: https://www.springer.com/gp/editorial-policies.

More information about this series at http://www.springer.com/series/15591

Jingfen Zhang

Tono-types and Tone Evolution

The Case of Chaoshan

Jingfen Zhang
Chinese Language and Literature
Foshan University
Foshan, China

ISSN 2522-5308 ISSN 2522-5316 (electronic)
Frontiers in Chinese Linguistics
ISBN 978-981-33-4869-1 ISBN 978-981-33-4870-7 (eBook)
https://doi.org/10.1007/978-981-33-4870-7

Jointly published with Peking University Press
The print edition is not for sale in China Mainland. Customers from China Mainland please order the print book from Peking University Press.

© Peking University Press 2020
This work is subject to copyright. All rights are solely and exclusively licensed by the Publisher, whether the whole or part of the material is concerned, specifically the rights of translation, reprinting, reuse of illustrations, recitation, broadcasting, reproduction on microfilms or in any other physical way, and transmission or information storage and retrieval, electronic adaptation, computer software, or by similar or dissimilar methodology now known or hereafter developed.

The use of general descriptive names, registered names, trademarks, service marks, etc. in this publication does not imply, even in the absence of a specific statement, that such names are exempt from the relevant protective laws and regulations and therefore free for general use.

The publishers, the authors, and the editors are safe to assume that the advice and information in this book are believed to be true and accurate at the date of publication. Neither the publishers nor the authors or the editors give a warranty, express or implied, with respect to the material contained herein or for any errors or omissions that may have been made. The publishers remain neutral with regard to jurisdictional claims in published maps and institutional affiliations.

This Springer imprint is published by the registered company Springer Nature Singapore Pte Ltd.
The registered company address is: 152 Beach Road, #21-01/04 Gateway East, Singapore 189721, Singapore

Acknowledgements

The present book is a refined version of my Ph.D. thesis. The process of developing this work has been an invaluable learning experience for me. Without the help from a large number of people, the completion of this book would never be possible. I would like to take the time here to thank them all.

Special thanks go to my supervisor, Prof. Zhu Xiaonong, a man of eminent sense. I benefit a lot from the discussions with him. His insights on phonetics and dialectology have always focused on the "big picture", which continuously urges me to think twice. Discussions with him have shaped my thinking about language evolution in general and many aspects of the present book in particular.

The members of my dissertation committee, Sun Jingtao, Zhang Min, Gan Yu'en and Yao Yao, are extremely generous with their advice, perspectives, and time. I owe a great intellectual debt to them. Prof. Sun helps me so much during my study in HKUST. I really miss those talks about life and study with him. Prof. Zhang not only guides me through the field of historical linguistic and dialectology, but also encourages me to devote into grammatical studies.

I would also like to thank Prof. Wang Hongjun, Chen Baoya, and Wangfeng, they recommend my thesis to compete for the "Frontier of Linguistics" doctoral thesis award. Many thanks are also due to two anonymous referees for their constructive comments, by which the present work was much improved.

This research is supported by a grant from the International Society of Teochew Studies and a postgraduate research grant from the Division of Humanities, HKUST. These grants supported my field trips and experiments for this study. The "Frontier of Linguistics" doctoral thesis award held by the Peking University-Hong Kong Polytechnic University Research Center and Peking University press generously sponsored the publication of this book.

My fellow linguistics students at HKUST, Shen Ruiqing, Wang Caiyu, Fan Xiaolei, Hong Ying, Jiao Lei, Li Dechao, Lin Qing, Lin Wenfang, Chen Limin, Zhang Ying, Zeng Yuyu, Zhou Yingyi, etc., share their friendship with me and have always been my side whenever I need their help.

I thank all the speakers that participated in my experiments. This book could not have been finished without their participation. They had provided me with the valuable raw phonetic materials. I will never forget their cooperation and patience during my investigations. Studying the language of real people from fieldworks is certainly not the easiest way of doing linguistics, but for me, it is the most essential and the most rewarding one.

I also owe a special debt to my family members who always support me selflessly. I would like to thank my husband, Wu Wenhao, for his support and encouragement during the period of my academic pursuit. Being a native Lugang speaker, he has been a perfect informant for me. Without his unconditional generosity and patience, the accomplishment of this work would be impossible. I thank my son, Wu Yehang, for being such an angel baby in the course of my writing of this work. Last but not least, I would like to express my thanks to my parents for their love and support.

Contents

1 **Introduction** 1
   1.1 General Introduction to Chaoshan Chinese 1
   1.2 Theoretical Background 4
      1.2.1 "Multi-register and Four-Level" Tonal Model 4
      1.2.2 Universal Tonal Inventories 5
      1.2.3 Tono-Type and Tonal Pattern 7
   1.3 Methodology 8
      1.3.1 Fieldwork Corpus 8
      1.3.2 Information of Informants 9
      1.3.3 Data Collection and Analysis 10
   1.4 Research Goals 11
   1.5 Statement of Significance 12
   1.6 Outline of the Book 13
   References 14

2 **Literature Review** 15
   2.1 Previous Studies on Chaoshan Chinese 15
      2.1.1 Descriptive Reports 15
      2.1.2 Comparative Studies 16
      2.1.3 Acoustic Phonetics 17
   2.2 The Development of Tonal Models Devised to Delineate
      Tones 19
   2.3 Tonal Typology and Tone Evolution 23
      2.3.1 The Mechanism of Sound Change 23
      2.3.2 Tonal Typology 26
      2.3.3 Tone Evolution 27
   2.4 Summary 29
   References 29

3	**Tonal Patterns Within the Chaoshan Area**	35
	3.1 Pattern A: Falling-Level-Level-Level-Low-Rising	36
	3.2 Pattern B: Falling-Falling-Level-Level-Low-Rising	37
	3.3 Pattern C: Falling-Level-Level-Low-Rising-Rising	41
	3.4 Pattern D: Falling-Falling-Level-Low-Rising-Rising	42
	3.5 Pattern E: Falling-Falling-Level-Low-Rising	45
	3.6 Pattern F: Falling-Level-Level-Low-Rising	47
	3.7 Pattern G: Falling-Falling-Level-Level-Low-High	48
	3.8 Pattern H: Falling-Falling-Level-Level-Level-Low	49
	3.9 Pattern I: Falling-Falling-Falling-Level-Low	51
	3.10 Pattern J: Falling-Falling-Level-Level-Low	54
	3.11 Pattern K: Falling-Falling-Level-Level-Rising	57
	3.12 Three Other Patterns	58
	3.13 Three Main Types: The Dialectical Classification of Chaoshan Chinese	63
	3.14 The Tono-Types of MC Tones Within the Chaoshan Area	68
	References	70
4	**The Tonal Chain Shifts in the Huipu Area**	73
	4.1 General Introduction to the Huipu Area	74
	4.2 The Special Phonation in T2a	75
	4.3 The Downward Chain Shift of Falling Tones	77
	4.4 The Upward Chain Shift of Rising Tones	78
	4.5 V-Shaped Tonal Shift	80
	4.5.1 From Jinghai to Liusha	80
	4.5.2 The Significant Role of the Pure Low Tone	83
	4.5.3 More Chain Shift Evolutions of Tone in Chinese Dialects	83
	4.6 Non-natural Merger of Tones Due to Language Contact	84
	4.7 The Downward Chain Shift of Level Tones	85
	4.8 The Further Development of T2a in Central Huilai County	87
	4.9 Summary	90
	References	91
5	**Tonal Changes in the Chaoyang Area**	93
	5.1 General Introduction to the Chaoyang Area	93
	5.2 Changes in the Production of T2a in the Chaoyang Area	96
	5.2.1 Age-Related Differences Parallel with Geographic Variations	96
	5.2.2 A Perceptual Experiment on T2a of Lugang Dialect	104
	5.2.3 Listener as an Initiator in Tonal Changes	107
	5.3 The Chain Shift of Tones in Miancheng Dialect	108
	5.3.1 Tones Involved in the Chain Shift	108
	5.3.2 A Pull Chain or a Push Chain?	108

	5.4	Tonal Changes in Haimen Dialect	111
	5.5	Tonal Changes in Dahao Dialect	112
	5.6	Tonal Changes in Guiyu Dialect	114
	5.7	The Motive Behind the Tonal Changes in the Chaoyang Area	117
	5.8	Summary	118
	References		119
6	**The Evolution of Checked Tones**		**121**
	6.1	General Introduction	122
	6.2	Different Stages in the Development of Checked Tones	122
	6.3	Different Phonation Types of Checked Tones	132
		6.3.1 Two Basic Forms of Checked Tone Syllables in Chaoshan Dialect	132
		6.3.2 What is the So-Called Glottal Stop?	133
		6.3.3 Different Phonetic Manifestations of T4a and T4b	134
	6.4	Experimental Measures of Acoustic Cues for Phonations in T4a and T4b	139
		6.4.1 Acoustic Measures	139
		6.4.2 Stimuli	140
		6.4.3 Informant	140
		6.4.4 Result	141
		6.4.5 Conclusion	147
	6.5	The Significance of the Yun'ao Case	147
	6.6	Summary	148
	References		149
7	**Conclusion**		**151**
	7.1	Summary of the Major Findings	152
		7.1.1 Phonetic Data Exploration	152
		7.1.2 Theoretical Explorations	156
	7.2	Future Research and Improvement	157

Appendix A: Wordlists for Analysis of Tonal System 159

Appendix B: Dialect Sites and Number of Informants 161

Appendix C: Informants From the Shanjie Type 165

Appendix D: Informants From the Huipu Type 169

Appendix E: Informants From the Chaoyang Type 171

Appendix F: Informants From Other Types 175

Appendix G: Tono-Types of Each Tonal Pattern 177

Bibliography 181

List of Figures

Fig. 1.1	A map of Southern Min dialects (adapted from Language Atlas of China, 1987: B12).	2
Fig. 1.2	Geographic distributions of Chaoshan subgroups	3
Fig. 1.3	The MRFL tonal model (cited from Zhu 2012a: Fig. 1)	4
Fig. 1.4	Three registers defined by six phonation types (cited from Zhu 2012a: Fig. 2)	5
Fig. 1.5	The syllabic-centric phonetic framework (cited from Zhu 2015: Fig. 2)	6
Fig. 1.6	Structure of tone (cited from Zhu 2015: Fig. 5)	6
Fig. 1.7	Gender, age and education backgrounds of 228 informants	10
Fig. 2.1	The eight tones of Chaozhou in Liu (1924/1951: 73, Fig. 96).	18
Fig. 3.1	Pattern A under MRFL	36
Fig. 3.2	The frequency curves of 30 dialect sites of Pattern A	38
Fig. 3.3	Pattern B under MRFL	40
Fig. 3.4	The frequency curves of 6 dialect sites of Pattern B	41
Fig. 3.5	Pattern C under MRFL	41
Fig. 3.6	The frequency curves of 4 dialect sites of Pattern C	42
Fig. 3.7	Pattern D under MRFL	43
Fig. 3.8	The frequency curves of 4 dialect sites of Pattern D	44
Fig. 3.9	The frequency curves of dialects in Eastern Street of Liusha District and Xishe Village of Zhanlong Town	44
Fig. 3.10	Pattern E1 under MRFL	45
Fig. 3.11	Pattern E2 under MRFL	45
Fig. 3.12	The frequency curves of 2 dialect sites of Pattern E1	46
Fig. 3.13	The frequency curves of 1 dialect site of Pattern E2	47
Fig. 3.14	Pattern F under MRFL	47
Fig. 3.15	The frequency curves of younger speakers in central Huilai County	48
Fig. 3.16	Pattern G under MRFL	49

Fig. 3.17	The frequency curves of Jinghai Town, older speakers, Pattern G	50
Fig. 3.18	Pattern H under MRFL	50
Fig. 3.19	The frequency curves of 2 dialect sites of Pattern H	51
Fig. 3.20	Pattern I under MRFL	51
Fig. 3.21	The frequency curves of 9 dialect sites of Pattern I	52
Fig. 3.22	The frequency curves of tones in Hongchang Town	53
Fig. 3.23	The frequency curves of tones in Shanpu Village of Zhanlong Town	54
Fig. 3.24	Pattern J under MRFL	54
Fig. 3.25	The frequency curves of Pattern J	55
Fig. 3.26	The frequency curves of the younger generations' tonal system in Guiyu and Dahao	56
Fig. 3.27	The frequency curves of Haimen Town, older speaker	56
Fig. 3.28	Pattern K under MRFL	57
Fig. 3.29	The frequency curves of Pattern K	58
Fig. 3.30	The frequency curves of Haimen Town, younger speakers	58
Fig. 3.31	Pattern L under MRFL	59
Fig. 3.32	The frequency curves of Xilu Town	60
Fig. 3.33	Younger speakers's tonal system in Xilu dialect	60
Fig. 3.34	Pattern M under MRFL	61
Fig. 3.35	The frequency curves of Houzhai Town	62
Fig. 3.36	Pattern N under MRFL	62
Fig. 3.37	The frequency curves of Pattern N	63
Fig. 3.38	The tri-length distinction of Yun'ao dialect	63
Fig. 3.39	The geographic distributions of the three tone types	64
Fig. 3.40	The geographic distributions of the three tonal types	65
Fig. 4.1	The geographic distribution of Huipu dialects	74
Fig. 4.2	Tonal systems of three older informants in Jinghai Town	76
Fig. 4.3	Comparison of T2a and T1b of Jinghai older speakers	77
Fig. 4.4	Downward shift of falling tones, from Jinghai (first two pictures) to Huicheng (the third picture)	78
Fig. 4.5	Downward shift of falling tones, from Jinghai (first two pictures) to Liusha (the third picture)	78
Fig. 4.6	The upward chain shift	79
Fig. 4.7	The tonal systems of Jinghai (the first two pictures) and Liusha (the third picture)	80
Fig. 4.8	The tonal system of Eastern Liusha Street	81
Fig. 4.9	The tono-types of T1a in the Huipu area	82
Fig. 4.10	The V-shaped tonal shift	82
Fig. 4.11	Tonal merger in central (second picture) and western (third picture) towns of Huilai county	84
Fig. 4.12	Age-related differences in Jinghai Town	86
Fig. 4.13	The two variations of T2a of informant SZX	86

List of Figures

Fig. 4.14	The changes of T1b and T1a from older to younger speakers in Jinghai	87
Fig. 4.15	Age-related differences in central Huilai County	88
Fig. 4.16	Two variations co-existing in one single tonal system	89
Fig. 4.17	The frequency curves of T2a's two variations	90
Fig. 4.18	The possible evolutionary routes triggered by the loss of fortis phonation in T2a	91
Fig. 5.1	Four tonal patterns distinctive from most Chaoyang dialects in the Chaoyang area	94
Fig. 5.2	Geographic distributions of towns and four tono-types in the Chaoyang area	95
Fig. 5.3	Age-related different tonal systems in Lugang dialect, suburban Chaoyang area	96
Fig. 5.4	Tonal acoustic space of four falling tones, older speakers	97
Fig. 5.5	The contrast of four falling tones in the group of older speakers in the suburban Chaoyang are	98
Fig. 5.6	Slope being the primary cue to the distinction of T2a and T2b/3a in younger speakers	100
Fig. 5.7	The pitch curves of four tones produced by younger speakers	101
Fig. 5.8	Scatter plot of slopes that vary with age in Chaonan District	101
Fig. 5.9	Relative duration of seven tones produced by 23 older speakers and 19 younger speakers	102
Fig. 5.10	Age-related tonal difference in Miancheng dialect	103
Fig. 5.11	Demo: Identification test	105
Fig. 5.12	T2a produced by the older speakers has an apparent bulge or level portion	106
Fig. 5.13	Tonal acoustic space of Miancheng dialect produced by one older speaker (left) and one younger speaker (right)	109
Fig. 5.14	Frequency trajectories of four tones produced by 12 Miancheng speakers	110
Fig. 5.15	The pull chain shift of Miancheng tones	111
Fig. 5.16	Pitch curves of seven tones of Haimen dialect	111
Fig. 5.17	T3b remains as low falling tone /42/ in Dahao dialect	112
Fig. 5.18	T1a is close to T3b in Dahao dialect	113
Fig. 5.19	The distributions of frequency curves of 1a and T3b in Dahao dialect	113
Fig. 5.20	The distributions of frequency curves of 1a and T3b in Dahao dialect	116
Fig. 5.21	Age-related differences of Guiyu dialect	116
Fig. 5.22	Tonal acoustic space of Guiyu dialect	117

Fig. 6.1	First stage, Quanzhou type: Yin-high versus Yang-low	123
Fig. 6.2	Second stage, Yun'ao type: Yin-falling and Yang-rising	124
Fig. 6.3	Third stage, Dahao type: Yin-low-falling and Yang-high-rising	124
Fig. 6.4	Fourth stage, Chaozhou type: Yin-low and Yang-high	125
Fig. 6.5	The pitch curves of T4a and T4b cross	126
Fig. 6.6	The starting points of T4a and T4b are the same	127
Fig. 6.7	The pitch height of T4b is slightly higher than that of T4a	127
Fig. 6.8	Pitch curves of 11 speakers from Dahao type dialects	128
Fig. 6.9	Average frequency and slope of T4a and T4b in Quanzhou type dialects	129
Fig. 6.10	Average frequency and slope of T4a and T4b in Yun'ao type dialects	129
Fig. 6.11	Average frequency and slope of T4a and T4b in Dahao type dialects	130
Fig. 6.12	Average frequency and slope of T4a and T4b in Chaozhou type dialects	130
Fig. 6.13	Absolute durations of checked tones in three types of dialects	131
Fig. 6.14	Waveform and spectrogram of T4a and T4b from four Yun'ao speakers	135
Fig. 6.15	Bar chart with error bar representing the standard error of the mean for H1−H2	142
Fig. 6.16	Bar chart with error bar representing the standard error of the mean for H2−H4	143
Fig. 6.17	Bar chart with error bar representing the standard error of the mean for H1−A1	143
Fig. 6.18	Bar chart with error bar representing the standard error of the mean for H1−A2	144
Fig. 6.19	Bar chart with error bar representing the standard error of the mean for H1−A3	144
Fig. 6.20	Bar chart with error bar representing the standard error of the mean for CPP	145
Fig. 6.21	Bar chart with error bar representing the standard error of the mean for ENERGY	145
Fig. 7.1	Two slight falling tones (T1b and T3b) in Houzhai dialect	153
Fig. 7.2	Frequency curves of five unchecked tones produced by two younger Lugang speakers	153
Fig. 7.3	Tonal acoustic space of five unchecked tones produced by two younger Lugang speakers	154
Fig. 7.4	Tonal patterns from Jinghai dialect to Liusha dialect	154
Fig. 7.5	Tonal patterns from older speakers of Jinghai to their younger counterparts	154

Fig. 7.6	Tonal patterns from Lugang dialect (older speaker) to Miancheng dialect (younger speaker)	155
Fig. 7.7	Tonal patterns from Rongcheng dialect to Jinping dialect	155
Fig. 7.8	Tonal patterns from Rongcheng dialect to Fenghuang dialect	156

List of Tables

Table 1.1	Universal tonal inventories.	7
Table 2.1	Tones and their features (cited from Wang 1967, Table 1).	20
Table 3.1	Tones transcribed under MRFL, Pattern A.	36
Table 3.2	Tones transcribed under MRFL, Pattern B.	40
Table 3.3	Tones transcribed under MRFL, Pattern C.	42
Table 3.4	Tones transcribed under MRFL, Pattern D.	43
Table 3.5	Tones transcribed under MRFL, Pattern E1.	46
Table 3.6	Tones transcribed under MRFL, Pattern E2.	46
Table 3.7	Tones transcribed under MRFL, Pattern F for younger generations.	48
Table 3.8	Tones transcribed under MRFL, Pattern G for the older generation	49
Table 3.9	Tones transcribed under MRFL, Pattern H for younger generations.	50
Table 3.10	Tones transcribed under MRFL, Pattern I	52
Table 3.11	Tones transcribed under MRFL, Pattern J	55
Table 3.12	Haimen tones transcribed under MRFL	56
Table 3.13	Tones transcribed under MRFL, Pattern K.	57
Table 3.14	Xilu tones transcribed under MRFL.	59
Table 3.15	Houzhai tones transcribed under MRFL.	61
Table 3.16	Tones transcribed under MRFL, Patter N.	62
Table 3.17	Districts and towns belonging to each pattern	66
Table 3.18	The phonetic realizations of four MC tones in type one.	68
Table 3.19	The corresponding rules between tono-types and MC tone categories.	68
Table 4.1	Various tonal patterns within the Huipu area.	75
Table 4.2	Tonal values of Jinghai and Liusha dialects transcribed under MRFL.	80
Table 4.3	Tonal values of Dezhou dialect.	83
Table 4.4	Downward tonal shift of level tones	87

List of Tables

Table 5.1	Anova test on duration and slope between T2a and T2b/3a produced by 23 older speakers in urban Chaoyang	99
Table 5.2	Anova test on duration and slope between T2a and T2b/3a produced by 19 younger speakers in urban Chaoyang	102
Table 5.3	Stimuli for the perceptual experiment on T2a	104
Table 5.4	Identification results of T2a for each group	105
Table 5.5	Tonal values of Miancheng dialect under MRFL	108
Table 5.6	Tonal values of Haimen dialect under MRFL	112
Table 5.7	Statistical results of phonetic cues in distinguishing T1a and T3b	115
Table 6.1	A classification of phonations, cited from Zhu (2015)	134
Table 6.2	Different phonation types in T4a and T4b	139
Table 6.3	Stimuli for the analysis of checked tones	141
Table 6.4	Informants for analysis of checked tones in Yun'ao and Shen'ao dialects	141
Table 6.5	The average values of each acoustic measure among ten speakers of Yun'ao type dialects	142
Table 6.6	The results of ANOVA on seven acoustic cues	146
Table 6.7	The different performances of employing acoustic cues to distinguish T4a and T4b by ten speakers	146

Chapter 1
Introduction

Abstract This chapter gives a brief introduction to the object of this research, Chaoshan Chinese, including its geographic location and linguistic classification. An outline of the theoretical background and methodology adopted, as well as the approach to data collection and data analysis are also provided, followed by the research goals and the significance of this book. The organization of this book is presented at the end of this chapter.

Keywords Research objects · Theoretical background · Methodology · Research goals · Research significance

This book investigates the tonal patterns and tone evolution of Chaoshan Chinese based on firsthand acoustic data from a wide range of dialectal varieties within the Chaoshan area. The tonal variations within speaker and across speakers are closely examined, as well as variations among dialects in different geographic regions.

This chapter gives a brief introduction to the object of research, Chaoshan Chinese, including its geographic location and linguistic classification. An outline of the theoretical background and methodology adopted, as well as the approach to data collection and data analysis are also provided, followed by the research goals and the significance of this research. The organization of this book is presented at the end.

1.1 General Introduction to Chaoshan Chinese

Southern Min is subdivided into three groups (namely, the Quanzhang group 泉漳片, Chaoshan group 潮汕片 and Datian group 大田片) on the basic of the number of consonant codas and the evolution of Middle Chinese (hereafter, MC) tonal categories (Language Atlas of China 1987: B12; Zhang Zhenxing 1985). The geographical distribution of southern Min dialect is shown in Fig. 1.1.

The most typical variety of Southern Min in Guangdong Province is Chaoshan Chinese. It is spoken widely around the world, and its uniqueness is manifested among Southern Min groups. Besides the Chaoshan area, Chaoshan speakers can also be found in Southeast Asia and Europe, as well as North America, Canada, etc.

Fig. 1.1 A map of Southern Min dialects (adapted from Language Atlas of China, 1987: B12)

Geographically, the term "Chaoshan" in its broad definition is often used to represent the area composed of Shantou City, Chaozhou City, Jieyang City, and Shanwei City, as well as their subordinate counties, revealing the close relationship of these four cities. According to Li Xinkui (1994), Chaoshan Chinese linguistically falls roughly into three subgroups:

(1) Shantou subgroup, including the urban areas of Shantou City, Chaozhou City and Jieyang City, as well as Chenghai District, Nan'ao County, Chao'an County, Raoping County, Jiexi County, etc.
(2) Chaopu subgroup, including Chaoyang District, Chaonan District, Haojiang District, Huilai County and Puning county-level City.
(3) Luhai subgroup, including Shanwei City, Lufeng county-level City and Haifeng County.

The geographic distributions of these three Chaoshan subgroups are shown in Fig. 1.2.

Administratively, Nan'ao County, Chaoyang District, Chaonan District, and Haojiang District belong to Shantou City; Huilai County, Jiexi County and Puning county-level City belong to Jieyang City; and Chao'an County and Raoping County belong to Chaozhou City. Some of the dialects in Puning and Chaoyang demonstrate

1.1 General Introduction to Chaoshan Chinese

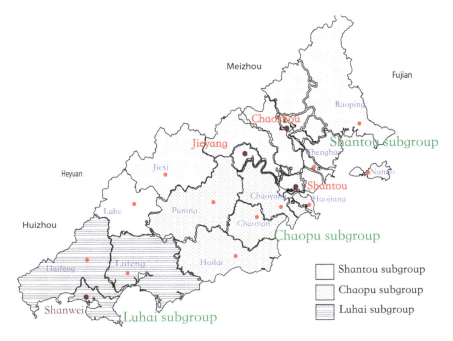

Fig. 1.2 Geographic distributions of Chaoshan subgroups

a similar phonology system with that of the Shantou subgroup, and are apparently not aligned with the Chaopu subgroup, for example, Hongyang dialect and Guanbu dialect (Hongyang is a town in Puning; Guanbu is a town in Chaoyang).

In this book, "Chaoshan" is adopted in its narrow and more widely accepted sense, being a cover term for the following three cities and their subordinate counties and towns only, namely Shantou, Chaozhou and Jieyang (Li 1959; Pan and Zheng 2009). That is to say, the chief research object of this book is limited to the above Shantou and Chaopu subgroups. According to Pan and Zheng (2009), the Luhai subgroup is more similar to Fujian Southern Min dialects. Yet we will also pay attention to the Luhai subgroup and other Southern Min dialects in Fujian province for comparison with Chaoshan Min dialects. It should be noted that some scholars may use "Chaozhou Chinese" 潮州话 to refer to the dialects throughout the whole Chaoshan area; however, in this book, Chaozhou Chinese only denotes a group of sub-Min dialects spoken in the Chaozhou City as defined by its administrative divisions.

1.2 Theoretical Background

1.2.1 "Multi-register and Four-Level" Tonal Model

The "Multi-register and four-level" model (hereafter, MRFL) (Fig. 1.3) proposed by Zhu (1999, 2005, 2012a) aims to incorporate phonation types into the tonal model and to remove the redundancy and insufficiency of the five-point scale model (Chao 1930). Zhu's model suggests that: "(a) a language may have more than one type of phonation, which defines up to three tonological registers; (b) each register should have its own pitch range, which is divided into four levels; and (c) each register will be one notch lower/higher in pitch than an adjacent one" (Zhu 2012a). Register Modal is defined by clear voice, like voiceless voice.[1] Register Upper and Lower are defined by falsetto and breathy voice, respectively. When fortis or creak voice contrasts with clear voice, they can define a register as well. Like the case in the Chaopu subgroup, fortis voice with an extremely high pitch value can define Register Upper. Otherwise, fortis voice belongs to Register Modal, and this is exactly what the dashed line in Fig. 1.4 denotes. MRFL model and the three registers defined by six major phonation types are shown in Figs. 1.3 and 1.4.[2]

In Zhu's framework, a tone consists of three components: pitch, length and register. Pitch is comprised of height and contour. Hence, a tone can be represented along four parameters: register, length, pitch height and pitch contour. These four parameters can be further sub-categorized. Register and length both show a tri-partite contrast, i.e. register (Upper, Modal and Lower) and length (Long, Mid-short and Short). Pitch contour can be categorized as level, rising, falling, dipping, and the less known but rather frequent type, the pure low tone (or contour unspecified low tone) (Zhu 2012b).

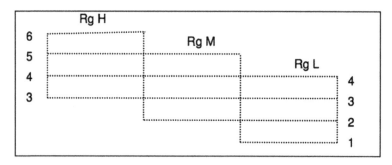

Fig. 1.3 The MRFL tonal model (cited from Zhu 2012a: Fig. 1)

---

[1] Clear phonation and non-clear phonation are introduced to refer to the overall phonation of syllables. Clear phonation is adopted to denote the moderate state of vocal cords in the production of speech sounds where they vibrate regularly in moderate tension as compared with that of non-clear phonation like the tense falsetto, fortis, creak and slack breathy.

[2] In Figs. 1.3 and 1.4, Zhu (2012a) uses Rg H, Rg M and Rg L to denote Register Upper, Register Modal and Register Lower, respectively.

1.2 Theoretical Background

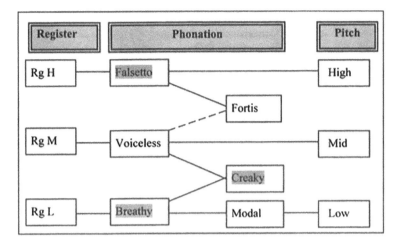

Fig. 1.4 Three registers defined by six phonation types (cited from Zhu 2012a: Fig. 2)

The MRFL model is adopted here for tonal presentation, not because it is a new model but because it is appropriate for the description of Chaoshan dialect, where length and phonation play a pivotal role in distinguishing different tones. The case of length distinction of tones can be found in Chaonan dialects, and fortis voice can be identified in Jinghai (Huilai) dialect. Moreover, checked tones of Chaoshan dialects are always accompanying with creaky voice or glottal stop. However, it should be noted that sometime creaky voice and breathy voice can be found in Chaoshan Chinese, but they only serve as free variants of clear voice. For another thing, the ambiguities in using the five-point scale model (see Sect. 2.2) could be considerably reduced to enable a more practical comparison of different tonal values. We can hopefully identify the evolutional path of tones in the Chaoshan area under the MRFL model.

1.2.2 Universal Tonal Inventories

To compare different tonal systems, we need not only a model to describe tones, but also an establishment of a universal tone inventory, so that every tone in each dialect can find its place in our tone model. The preconditions of establishing the "universal tonal inventories" are two-fold: (a) data collection and (b) theoretical considerations. The most essential prerequisite is the syllabic model. Zhu (2008, 2011, 2015) proposes the syllabic-centric theory, which sets the syllable as the basic unit (Fig. 1.5).

In this framework, the "phonational" as the first-level non-linear syllabic constituent can also be called tone. As illustrated in Sect. 2.1, tone consists of three components: register (Rg), length (Leng) and pitch (P). Since pitch is comprised

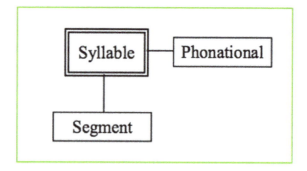

Fig. 1.5 The syllabic-centric phonetic framework (cited from Zhu 2015: Fig. 2)

of height (Ht) and contour (Cnt), tone can be represented along four parameters: register, length, pitch height and pitch contour. These components are hierarchically structured under the syllable as in Fig. 1.6.

Based on the syllable model (Fig. 1.5) and a series of studies (Peng and Zhu 2010; Zhu 2012b, 2014; Zhu et al. 2012; Mai 2014; Shen et al. 2016) develops a more comprehensive classification system for tones, namely "universal tonal inventories". A classification of the tono-types will benefit us both in identifying a tonal variant, and in discovering the direction of sound change. Table 1.1 shows the latest version of "universal tonal inventories", developed from Zhu (2014). Take tono-type "Mid-level" /44/ as an example. Its values along the four parameters are as follows: register is modal with clear voice, length is long, pitch height is middle and pitch contour is level.

On the basis of the MRFL model and the "universal tone inventory", we can further explore tono-types in different languages. Cun and Zhu (2013) conduct a pioneering

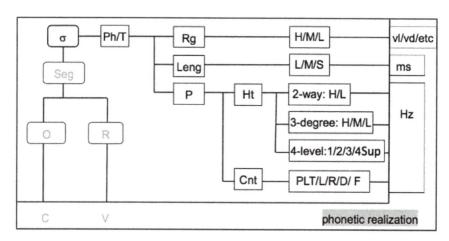

Fig. 1.6 Structure of tone (cited from Zhu 2015: Fig. 5)

1.2 Theoretical Background

Table 1.1 Universal tonal inventories

Cnt		Long			Half		Short	Allotype
Cnt	Tonotype	*RgH*	RgM	**RgL**	*RgH*	RgM	**RgL**	RgM, Long
~Cnt	CULT/LoT		/22/	/11/				{32,323,23}
Level	H	/66/	/55/		/66/	/55/		{45,55⁴,54}
	M		/44/	/33/		/44/		{33²,32}
	L		/33/	/22/		/33,33/		{44³,43}
Rising	H	/46/	/35/	/24/	/46/			{25}
	M	/35/	/24/	/13/		/24/	/13/	{243}
	SlightR		/45/	/23/				{34}
	Back convex		/354/					{353,243}
Dipping	Front		/324/	/213/				{325}
	Central	/404/	/323/	/202/				{303,223,324}
	Back		/523/					{423}
	DCT		/4242/					{5232,3242}
Falling	H	/63/	/52/	/40/	/64/	/52/		{53}
	M		/42/	/31/		/42,42/		{43}
	SlightF-H		/54/					{43}
	SlightF-L		/43/					
	DeferredF-H		/552/	/341/				{553,452}
	DeferredF-L		/342/	/231/				{442,332}
Sum	47	5	18	12	3	6+2	1	

Cnt=Contour. H=High, M=Mid, L=Low. F=Falling, R=Rising. CULT/LoT=Contour Unspedified Low Tone.

study by examining the tono-types of 16 varieties of Southwest Mandarin in Chengdu and Chongqing. Two tonal patterns, Chengdu and Chongqing, have been identified in their research. Tono-types in Chaoshan dialects can significantly enrich the "universal tone inventories" by providing more unreported tonal distinctions. These include, for instance, the two slight falling tones in Houzhai dialect, the tri-division of length in Chaonan dialect and the distinction of two rising tones in Puning dialect, etc.

1.2.3 Tono-Type and Tonal Pattern

"Tono-type" is used in this book as the basic unit in describing tones. The model of "universal tonal inventories" integrates acoustic features and perceptual characteristics to classify tones along four parameters, with the aim of describing tones from the perspective of typology. In this sense, "tono-type" is a typological term related to typology across different languages and dialects. It is distinguishable from "toneme", which is a distinctive phonological term within a mono-tonal system.

"Tono-type" can be identified by scrutinizing along the following three respects: firstly, every tono-type has its own unique acoustic and perceptual manifestations. Secondly, there is at least one language or dialect that has a contrast between the specific tono-type and its counterpart in the same contour category. Lastly, the overall tono-types in "universal tonal inventories" are sufficient and necessary (with the least redundancy) to describe and incorporate tones found in all tonal languages. However, the most important feature of tono-type is its contrastive role in languages.

By "tonal pattern", I mean the combination of different tono-types occurring within one language or dialect. For example, the tonal patter of Mandarin is "falling-level-low-rising".[3] Apart from the different correspondences between tono-types and MC tonal categories, Tianjin dialect presents the same tonal pattern as Mandarin, which is quite astonishing and shows the similarity between dialects seen from the perspective of tonal pattern. In this regard, we can seek more similarities between dialects and generalize the universal pattern behind those similarities.

Based on the tonal patterns of six Mandarin dialects, Zhu (2014) supposes that the pattern of "falling-level-low-rising" is probably the optimal pattern for a four-tone system. Wang (2015) demonstrates that an efficient distributive pattern with a uni-register system of four tones is the destination of tonal change for most Jianghan dialects. Without the insight of tonal pattern and tonal typology, such conclusions cannot be reached.

By converting the raw acoustic data into pitch curves and taking perceptual impressions into account, we can decide the tono-type for one specific tone and further generalize the tonal pattern for the language or dialect in question. What is pertinent in this book is the notion of "tono-type", leading to the lesser importance of the numeral representation of tones.

1.3 Methodology

The following section will briefly introduce the procedures of phonetic experiment as well as the process of data analysis in this book.

1.3.1 Fieldwork Corpus

In order to obtain firsthand acoustic data and elicit the acoustics of tones of Chaoshan Chinese, several fieldwork investigations were conducted. The phonetic experiments were mainly conducted in the Chaoshan area, as well as in Guangzhou city, Foshan city and Hong Kong. The fieldwork corpus consists of four wordlists.

The first wordlist contains four groups of syllables with same initials and finals, and each group has eight words from different MC tonal categories. It is designed

---

[3] "Falling-level-low-rising" pattern means that there are four citation tones of one dialect, and the tono-types are falling tone, level tone, the pure low tone and rising tone, respectly. The tonal pattern is presented according to the sequence of tono-types, namely "falling-level-low-rising-concave-high", where "low" stands for "the pure low tone" and "high" stands for tones in upper register.

to help the investigator quickly gain some understanding of the tone system of the dialect in question and find out minimal pairs of tones.

For the selection of syllables for the second wordlist, priority was given to monophthongs initiated with voiceless unaspirated consonants [p-, t-, k-]. The reason behind this preference is that the pitch perturbation is smaller caused by the preceding voiceless unaspirated consonant compared with that caused by voiced or nasal consonants. The MC eight tonal categories are scattered in order to avoid inertia when reading the same tonal class. Informants are required to read the characters shown in the PowerPoint slide presentations one by one. There are about 100 syllables in this wordlist and it is recorded twice, so we collect around 200 syllables by using this wordlist.

The third wordlist is made up of around 120 checked tone syllables. Chaoshan dialect is famous for its "flip-flop" of checked tone values. "Flip-flop" is a widely accepted notion in describing tonal alternations in which two tones exchange their tonal values. By conducting an overall investigation of checked tones, we can further explore the development of checked tones.

The fourth wordlist is designed to investigate the tonal sandhi of disyllabic words. However, tone sandhi is beyond the scope of this book, thus we just use them for reference when necessary and reserve them for further research.

The above corpora are all put into PowerPoint slide presentations and shown to the informants one by one controlled by the author during the recording. The first two wordlists are used to analyze the tonal system and the details of stimuli are given in Appendix A. The details of the third wordlist will be given in Chap. 6. In addition, there are selected wordlists for examining minimal pairs of the tonal categories that have subtle differences. For this reason, the total number of syllables used for analysis varies with dialect.

1.3.2 Information of Informants

The central concern of this book is to provide a thorough typological study on tones of Chaoshan Chinese, so it is ideal to have informants from every town (镇). However, due to the limits of time and funds, it is impossible for us to cover every town. We finally recruited 255 informants from more than 65 different localities of the Chaoshan area to conduct face-to-face interviews; their ages ranged from 13 to 84 at the time when they were recorded. In order to explore tone evolution based on age-related difference, we recruited informants from different age groups within one dialect. For example, in the cases of Lugang 泸岗镇 and Miancheng 棉城镇 dialects, we have recruited sufficient informants from different age groups. Ample tonal variations within speaker and across speakers are collected as well as variations across different geographic regions, so an in-depth study on tonal development can be guaranteed.

Appendix B Shows the Dialect Sites We Investigated and the Number of Informants for Each Site. Not All Informants' Data Are Presented in This Book. We

Fig. 1.7 Gender, age and education backgrounds of 228 informants

Choose Those with Good Quality of Vocal Folds, Relative Steadiness and Confidence in Their Mother Tongue as Our Subjects for Experimental Analysis. 228 Speakers in My Database Have Been Recorded with Detailed Linguistically Relevant Background Information and They Are Summarized by Mosaic Plot Using R in Fig. 1.7. In Terms of Sex, Our Pool of Sample Contains 127 Male Speakers and 101 Female Speakers. Regarding Age, There Are 106 Speakers Below the Age of 30, 88 Between the Age of 31 and 50, and 34 Speakers Above the Age of 51. In the Level of Education, 105 Have College Degree or Above (Label as "High"), 71 Receive High School or Technical Secondary School or Junior College School Education (Label as "Intermediate"), and 52 Speakers Have Education at or Lower Than the Junior Middle School Level (Label as "Primary"). Detailed Information About the Informants Will Be Given in the Appendixes C Through F.

Every individual offers a profile of the tonal system and displays some variations. When we examine a community closely enough, it will inevitably appear that each individual's linguistic pattern differs in some respects from that of everyone else. It is these synchronic variations that can shed light on the diachronic change of tone.

1.3.3 Data Collection and Analysis

When possible, a quiet room without too much noise from outside was chosen to record the wordlists. The recordings were made using a TASCAM Recorder and a Shure PG42 Microphone at the sampling frequency of 44,100 Hz. The data were then transferred directly to computer for further analysis. The whole recording process of the four wordlists took about 50 min. For the sake of consistency, all the raw acoustic data are analyzed by the author adopting the same criteria, including using Praat for annotation and pitch extraction, and applying Excel and R for normalization, statistical analyses and graphic representation. Some acoustic data are extracted by using Voicesauce, see chapter 6 for more details.

The most important step in the process of tonal measurement is to decide the onset and offset of each token. As a common practice, the final is the main-bearing portion of tones within the syllable. We employ the criteria in Zhu (2010: 281–282) to determine the onset and offset. For the decision of the onset point, the second obvious pulse is set as the onset for those without sonorant consonants; and for those with a pre-nasal initial, we start at the point where F2 appears to be stable. There are two general principles for determining the offset of various contours: (1) the amplitude of the waveform declines dramatically; (2) F2 becomes faint. Zhu (2010: 282) also sums up the strategies for deciding the offset of rising and falling tones. When there is glottalization, especially creaky voice, the pitch data sometimes can not be extracted very well, therefore, under this circumstance, we will remove this token and only use the tokens that display complete pitch curve.

F0 values at Every 10% Point of the Entire Time Course Are Obtained by Using Praat, and Thus There Are 11 Pitch Data Points for Each Token. The Raw Data Are Normalized Following Zhu's Logarithm Z-score (LZ) Method (Zhu 2010: 286–288), Which Involves Calculating the Log Values of Each speaker's Mean F0 at 0, 10, 20, 30, 40, 50, 60, 70, 80, 90, and 100% of the Whole Duration. The LZ Formula is: $Z = (X_i - \mu) / \Sigma$, Where Z is the Z-score, X_i is the Raw Data, M is the Log Mean Value, and Σ is the Log Standard Deviation. When We Calculate the Mean and Standard Deviation of the Logarithms, the Value at the Onset (0%) of Various Contour Tones, as Well as the Offset (100%) of Falling Tones Are Omitted. The Purpose of Normalization is to Reduce Between-Speaker Variance and Make Comparison Across Speakers Possible.

Meanwhile, speakers may vary greatly from each other in absolute duration of tones. Hence, the duration may also be normalized using the following formula (Zhu 2005: 67–69): normalized duration = (duration of individual tone) / (grand mean duration of all tones). Normalization of durations can filter out the differences between speakers, providing comparable data for the study of tonal durations. However, absolute duration may paly a pivotal roal in distinguishing different tones. In this regard, we prefer to present the normalized F0 curves by plotting the absolute time along the abscissa and the LZ score of pitch value along the ordinate in this book.

1.4 Research Goals

The present study intends to present an all-round investigation of tones in a variety of Chaoshan dialects by describing the phonetic features of tones, identifying their tono-type and generalizing tonal pattern of each dialect, upon which the evolution of tones can be further explored. Three case studies of tone evolution in Chaoshan Chinese are provided and mechanisms behind tone evolutions are illuminated too. We also delve into the various kinds of tonal merges in Chaoshan dialects. As is well known, maintaining the contrast of eight tones is a salient characteristic of Chaoshan dialects. However, some of the dialects have reduced to seven tones. How does this change happen? What are the directions of tonal merges in those dialects?

To summarize, the goals of this book are as follow:

(1) To present firsthand acoustic data of citation tones from a large number of Chaoshan Chinese speakers and probe the phonetic details such as fundamental frequency, contour, length, and phonation type.
(2) To identify tono-type from the perspective of typology, referring to the theory of "universal tonal inventories" and to further discuss the significance of Chaoshan dialects in enriching the whole tonal inventory.
(3) To demonstrate the tonal patterns of different dialects within the Chaoshan area and point out their uniformity and discrepancy.
(4) To depict the evolution of tones by examining the synchronic variations within and between individual speakers and dialectal varieties, with special focus on age-related differences and regional differences.

This tentative study mainly focuses on citation tones. Tone sandhi is another important topic that goes beyond the research scope of this book and awaits further exploration.

1.5 Statement of Significance

Previous studies on Chaoshan dialect are sketchy and far from full-scale. Up till now, a large number of the phonological descriptions of Chaoshan varieties are auditory-based. Studies employing experimental phonetics on Chaoshan dialects are relatively few. In addition, many attempts mainly focus on the standard dialects, like Chaozhou and Shantou dialect, leaving quite a few dialects unexamined. In this sense, this book is the first holistic and comprehensive study employing the approach of experimental phonetics to describe the acoustic features of tones and their evolution across the whole Chaoshan area.

To sum up, there are four aspects that make this book significant:

(1) Accurate: we collect substantial firsthand acoustic data in a variety of Chaoshan dialects using instrumental method, providing the study of tones with greater accuracy and preciseness.
(2) Complete: we cover a huge number of dialects in the Chaoshan area so as to facilitate a typological study on tones of Chaoshan Chinese.
(3) Theoretical: the tono-types identified in the Chaoshan area can further enrich the "universal tonal inventories". At the same time, this research verifies that tone can be defined along four parameters proposed by Zhu (1999, 2005, 2012a).

1.5 Statement of Significance

Length and phonation have been proven to serve at the phonemic dimension to distinguish different tones in Chaoshan Chinese, especially in the Chaopu subgroup.
(4) Innovative: last but not least, tonal variations within and across speakers in one dialect (especially age-dependent differences) and variations among different dialectal varieties are incorporated together to indicate the diachronic change of tones, proving the efficiency of the perspective of variation in the studies of tone evolution.

1.6 Outline of the Book

This book consists of seven chapters. Following this introduction, Chap. 2 reviews the extant literature. It is divided into four sections. The first one reviews the literature on Chaoshan Chinese, which can be grouped into three sub-sections, including traditional phonological descriptions, comparative studies, and phonetic research. The second section introduces the development of tonal models. The third part briefly reviews the literature on the mechanism of sound change, with special focus on the tone typology and tone evolution. The fourth part gives a short summary.

Chapter 3 presents fourteen tonal patterns identified in Chaoshan Chinese. Detailed acoustic analyses of tones along the four parameters (pitch height, pitch contour, phonation and length) are given. The overall impression of tones in Chaoshan Chinese, including the correspondences between synchronic tone values and MC tonal categories, is demonstrated in this chapter as well.

Chapters 4–6 illustrate the tone evolution of Chaoshan Chinese with three case studies.

Firstly, based on firsthand acoustic data from 12 Southern Min varieties in Huilai and Puning counties (Huipu area), five tonal patterns are identified in the Huipu area. Two kinds of chain shift, (1) V-shaped shift that is made up of the downward shift of falling tones and the upward shift of rising tones, and (2) the downward shift of level tones, have been verified, which can account for the diversified tonal patterns in this area. We also spot different kinds of tonal merger that have interrupted tonal chain shifts.

Secondly, on the basis of age-related differences of tones and variations across geographic regions, the evolutionary path of T2a in the dialects of Chaoyang area (including Chaoyang, Chaonan and Haojiang districts) has been established. We also probe the phonetic variations of other tones in this area. Three tonal patterns in Miancheng dialect can be identified among different age groups; the number of falling tones reduces with decreasing age. This kind of age distribution reflects a diachronic development of tones in time.

Thirdly, the phonetic realizations of checked tones in Yun'ao and Dahao dialects suggest the existence of an intermediate stage in the phenomenon of "flip-flop" of checked tones in the Chaoshan area. By referring to the different pitch relationships of T4a and T4b in various Southern Min dialects, four stages with regard to the development of checked tones are identified. Chapter 6 further presents the acoustic properties of checked tones in Yun'ao dialect. The Yun'ao case is of great typological significance for it signals that phonetically short tone syllables can have contour distinctions as well.

Chapter 7 sums up the major findings of this book and puts forward several crucial yet unsolved questions for further research.

References

Chao, Yuen-Ren. 1930. A system of tone letters (in IPA). *Le Maitre Phonetique* 45: 24–27.
Cun, Xi, and Zhu, Xiaonong. 寸熙 & 朱晓农. 2013. 成渝官话的声调类型 [Tonotypes of Chengdu(成都)-Chongqing(重庆) Mandarins]. 语言研究, 4: 1–11.
Language Atlas of China. 1987. *Jointly compiled by the Chinese Academy of Social Sciences and the Australian Institute of Humanities*. Hong Kong: Longman (Chinese version).
Li, Yongming 李永明.1959. Chaozhou Fangyan 潮州方言. Beijing: Zhonghua Shuju 中华书局.
Li, Xinkui 李新魁. 1994. Guangdong de fangyan 广东的方言. Guangzhou: Guangdong Renmin Chubanshe 广东人民出版社.
Mai, Yun. 麦耘. 2014. 湘语冷水江毛易镇方言声调系统——一个方言内部的两种"两域四升调"格局. [Two RL models of Maoyi Dialect in Lengshuijiang City]. 方言, 4: 289–295.
Pan, Jiayi, and Zheng, shouzhi 潘家懿, & 郑守治. 2009. 粤东闽语的内部差异与方言片划分的再认识.语文研究, 03: 55–59.
Peng, Jianguo, and Zhu, Xiaonong 彭建国,朱晓农. 2010. On the falsetto voice in Yueyang dialect 岳阳话里的假声. In Contemporary Linguistics 当代语言学1: 24–32.
Shen, Ruiqing. Hong, Ying. Lam, Monfong and Zhu, Xiaonong. 沈瑞清、洪英、林文芳、朱晓农. 2016. 建阳闽语的声调模式: 兼论五条降拱的类型学意义 [The five falling contours in Jianyang Min: Typological significances]. *Bulletin of Chinese Linguistics*. 9: 250–263.
Wang, Caiyu. 2015. Multi-register tone systems and their evolution on the Jianghan plain (A dissertation for the degree Doctor of Philosophy). The Hong Kong University of Science and Technology.
Zhang, Zhenxing 张振兴. 1985. 闽语的分区 (稿) [On the Subgrouping of Min Dialects]. 方言 [Dialects]. 3: 171–180.
Zhu, Xiaonong. 朱晓农. 1999. Shanghai Tonetics. ANU dissertation, Published by Lincom Europ.
Zhu, Xiaonong. 朱晓农. 2005. 上海声调实验录An Experimental Study of Shanghai Tones. 上海教育出版社 Shanghai: Shanghai Educational Press.
Zhu, Xiaonong. 朱晓农. 2008. 音节和音节学 [Syllable and syllabics]. *Oriental Linguistics* 4: 142–164.
Zhu, Xiaonong. 朱晓农. 2010. 语音学. *Phonetics: An Introduction*. Beijing: Commercial Press.
Zhu, Xiaonong. 朱晓农. 2011. 语言语音学和音法学:理论新框架 [Linguistic phonetics and pan-chronic phonology: A new theoretical framework. 语言研究 31.1: 4–85.
Zhu, Xiaonong. 朱晓农. 2012a. Multiregisters and four levels: a new tonal model. *Journal of Chinese Linguistics* 40(1): 1–17.
Zhu, Xiaonong. 朱晓农. 2012b. 降调的种类 [A classification of falling tones]. 语言研究, (02): 1–16.
Zhu, Xiaonong. 朱晓农. 2014. 声调类型学大要[An outline of tone typology]. 方言 [Dialects]. 3: 193–205.
Zhu, Xiaonong. 朱晓农. 2015. Phonetics, Articulatory. International Encyclopedia of the Social and Behavioral Sciences, 2nd edition/Edited by James D. Wright. Elsevier, 65–74.
Zhu, Xiaonong. Zhang, Ting and Yi, Li. 朱晓农, 章婷, 衣莉. 2012. 凹调的种类. [A classification of dipping tones].中国语文, (5): 420–436.

Chapter 2
Literature Review

Abstract This chapter first outlines the early phonetic and phonological descriptions of Chaoshan Chinese. The tonal models that are devised to delineate tones, the typology and evolution of tones, and the general views of sound change are also discussed in this chapter.

Keywords previous studies · tonal models · tonal typology · tone evolution

This chapter is composed of four sections. In Sect. 2.1, I outline the early phonetic and phonological descriptions of Chaoshan Chinese. In Sect. 2.2, I review the tonal models that are devised to delineate tones. In Sect. 2.3, I concentrate on the studies concerning the typology and evolution of tones, and discuss the general views of sound change. Section 2.4 is a summary of the issues discussed in this chapter.

2.1 Previous Studies on Chaoshan Chinese

Previous studies on Chaoshan Chinese can be categorized into three types according to their goals and methodologies: (1) descriptive reports; (2) comparative studies and (3) acoustic phonetics.

2.1.1 Descriptive Reports

Karlgren (1915–1926) is the first descriptive study of Chaozhou (called Swatow in his book), while Chao Yuen Ren is the first Chinese linguist to employ scientific methods to investigate Chaoshan dialect. Prof. Chao investigated Jieyang and Chao'an dialect in his LiangYue Fangyan Diaocha, which Prof. Chao undertook single-handed in 1928 and 1929 (see Yue 1970). Yue-Hashimoto (2001) further cites Chao'an examples drawn from Prof. Chao's materials and illustrates the key role of these materials in contributing to our understanding of the history of the dialect in question, thus providing us with more detail about Chao'an dialect in that time. In the 1950s, a large-scale survey of Chinese dialects was carried out in China. Li (1959) and Zhan (1959) are two of these studies concerning Chaozhou dialect. After that, a vast number of phonological researches were published on various Chaoshan dialects, Lin (1973, 1994a, b, 1995, and 1996), Zhang (1979a, b, c, 1980, 1981 and 1994), Cai (1991), Li (1994), Lin and Chen (1996), Lin and Lin (2007), Chen (2008), Wu (2009), Xu (2010) and the Dialect Survey Team of Peking University (2011), just to name a few. These studies are mainly based on traditional dialectology methods by providing the phonological systems and a comparison between the synchronic system and the Qieyun system. Their practice leaves us with an abundance of valuable linguistic data for further comparison.

Compared to Chaozhou and Shantou dialect, Chaoyang dialect and other Chaoshan dialects have not received much attention and studies on them are relatively rare. The most remarkable study is Zhang Shengyu's work on Chaoyang dialect, which thoroughly investigates the initial, final and tone systems as well as tone sandhi in the Miancheng variety of Chaoyang. Although his studies do not use acoustic data and the author bases his phonological transcriptions on auditory impressions, it is still worth noting for they record the earlier stage of Chaoyang dialect and may shed light on the development of tones in this area. Regarding Huilai 惠来 and Puning 普宁 dialect in Jieyang City, they have not yet received any systematic surveys. Li (1994) only gives a general introduction to them.

2.1.2 Comparative Studies

There is a plenty of studies comparing different Min dialects according to MC categories, such as Dong (1960) and Chang (1985, 1991). Dong (1960) demonstrates the phonological differences of four selected Southern Min dialects (Xiamen 厦门, Jinjiang 晋江, Longxi 龙溪 and Jieyang 揭阳) by giving their corresponding phonetic forms of certain words, but he does not probe into the sound changes behind the scenes. Chang (1985) reconstructs the proto-forms of some phonological categories in three Min dialects (Xiamen 厦门, Chaoyang 潮阳 and Fuzhou 福州) by distinguishing the colloquial and literal readings according to MC categories and explains their evolution. Chang (1991) pays more attention to clarifying the different layers of Min dialects by referring to the Qieyun system. Generally speaking, previous analyses of comparative studies rely heavily on the phonological system of Qieyun.

Since the late 1960s, there have been a number of foreign scholars focusing their research on applying the comparative method to Chinese dialects. In the groundbreaking work done by Norman (1973, 1974, and 1981), he outlines the tonal, initial and final systems of Proto-Min, respectively. He bases his reconstruction on the corresponding rules of spoken words, and the result is quite distinct from the Qieyun system, especially the syetem of initials. Based on Norman's studies, Handel (2003,

2.1 Previous Studies on Chaoshan Chinese

2009) examine the reconstruction of Proto-Min using Northern Min dialects, especially the softened initials, and his studies support Norman's reconstruction of softened initials. On the contrary, other studies like Wang (1999, 2004, 2005), dissent from Norman's reconstruction (1973) of softened initials in Proto-Min and offer another explanation of the relevant data by asserting that borrowing from Wu dialects is the key point.

Furthermore, Wang (2012) asserts that the proto-form of voiced softened initials in Northern Min should be a voiced obstruent like *–d in Qieyun and the unconditional multi-split of the voiced obstruent has been caused by the mixture of different dialects. However, the solution of unconditional split is inconclusive and unconvincing.

Consequently, whether we can rely merely on the comparative method to reconstruct the proto-language of Chinese dialects is still controversial. In order to test the validity of the comparative method in Chinese, Zhang (2013) applies historical comparative methods to reconstruct the proto-language of the Southern Min dialect by comparing six dialects including two Chaoshan dialects, namely Chaonan and Chenghai dialects. Of course, a detailed and sufficient comparison among Southern Min dialects will certainly lay the foundation for a comprehensive study of Min dialect.

2.1.3 Acoustic Phonetics

In a nutshell, previous researches give us little detail about the phonetic realization of the initials, finals and tones. In this section, I present acoustic studies of Chaoshan Chinese. In the last ten years, more and more scholars are paying attention to the acoustic phonetics of Chaoshan Chinese and have gained valuable insights into Chaoshan phonology.

Liu (1924/1951) was the first experimental phonetic study using a kymograph ("wave writer") to give graphical representations of twelve Chinese dialects' tones, including Chaozhou dialect. This attempt not only provided us with visual impressions of tones, but also opened a new domain for Chinese phonetics at that time. He recorded a male Chaozhou speaker with eight words representing eight tones, and presented the tones by stave and kymograph as illustrated in Fig. 2.1.

As can be seen from Fig. 2.1, although the pitch curve of Yinping (Shangping 上平 in the figure) and Yangping (Xiaping 下平) have a decline at the end, they are also regarded as level tones. The situation of Yinshang (Shangshang 上上), Yangshang (Xiashang 下上), and checked tones are the same as those in our current research. The contours of Yinqu (Shangqu 上去) and Yangqu (Xiaqu 下去) are somehow reversed compared with modern Chaozhou dialect we investigte. That is to say, the contour of Yinqu in Liu's experiment is the contour of Yangqu in today's Chaozhou dialect. We have no idea what happened to these two tones. Due to the lack of acoustic data from that time, it remains unexplainable. But it is nevertheless true to say that Liu's pioneering work is the first study exploring experimental methods to describe Chaozhou tones.

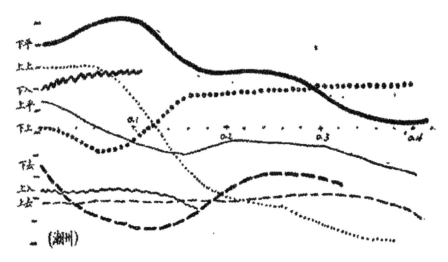

Fig. 2.1 The eight tones of Chaozhou in Liu (1924/1951: 73, Fig. 96)

The phonetic realization of checked tones and their evolution in Chaoshan Chinese have received much attention, such as Zhu et al. (2008), Chu (2009), Hong (2009), and Zhu and Hong (2010). Zhu et al. (2008) use data from Wu, Yue, Min and Gan to explore checked tones from the perspectives of field phonetics and phonology, proposing three modes of evolution: syllable opening, lengthening and phonation changing. Inspired by Ohala (1987, 1993)'s claim that the source of sound change lies in the misperception of the listeners, Chu (2009) conducts two perceptual experiments to explore the correlations between the misperception and the loss of the alveolar stop coda [–t] of Chaoshan Chinese. Chu's study is in accord with Ohala's proposal and has confirmed that the listeners have taken the role in losing the [–t] coda of Chaoshan dialect. An attempt to explain the evolution of checked tones in Chaozhou dialect is put forward in some detail in Hong (2009), as well as in Zhu and Hong (2010). Zhu and Hong (2010) examine the spectrogram, spectral tilt and HNR (Harmonics to Noise Ratio) between the corresponding checked tones and unchecked tones, and determine that phonation types are the triggers for the phenomenon of "flip-flop" in checked tones. Two types of phonation, namely creaky voice and glottal stop, have caused two distinctive phonological phenomena with the former becoming low-pitch tones and the latter becoming high-pitch tones. Creaky-falsetto also occurs in the Yang checked tones according to their field data.

Up to now, more and more studies on the tones of Chaoshan dialects are adopting phonetic experimental methods. For example, Phadungsrisavas (2008) examines the tone system and tone sandhi pattern of Swatow dialects in five regions of Thailand using both auditory- based depiction and acoustic survey. Li and Zheng (2010) probe the acoustic properties of eight Chaozhou citation tones. Jin and Shi (2010) report that there are four falling tones in the Gurao variety of Chaoyang with acoustic data, and they point out that the four falling tones are too subtle to describe using the traditional five-point scale model. They also conduct identification experiments to find out the distinctive features of these four falling tones. Hong et al. (2013) further verify this phenomenon and propose that length and phonation also play a pivotal role in distinguishing four different falling tones.

In her pioneering work, Cun (2009) explores the phonetic and phonological characteristics of the implosive found in a variety of Chinese dialects, and she demonstrates that the implosive often appears as a free variation of voiceless plosive in Chaoshan dialects. Zhu and Hong (2010) verify the existing of implosives in Chaozhou dialect. They assert that two kinds of implosives [ɓ ɗ] are often discovered to serve as the allophones of /p t/ in the initial position. Zhu et al. (2009) illustrate that the implosive can not only serve as a phonetic variant of voiceless stops in Chaozhou dialect, but also as a variant of the stops with breathy voice in Gan and Xiang dialects.

Hong (2013) is the first comprehensive attempt to apply phonetic experiments to explore the phonetic characteristics of initial, final and tonal systems of Chaozhou dialect, such as implosives, glottal stop, citation tones and phonation types. She also provides a comparison of tonal systems within the whole Chaoshan area. Although the tonal data Hong uses for comparison are somewhat limited, it is still very inspiring in that it provides us with the outline of potential evolution of tones in the Chaoshan area.

2.2 The Development of Tonal Models Devised to Delineate Tones

Before entering the discussion of tonal typology and tone evolution, first we need to know how to characterize different tones. In this section, theories or models that have been devised to formalize the features and organization of tones are introduced.

Just as stated in Yip (2002: 1), most people assume that languages that use pitch to distinguish one word from another are rare. Yet according to Crystal (1987/1997: 174), more than half of the languages in the world are tonal languages. Ashby and Maidment (2005: 163) claim that nearly half the world's languages are lexical tone languages that use pitch patterns to distinguish between one word and another. It is not surprising, then, that the study of tone languages is crucial to a complete understanding of sound patterns in linguistics.

In the early literature, tone is simply treated as a pitch-manipulating entity used in language to distinguish lexical or grammatical meaning (Pike 1948; Abramson 1962, 1976). Pike (1948) is an epitome in this regard. He explicitly defines tones and classifies different types of tones around the world into two types: level-pitch register system (register-tone) and gliding-pitch contour system (contour-tone) (Pike 1948: 3–15). The example for the first one is African languages, while modern standard Chinese is an example for the latter one.

At the same time, Pike also reminds us that the dichotomy between register-tone type and contour-tone type is not clear-cut. Combinations of register and contour types also exist: one is register-tone language with contours overlap; the other is

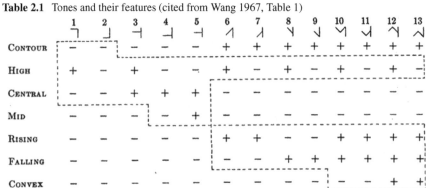

Table 2.1 Tones and their features (cited from Wang 1967, Table 1)

contour-tone language with registers overlap (for instance, when two or more glides occur which move in the same direction but are of different heights). The second type is more prevalent in Asian languages; Pike points out that various languages of China appear to be of a contour type with some strong register overlap (Pike 1948:13). Abramson (1962: 112) suggests that the physical parameter usually associated with change of pitch is variation in fundamental frequency. Abramson admits that although some tones may have additional phonetic features, the major characteristics of a tone system are fundamental frequency states and movements (Abramson 1976).

Many phonologists have attempted to analyze contour tone systems in Asia under the framework of generative phonology (Wang 1967; Yip 1980, 1989; Bao 1990, 1999; Chen 1992, 1996; Tsay 1994, among others). I briefly mention just two here for review since they all shed light on our understandings about the features of tone. Wang (1967) for the first time proposes using seven features (three-way pitch height and four-way distinction of contour) to depict tones, and outlines thirteen tono-types, as shown in Table 2.1. He also proposes the famous rule of the Southern Min tone circle (based on the alternations between citation and sandhi form in Xiamen dialect).

Tsay (1994) argues the "Phonology Pitch" model, a theory of the phonological representation of lexical tone, which claims that what is crucial about tone is relative pitch. "Phonology Pitch" uses a single multivalued pitch-based tone feature whose behavior is constrained by extra-grammatical factors such as learnability, perception and physiology, so it contains both grammatical mechanisms and extra-grammatical constraints. This model does not stipulate the universal upper limit on the number of tone levels or universal set of natural tone classes. However, contour tones in this model are analyzed as sequences of level tones, which has been seriously chanllenged in the field of Asia languages. Nowadays, most linguists have reached a consensus that contour tone is unitary. Yet Chen (1996) notes that we should not overstate this. While he mentions that Danyang and Wuxi dialects treat contour tones as indivisible, atomic melodic shapes, he also demonstrates the compositional nature of contour tones in Wenzhou and Zhenhai dialects. However, from the perspective of diachronic change of tones, it has been verified that contour tones in Vietnamese, Thai

2.2 The Development of Tonal Models Devised to Delineate Tones

and Mandarin have undergone a gradual phonetic evolution, illuminating the non-composite characteristic of contour tones (Michaud 2008; Michaud and Vaissiere 2015).

In addition, evidence is mounting from psycholinguistic that one can further verify the non-composite feature of contour tones. For example, Wan and Jaeger (1998: 427) collect speech errors between 1995 and 1998 in naturalistic settings from native speakers of the dialect of Mandarin spoken in Taiwan. Their data strongly support the hypothesis that Mandarin contour tones are underlyingly unitary, and they find no evidence from the data to support a claim that at some level of representation they consist of a sequence of level tones. In this regard, contour tone in Chinese should be treated as possessing non-decomposable integrity, not clusters of level tones.

Returning to the definition and representation of tones in Asian languages, there are a few milestones. In his pioneering work, Chao (1930) proposes the method of the five-point scale (FPS) to transcribe tone values, with 1 representing the lowest pitch and 5 the highest. Contour tones are denoted by number concatenations. This has been extensively used for Asian languages, particularly Chinese. FPS defines the simple and complex tone systems within a uni-register language, making comparative studies of tones possible. Many scholars treat the FPS model not at face value, but as a proxy for appropriately precise tonal contour descriptions; for example, "55" denotes the level contour at the highest pitch value. However, due to the redundancy of FPS in depicting tonal contrast, differences in the tone values are sometimes unspecified. For instance, the difference between values 51 and 41 or 41 and 31 is ambiguous within or between languages/dialects. Moreover, FPS has been demonstrated to be insufficient when dealing with tonal languages in which not only pitch height and pitch contour, but also length and phonation, carry tonal information (Zhu et al. 2012; Hong et al. 2013; Zhu 2014, ect.). Nevertheless, the invention of FPS is a significant milestone in the development of tonal models for the convenience it offers in transcribing tones and its broad application in Chinese tonal studies. It is still the most-used model for transcribing tones in practice.

The MRFL model proposed by Zhu (1999, 2005, 2012) aims to incorporate pitch (height and contour), length and phonation into one model. It is refined in terms of register (determined by phonations), yet simplified in terms of pitch height level (see Sect. 1.2.1 for more details). It is a further development of FPS. The main difficulty in typology studies of tones is that phonetic transcriptions under FPS from different scholar are not mutually consistent. While transcriptions under MRFL can eliminate such inconsistencies to a large extent.

Kuang (2013) argues that there are two modes of relationship between pitch and phonation: one is pitch-driven phonation, and the other is pitch-independent phonation. She further claims that since pitch-driven phonations are related to the realization of extreme pitch targets, they can be found in low tones or high tones. For instance, creaky voice in low tones is very common in Mandarin and Cantonese, while fortis voice in high tone is usual. On the other hand, pitch-independent phonations serve as independent phonemes in distinguishing different sounds and are normally deemed as a phonemic dimension in languages. In my point of view, pitch-driven phonations correspond to those phonations that cannot independently define a register in Zhu's model, while pitch-independent phonations is equivalent to those that can define a register by themselves, like breathy, voiceless (modal) and falsetto (Zhu 1999, 2005, 2012).

In previous literature on the acoustic study of contour tones, the model proposed by Liu (1924/1951) has usually been used to represent the dynamic change of F0 of different tones by plotting F0 values along the Y-axis and the time-course along the X-axis. However, this conventional model only captures the average figures of F0 data, but fails to describe other tonal features. MRFL is a new tonetic representation that utilizes four parameters, namely pitch height, pitch contour, length and phonation. Although this new model can facilitate a better understanding of tones, especially when it comes to the evolution of tones; but it still omits some important dimension of tones, like slope. The F0 curve only shows us the average pitch and length, and the actual slope is frequently ignored. The slope is verified to be a very useful indicator for different contours and is of great importance to differentiate different falling tones, like Jianyang dialect (Shen et al. 2016) and Gurao dialect (Hong et al. 2013). In addition, the representation of tone under MRFL still follows Liu (1924/1951)'s convention, so we can hardly get any particulars about tonal variations by its graphic representations.

Different from Liu (1924/1951)'s convention, Peng (2006) analyzes the tones of Mandarin and Cantonese by two parameters, namely F0 height and F0 slope, and further draws minimum ellipses of varying areas to cover 90% of the tonal variations. In this way, he can show the distributions of each tone of Mandarin and Cantonese, and predict the potential tonal merger. Peng et al. (2012) also show the perceptual center gravity of Mandarin and Cantonese tones plotted in a two-dimensional space (height and slope), and they find that inter-talker variations introduce difficulties in the identification of tones that rely mainly on pitch height but less so for tones having distinctive F0 contours (i.e., those that can be represented by slope). Although the calculation of average height and slope await more discussion, it is nevertheless a useful way to demonstrate the dispersions of each tone at the present time. Barry and Blamey (2004) plot F0 offset versus F0 onset of a series of tokens for each of the six tones of Cantonese, and group the same tone into an ellipse, thus forming a tonal production space. The authors can therefore further examine the general tendencies in F0 usage for different tono-types.

Inspired by the vowel formant chart and previous attempts, Shen (2016) invents a totally new quantitative model—tonal acoustic space (TAS)—a four-dimension tonal space model with the information of pitch, slope, length and phonation shown in the same graph. It demonstrates the tonal variations along four dimensions. These four dimensions are height, represented by average pitch (longitudinal axis); contour, represented by slope (horizontal axis); duration (figure size); and phonation (color). It is superior to previous models in that we can plot all the tokens of each tone at one time, and the distributive range of each tone can be shown as well as the relative location between two tones. Shen (2016) argues that the acoustic distance can represent the perceptual distance, and his proposed model could better map the perceptual distance. Thus, the TAS model is a perceptual space as well. Shen's study is insightful and inspiring for at least two reasons. For one thing, it offers a new approach to capture tonal variations; and for another, it indicates that perception could be a key factor in the evolution of tones.

With regard to the perceptual characteristics of tones, one may refer to the following studies (Gandour and Harshman 1978; Gandour 1978, 1981, 1983; Brunelle 2009). By using a multidimensional scaling analysis of data for tonal groups, Gandour and Harshman (1978) suggest that five dimensions, namely average pitch, direction, length, extreme endpoint and slope, can best summarize the perceptual structure underlying the dissimilar data. Three dimensions, including contour, direction and height, underlie the perception of six long unchecked tones in Cantonese (Gandour 1981). Gandour (1983) confirms the fundamental importance of average frequency and direction of movement in the perception of tone. The discrepancy in the number of dimensions among the above studies may be partly attributed to differences in the stimulus sets. Brunelle (2009) reveals that voice quality and pitch mainly determine the perception of the Northern Vietnamese.

By and large, we can better dig into the details of tone evolution powered by MRFL and TAS, and figure out the key factor among the different parameters of tones in a specific change. At the same time, statistic analysis is needed before we exploit the proper tonal model. Without the quantification methods and the tonal descriptive models, we are constrained by the limits of our eyeballs. As the saying goes, "sharp tools make good work" (工欲善其事，必先利其器). With the development of tonal models, our understanding about tones also progresses.

2.3 Tonal Typology and Tone Evolution

A large variety of work in phonetics is concerned with or related to tonal typology and tone evolution. These include tone typology (Cheng 1973; Maddieson 1978; Zhu 2012b; Zhu et al. 2012; Zhu 2014), tonogenesis (Haudricourt 1954a, b; Mei 1970; Hombert et al. 1979; Thurgood 2002; Abramson 2004; Svantesson and House 2006; Zhu 2007, 2009; Kirby 2014), tone evolution (Zhu et al. 2008; Xu and Zhu 2011) and tone with different phonation types (Zhu 1999; Mai 2007; Peng and Zhu 2010; Zhu and Hong 2009; Kong 2001). In order to facilitate more in-depth research about tone evolution in the Chaoshan area, a review of tonal typology and tone evolution is needed here. Before we come to our main concern, a few words on the mechanism of sound change are in order.

2.3.1 The Mechanism of Sound Change

(1) Listeners are the source of sound change

It has long been pointed out that listeners play a key role in sound change (Ohala 1981, 1986, 1987, 1992, 1993). In the above studies, Ohala emphasizes that listeners are one of the sources of sound change and he outlines three scenarios of variations resulting from listeners: (1) confusion of similar sounds, (2) hypo-correction and (3) hyper-correction. Firstly, those sounds shown to be similar by acoustic analysis and/or the perceptual data are those that figure often in sound changes. Secondly, confronted with a potential distortion, the listener can acquire sufficient experience to be able to factor it out. The failure to implement the corrective rules is labeled "hypo-correction", while implementing the rules when they are not called for is "hyper-correction".

The idea that listeners as a source of sound change has been proved to be a very effective perspective to explore the mechanism behind sound change in Chinese dialects. Chu (2009) finds that the coda [–t] is disfavored by the vowel [a] and [a] is preferred in the company of the coda [–k]. She further claims that the loss of the coda [–t] may possibly initiate from the rhyme [at] because of listeners' misperceiving it as [ak]. Chu's study supports Ohala's proposal about the role of listeners in the sound change and also provides a plausible explanation for the derivation of codas of Chaoshan dialects. Shen (2013) demonstrates an asymmetry of pitch differences in languages with both short and long checked tones: the "short-high versus long-low" pattern is much more prevalent than the "short-low versus long-high" one. He adopts Ohala's hypothesis of "hyper-correction" to explain this asymmetry and reconstructs an evolution path from "short versus long" to "high versus low".

However, if we assume that sound change is first initiated by listeners, it is better to observe this kind of change from the perspective of perception. The claim that listeners play a pivotal role in sound change just remains as a hypothesis based on some empirical observations. It is necessary for us to conduct perceptual experiments to further verify this hypothesis. Hawkins (2004) makes a good summary of some perceptual experiments. He uses selected experiments in a number of different areas to trace the development of ideas about speech perception between the early 1950s and 2004.

There are some other studies focusing on the relationship between sound change and perception. For example, Beddor (2012) finds that different listeners systematically accessed a given lexical item through different acoustic information; and the perception grammars of innovative listeners have strong potential to contribute to sound change in that they are likely manifested in conversational interactions either through their expectation about co-articulated speech or through their own production. Pharao and Thøgersen (2015) explore the effect of speaker and listener age on the placement of the phoneme boundary between /ɛ/ and /a/ in Copenhagen Danish by conducting a forced choice word identification task. In their experiment, the younger listeners accept a greater range of vowels as tokens of /a/ which conforms to the production change of this phoneme (younger speakers tend to realize /a/ with a lower F1 and higher F2 than older speakers do).

At this point, we are now at the early stage of designing proper perceptual experiments concerning Chinese tonal development.

2.3 Tonal Typology and Tone Evolution

(2) Sound change is drawn from a pool of synchronic variation

Ohala (1987) suggests that one of the most important discoveries of modern instrumental phonetics is the incredible amount of variation that exists in pronunciation, not only between speakers but also in the speech of a single speaker. In the same paper, he also asserts that variations between and within speakers are the origin of language changes. From the perspective of evolution, the route of diachronic change can be derived from the synchronic variations. As noted in Ohala (1997: 686): "The synchronic variation in many cases is understandable by reference to known physical principles. From this one may conclude that (a) many sound changes arise first as non-distinctive synchronic variation and (b) that it is physical principles that determine the direction of this variability, including articulation (the typological geometry of the vocal organs as well as their inertia and elasticity), aerodynamics, how given vocal tract configurations give rise to sound, and auditory principles."

Most often, diachronic variation (sound change) parallels synchronic variation. One thing that needs to be noted is that synchronic variation may serve as a candidate for sound change, but in most cases, it just remains as it is. Ohala (1987, 1993) also comments that sound change can be replicated in the laboratory either from the diachronic or synchronic point of view. When faced with a tonal system, one may wonder what its historical origins are. Although the question is assumed to be addressed in a diachronic manner, the answer may lie in the synchronic variations of tones presented within or between speakers and communities, for many sound changes arise first as non-distinctive synchronic phonetic variations.

Wang (2015) investigates five towns on the Jianghan plain and has proved the effectiveness of the method in question, namely by inferring changes from variations. In the following sections of this book, the approach we adopt in identifying potential sound changes that either took place or will take place is drawing changes from the pool of synchronic variations.

(3) Lexical diffusion theory

Wang (1969) proposes the lexical diffusion theory; it assumes that sound change may occur in a way that is phonetically abrupt and lexically gradual. Indeed, empirical evidence confirms that many types of change are phonologically abrupt and take time to diffuse across the lexicons.

Some extraordinary work based in lexical diffusion theory has emerged on the phenomenon of lexical split in the reflexes of MC Yangqu tones (T3b) in Chaozhou dialect. The most disputed question is why some Yangqu tones have merged with Yangshang (T2b) tones. There is a long debate on this unique tonal change of Chaozhou dialect. Cheng and Wang (1971/1977) delve into this phenomenon from the perspective of lexical diffusion. However, it has been verified that the most likely explanation is the co-existence of the colloquial and literary strata (Egerod 1976, 1982). Wang and Lien (1993), as well as Lien (1993), emphasize that the case of Chaozhou is of great significance for lexical diffusion theory since it provides the overall picture of "bidirection diffusion". They claim that there is strong evidence in Chaozhou that after the initial period of mixture, two linguistic systems (namely colloquial and literal systems) entered a symbiotic relationship in which they interacted with each other.

Yet, discussion on tone evolution in Chaoshan dialects based on acoustic data from multiple speakers and from different dialects is hardly seen. Our acoustic data from field investigations can serve as potent evidence for lexical diffusion by demonstrating that some speakers have two reflexes of one tonal category while other speakers only possess one of these two reflexes. Let's take the change of T2a in some Chaoshan dialects as an example, the process of this change occurs through diffusion among lexicon and its progress varies from speaker to speaker.

2.3.2 Tonal Typology

Based on tonal patterns from 737 Chinese dialects, Cheng (1973) demonstrates that high tones predominate in most dialects and the falling tone occurs more frequently than any other tonal contours. Maddieson (1978: 345) claims that "five" is the maximum number of phonemic tone levels that may contrast. In addition, he indicates that contour tones do not occur unless at least one level tone occurs in the system and bidirectional contours only occur if simple contours also occur. By saying this, he means that if a language has a falling tone or other contour tones, it entails that this language must at least have a level tone. Yet this hypothesis needs to be verified and awaits more investigation. The number of uncheck tones in Chaoshan dialects is 5 or 6, and the implication relations among tones are in line with what Maddieson hypothesized above.

On the basis of a large amount of acoustic data of Chinese dialects as well as minority languages, Zhu (2012b) points out that the most frequent contour in tonal languages is the falling tone (level tone is treated as a kind of contour tone too). He identifies three major falling tones: long, short and deferred falling, and each of which is sub-categorized as high and low. Furthermore, there is a slight falling tone in the category of long falling tone. The long and the deferred types, both high and low, also occur in Register L with non-clear phonation; examples of this kind of falling tone can be found in Wu Chinese. In total, eleven falling tones are found.

In our tentative study on Houzhai dialect, we discover there are also two sub-types, namely high slight and low slight, in the slight falling category. As a result, we can identify at least twelve types of falling tones when comparing different tonal languages.

Regarding the bidirectional contour tones, four distinctive dipping tones are recognized in Zhu et al. (2012), two in Register M and two in Register L. The former includes the common low dipping {323},[1] back dipping {523}, and the latter creaky dipping {202} and breathy dipping {213}. The double circumflex tone {3232} is

---

[1] Please note that the number in the brace ({}) means the specific phonetic manifestation of tones, and the number between the two slashes (//) denotes the tono-type.

originally regarded as a rare pitch pattern, but has gradually been recognized as a rather common one. Zhu and Yi (2011) examine different pitch contours of the "double circumflex tone" in Chinese dialects in detail.

2.3.3 Tone Evolution

An overwhelming majority of existing researches on tone evolution discuss the problem of tonogenesis. The discussions of tonogenes not only cover the rise of tones in the first place but also deal with the subsequent splitting of tones into more tones. Starting from the 1950s, various hypotheses have been proposed to pinpoint tone-triggering factors. The most influential one put forward is that of Haudricourt (1954a, b), which indicate that tone is induced by the syllable-final and initial consonants. Three types of codas determine three kinds of contour. Namely, (1) a final stop (including glottal stop [(-ʔ)]) leads to a rising tone; (2) a final voiceless fricative results in a falling tone; and (3) an open or ended in a nasal induces a level tone. Subsequently, the voicing distinction of the initial consonants will lead to the split of these tones into different pitch heights. This theory became widely accepted latter when the hypothesis was verified phonetically (Hombert et al. 1979).

In Thurgood (2002)'s revised model, the three-way tonal split that Haudricourt attributes to three classes of finals has been reanalyzed as due to three types of laryngeal configuration. In Haudricourt's model, the distinctions of pitch height are attributed directly to the distinction between the proto-voiceless and the proto-voiced initials. However, Thurgood (2002) attests that there is strong evidence that it was the distinction between clear and breathy voice that split each of the three earlier categories into a high-pitched and a low-pitched variant in Vietnamese. In a nutshell, Thurgood's laryngeal model of tonogenesis proposes that the laryngeal feature of initial and final consonants determines the F0 perturbations and further develops into tones in Chinese and other Southeast Asian languages.

Silva (2006) argues that contemporary Seoul Korean may be developing a tonal system. The underlying contrast between lax and aspirated stops is maintained by younger speakers not by VOT difference as among older speakers, but by differentiated tonal melodies that are phonetically manifested: laryngeally unmarked (lax) stops trigger the introduction of a default L tone, while laryngeally marked stops (aspirated and tense) introduce H tone, triggered by a feature specification for [+stiff]. Svantesson and House (2006) report that some dialects of Kammu (Mon-Khmer language) have developed a tone contrast which corresponds to a contrast between voiceless and voiced initial consonants in other dialects, thus providing us with a particularly interesting object of study for the development of tone. Kirby (2014) provides another example of tonogenesis in Khmer.

Confining our discussion to the origins of Chinese tones, there is still no consensus on this issue. Many plausible explanations have been put forward (Mei 1970; Sagart 1986, 1999; Zhengzhang 1994; Zhu 2007, 2009; among others). Mei (1970) argues that the rising tone in MC developed through the loss of a final glottal stop and probes the phonetic basis of the four tones of MC, such as the rising tone of MC being short and high. Sagart (1986) claims that the departing tone in Chinese arose not through the loss of final [–h], but through a glottalized phonation stage that is still observable. He further concludes that, at the phonetic level, Chinese tones are defined by characteristic evolutions of pitch and amplitude, and sometimes accompanied by specific voice qualities such as breathiness, creaky, whisper or ventricular voice (Sagart 1999). Zhu (2007) suggests that the MC rising tone originated from a combination of falsetto and glottal stop, which can be found in the modern Wenzhou dialect and regards phonation types (a property of the syllable rather than the consonants) as the main phonetic cause for tonogenesis (Zhu 2009).

Up to now, the role of phonation type in tonogenesis has been widely recognized in various languages. Kingston (2011), through a number of case studies in several language families, also suggests that tone emerged from consonant phonation contrasts. After the emergence of tones, they gradually get rid of their original restrictions and start to evolve (for example, lower pitch starts to change their pitch height when the associated breathy voice fades away).

Hong et al. (2013) disclose that the four falling tones in Gurao dialect and Fuqing dialect occur in the same tonal categories of MC. They claim that this kind of correspondence cannot be simply treated as accidental. Accordingly, they hypothesize that these four falling tones should have existed in the ancient Min dialect before Gurao dialect and Fuqing dialect split. However, they do not offer any other appropriate proofs. We still need more acoustic data from other Min groups to verify this argument that four falling tones existed in Proto-Min. Nevertheless, their perspective on this problem is very instructive. If we take the stage of four falling tones as a starting point, then we can depict their evolutionary path in other dialects whose ancient falling tones have changed into other contours.

Rose (2006) provides us with a new perspective to conduct tonal research about Chinese dialects. He points out that the normalized tonal acoustics can be interpreted historically by a reconstruction of proto-language tones and presents us with an example from Oujiang Wu dialect. After collecting enough acoustic data on tones in one area, we can reconstruct the proto-tones based on the tonal homogeneity or the analysis of tonal evolution. Steed and Rose (2009) demonstrate a more complicated situation, where the same MC tone category may have complex representations among different dialects, such as the Chuqu Wu dialects. The phenomenon of one MC tonal category corresponding with complex reflections among different dialects is not uncommon, especially in the Huipu area of Jieyang city in our study.

As stated in the previous review, by describing different tonal systems in the same tone model (MRFL) and referring them to the "universal tone inventory", we can further reveal their evolutionary process. The direction of sound change can be determined by setting up correspondences among different dialects (historical comparative method) and taking the perspective that synchronic variations parallel diachronic changes.

In short, in this book, when considering the evolution of tones in Chaoshan Chinese, we will adopt the historical comparative method and the method of drawing sound changes from the pool of synchronic variations.

2.4 Summary

The purport of this literature review is threefold: Firstly, it aims to give a brief review on the previous research on Chaoshan dialects. Secondly, we introduce some typical tonal models and choose the one that is most suitable for our research goal. Lastly, previous studies on tonal typology and tone evolution may shed some light on the evolution of tones in the Chaoshan area. We will refer to the theories mentioned above when necessary.

As can be seen from the above sections, studies on Chaoshan dialects are mostly concerned with the phonological system either from the perspective of traditional dialectology or that of phonetics. Only few investigations have been concerned with the tonal patterns in this area, let alone tonal research using firsthand acoustic data from a large number of dialectal varieties of Chaoshan Chinese.

What is more, although phonological descriptions of Chaoshan dialects are in abundance, many of them simply focus on the Shantou sub-group, especially Chaozhou dialect and Shantou dialect. Although Chaoyang dialect has received some attention too, it still needs further elaboration. Unfortunately, detailed descriptions of Huilai and Puning dialects are still non-existent, except for a brief aside in the county gazetteer. There are still a great number of unexamined dialects in the Chaopu sub-group, not to mention the collection of firsthand acoustic data. Therefore, we put more effort into collecting acoustic data of the Chaopu sub-group in our field work. A database of tonal patterns in Chaoshan dialects will also be constructed in the following chapter, providing authentic firsthand acoustic tonal data for further comparison.

The research of tone evolution based on the acoustic data of Chaoshan dialects was also rare in the past. Ohala (1987)'s claim that sound change can be drawn from a pool of synchronic variations will serve as the basic assumption in this book, and we will closely examine the variations within the same speaker and between speakers, as well as variations within one dialect and across dialects. Phonetic tonal variations are the precursors of diachronic tonal change. In addition, the direction of tonal change will be extrapolated from data on widely dispersed age groups assuming that the older generation is more conservative in general. The theory of lexical diffusion, tonal typology and tone evolution can also shed light on the tone evolution of Chaoshan Chinese and facilitate in-depth research.

In the following chapters, I present an in-depth investigation on Chaoshan Chinese, providing the tono-types and tonal patterns identified in the area of Chaoshan, and offer three case studies on tone evolution. I propose several tonal chain-shifts to account for the diversified tonal patters discovered in this area.

References

Abramson, A.S. 1962. Vowels and tones of Standard Thai: Acoustical measurements and experiments. *International Journal of American Linguistics* 28: 2.

Abramson, A.S. 1976. Static and dynamic acoustic cues in distinctive tones. Haskins Laboratories Status Report on Speech Research. SR-47, 121–127. New Haven, Connecticut.

Abramson, A.S. 2004. The plausibility of phonetic explanations of tonogenesis. In *From Traditional Phonology to Modern Speech Processing: Festschrift for Professor Wu Zongji's 95th Birthday*, ed. G. Fant, H. Fujisaki, J. Cao, and Y. Xu, 17–29. Beijing: Foreign Language Teaching and Research Press.

André-Georges, Haudricourt. 1954a. De l'origine des tons en vietnamien. *Journal Asiatique*. 242: 69–82.

André-Georges, Haudricourt. 1954b. Comment reconstruire le chinois archaïque. *Word*. 10: 351–364.

Ashby, M., and Maidment, J. 2005. *Introducing Phonetic Science*. Cambridge: Cambridge University Press.

Bao, Zhiming. 包智明. 1990. On the nature of tone. Doctoral dissertation, MIT.

Bao, Zhiming. 包智明. 1999. Tonal Contour and Register Harmony in Chaozhou. *Linguistic Inquiry* 30: 485–492.

Barry, J.G., and P.J. Blamey. 2004. The acoustic analysis of tone differentiation as a means for assessing tone production in speakers of Cantonese. *the Journal of the Acoustical Society of America* 116(3): 1739–1748.

Beddor, P.S. 2012. Perception grammars and sound change. In *Current Issues in Linguistic Theory*, vol. 323, ed. M.-J. Solé and D. Recasens, 37–56. Amsterdam: John Benjamins Publishing Company.

Brunelle, M. 2009. Tone perception in Northern and Southern Vietnamese. *Journal of Phonetics* 37(1): 79–96.

Cai, Junming. 蔡俊明. 1991. Chaozhou fangyan cihui 潮州方言词汇. Hong Kong, The T. T. Ng Chinese Language Research Center, Institute of Chinese Studies, The Chinese University of Hong Kong.

Chang, Kun. 张琨. . 1985. Lun Bijiao Minfangyan 论比较闽方言. *Yuyan Yanjiu* 语言研究 1: 107–138.

Chang, Kun. 张琨. . 1991. Zailun Bijiao Minfangyan再论比较闽方言. *Yuyan Yanjiu* 语言研究 1: 93–117.

Chao, Yuen-Ren. 1930. A system of tone letters (in IPA). *Le Maitre Phonetique* 45: 24–27.

Chen, Matthew. 1992. Tone rule typology. In Proceedings of the Eighteenth meeting of the Berkeley Linguistics Society (Special Session), 54–66. Berkeley Linguistics Society, Berkeley: University of California.

Chen, Matthew. 1996. Tonal geometry: A Chinese perspective. In *New horizon in Chinese linguistics*. ed. C- T. James Huang and Yen-hui Audrey Li. Volume 36 of the series Studies in Natural Language and Linguistic Theory. 21–48. Dordrecht: Kluwel.

Cheng, Chin-Chuan. 1973. A quantitative study of Chinese tones. *Journal of Chinese Linguistics* 1: 93–110.

Cheng, Chin-Chuan & Wang, William S-Y. 1971/1977. Tone change in Chao-zhou Chinese: a study in lexical diffusion. in *The lexicon in phonological change*. Ed by Wang William S-Y. Walter de Gruyter. 86–100.

Chen, Xiaoqi. 陈筱琪. 2008. A study on the phonology of Southern Min in Lufeng, Guangdong 广东陆丰闽南方言音韵研究, 台湾大学中国文学研究所硕士学位论文.

Chu, Man-ni. 朱曼妮. 2009. Motivating the Change of Stop Codas in Chaoshan: A Perceptual Study 从语言感知探究潮汕入声韵尾的变迁. Ph.D. Thesis, National Tsing Hua University, Taibei.

Crystal, D. 1987/1997. *The Cambridge Encyclopedia of language*, 2nd edn. Cambridge: Cambridge University Press.

Cun, Xi. 寸熙. 2009. A Phonetic Study on Implosives in China. Ph.D. Thesis, The University of Hong Kong Science and Technology, Hong Kong.

Dialect Survey Team of Peking University. 北京大学方言调查队. 2011. 潮州(潮安)方言同音字表. Unpublished.

Dong, Tonghe. 董同龢. 1960. 四个闽南方言. 中央研究院史语所集刊. 第30本下册. 729–1042页.
Egerod, S. 1976. Tonal splits in Min. *Journal of Chinese Linguistics* 4: 108–111.
Egerod, S. 1982. How not to split tones—the Chaozhou case (《论潮州方言古去声浊声母字今调类的分化》). *Fangyan* 方言 3: 169–173.
Gandour, J. 1978. The Perception of Tone. In *Tone: A linguistic survey*, ed. V. Fromkin, 41–76. New York: Academic.
Gandour, J. 1981. Perceptual dimensions of tone: Evidence from Cantonese. *Journal of Chinese Linguistics.* 9: 20–36.
Gandour, J. 1983. Tone perception in far eastern-languages. *Journal of Phonetics* 11(2): 149–175.
Gandour, J.T., and R.A. Harshman. 1978. Crosslanguage differences in tone perception: A multidimensional scaling investigation. *Language and Speech* 21(1): 1–33.
Handel, Zev. 2003. Northern Min Tone Value and the reconstruction of 'Softened Initials.' *Language and Linguistics* 4(1): 47–84.
Handel, Zev. 2009. Reflections on the Historical Origin of the Northern Min 'Softened Initials.' *Language and Linguistics* 10(1): 1–16.
Hawkins, S. 2004. Puzzles and patterns in 50 years of research on speech perception. From sound to sense: at MIT.
Hombert, J.M., J.J. Ohala, and W.G. Ewan. 1979. Phonetic Explanations for the Development of Tones. *Language* 55: 37–58.
Hong, Ying. 2009. Phonation Types in the entering tone syllables of Chaozhou dialect. M.Phil Thesis, Hong Kong: The Hong Kong University of Technology and Science.
Hong, Ying. 2013. A phonetic study of Chaozhou Chinese. Ph.D. Thesis, Hong Kong: The University of Hong Kong Science and Technology.
Hong, Ying. Lam, Man Fong, and Zhu, Xiaonong. 洪英, 林文芳, 朱晓农. 2013. Gurao Fangyan de Sige Jiangdiao 谷饶方言的四个降调. In *Festschrift in Honor of Professor William S-Y. Wang on his 80th Birthday*, ed. Shifeng, Penggang. 219–233. HongKong: City University Press.
Jin, Jian, and Shi, Qisheng. 金健 & 施其生. 2010. 汕头谷饶方言多个降调的声学分析和感知研究 [An acoustic analysis and perception research on the falling tones in the Shantou Gurao dialect]. *Zhongguo Yuwen* 中国语文. 6: 544–556.
Karlgren, Bernhard. 1915–1926. Études sur la Phonologie Chinoise. Chinese version. 1948. Chao Yuen Ren, Li Fang Kuei and Luo Changpei, trans., Zhongguo Yinyunxue Yanjiu 中国音韵学研究. Beijing: Shangwu yinshuguan 商务印书馆.
Kingston, John. 2011. Tonogenesis. In *The Blackwell Companion to Phonology*, 2304–2333.
Kirby, J.P. 2014. Incipient tonogenesis in Phnom Penh Khmer: Acoustic and perceptual studies. *Journal of Phonetics* 43: 69–85.
Kong, Jiangping. 孔江平. 2001. *Lun Yuyan Fasheng* 论语言发声. Beijing: Zhongyang Minzu Daxue Chubanshe 中央民族大学出版社.
Kuang, Jianjing. 2011/2013. *Phonation in Tonal Contrasts (A dissertation for the degree Doctor of Philosophy)*. University of California Los Angeles.
Li, Yongming. 李永明.1959. Chaozhou Fangyan 潮州方言. Beijing: Zhonghua Shuju 中华书局.
Lien, Chin-fa. 连金发. 1993. Bidirectional diffusion in sound change Revisited 再论语音变化的双向扩散. *Journal of Chinese Linguistics* 21: 255–276.
Lin, Lien Hsien. 1973. Give a comparative study of Chaozhou dialect with special reference to Guangyun 潮州方言比较研究——从潮州方言与广韵的比较论潮语在汉语方言中的地位. Ph. D. dissertation. Hong Kong: Hong Kong University.
Lin, Lunlun, and Lin, Chunyu (2007). Guangdong Nan'aodao Fangyan Yuyin Cihui Yanjiu 广东南澳岛方言语音词汇研究. Zhonghua Book Company.
Lin, Lunlun, and Chen, Xiaofeng. 林伦伦, 陈晓枫. 1996. *Guangdong Minfangyan yuyin yanjiu* 广东闽方言语音研究. Shantou: Shantoudaxue chubanshe 汕头大学出版社.
Lin, Lunlun. 林伦伦. 1994a. Guangdongsheng jiexixian fangyin yanjiu 广东省揭西县方音研究. *Journal of Shantou University* 汕头大学学报 3: 82–89.

Lin, Lunlun. 林伦伦. 1994b. Guangdong chenghai fangyan yinxi jilue 广东澄海方言音系记略. *Journal of Shantou University* 汕头大学学报 1: 82–91.

Lin, Lunlun. 林伦伦. 1995. Chaoshan fangyan shengdiao yanjiu 潮汕方言声调研究. *Yuwen Yanjiu* 语文研究 1: 52–59.

Lin, Lunlun. 林伦伦. 1996. *Chenghai fangyan yanjiu* 澄海方言研究. Shantou: Shantoudaxue chubanshe 汕头大学出版社.

Liu, Fu. 1924/1951. 四声实验录[Sisheng Shiyanlu]. 中华书局.

Li, Xinkui. 李新魁.1994. Guangdong de fangyan 广东的方言. Guangzhou: Guangdong Renmin Chubanshe 广东人民出版社.

Li, Dongfeng and Zheng, Guimin. 李东风, 郑桂敏. 2010. Chaozhou fangyan danzidiao de shiyan yanjiu 潮州方言单字调的实验研究. *Liaoning Shifan Daxue Xuebao* 辽宁师范大学学报 3: 369–373.

Maddieson, Ian. 1978. Universals of tone. In *Universals of Human Language: Phonology*, eds. Greenberg, J.H., Ferguson, C.A., and Moravcsik, E.A. 335–365. Stanford University Press.

Mai, Yun. 麦耘. 2007. Guangxi hezhou babuqu baduhua Rusheng de yuyin fenxi 广西贺州八步区八都话入声的语音分析. *Journal of Guilin Teachers' College* 1: 1–7.

Mei, T. 1970. Tones and Prosody in Middle Chinese and The Origin of The Rising Tone. *Harvard Journal of Asiatic Studies* 30: 86–110.

Michaud, A. 2008. Tones and intonation: some current challenges. In *Proceedings of the 8th International Seminar on Speech Production* (ISSP'08), 13–18.

Michaud, A , and Vaissiere, J. 2015. Tone and intonation: introductory notes and practical recommendations. in Volume 3 of KALIPHO - Kieler Arbeiten zur Linguistik und Phonetik 2014.

Norman, Jerry. 1973. Tonal Development in Min. *Journal of Chinese Linguistics* 1(2): 222–238.

Norman, Jerry. 1974. The Initials of Proto-Min. *Journal of Chinese Linguistics* 2(1): 27–36.

Norman, Jerry. 1981. The Proto-Min Finals. In Guoji hanxue huiyi lunwenji 国际汉学会议论文集: 35–73.

Ohala, J.J. 1981. The listener as a source of sound change. In *The Parasession on Language and Behavior*, eds. C.S. Masek, R.A. Hendrick, and M.F. Miller, 178 – 203. Chicago: Chicago Ling. Soc.

Ohala, J.J. 1986. Against the direct realist view of speech perception.pdf. *Journal of Phonetics* 14: 75–82.

Ohala, J.J. 1987. Sound change is drawn from a pool of synchronic variation. *Presented at the Symposium on The causes of Language Change, Do We Know Them Yet?* Norway: University of Troms.

Ohala, J.J. 1993. Sound change as nature's speech perception experiment. *Speech Communication* 13: 155–161.

Peng, G. 2006. Temporal and tonal aspects of Chinese syllables: A corpus-based comparative study of Mandarin and Cantonese. *Journal of Chinese Linguistics* 34(1): 134–154.

Peng, Jianguo. and Zhu, Xiaonong. 彭建国 & 朱晓农. 2010. On the falsetto voice in Yueyang dialect 岳阳话里的假声. In Contemporary Linguistics 当代语言学1: 24–32.

Peng, G., C. Zhang, H.Y. Zheng, J.W. Minett, and W.S.Y. Wang. 2012. The Effect of Intertalker Variations on Acoustic-Perceptual Mapping in Cantonese and Mandarin Tone Systems. *Journal of Speech, Language, and Hearing Research* 55(2): 579–595.

Phadungsrisavas, V. 2008. *An acoustical comparative study of Swatow Chinese tones spoken in five regions of Thailand*. Bangkok, M.A: Thesis, Mahidol University.

Pharao, N., and Thøgersen, J. 2015. Raising of /a/ in Copenhagen Danish—perceptual consequences across two generations.

Pike, K.L. 1948. *Tone Languages: A Technique for Determining the Number and Type of Pitch Contrasts in a Language, with Studies in Tonemic Substitution and Fusion*. University of Michigan Press.

Rose, Phil. 2006. *Zooming-in on Oujiang Wu: Tonal homogeneity and acoustic reconstruction in a small subgroup of Chinese dialects*. Presented at the CRLC Seminar Series: Australian National University.

Sagart, L. 1986. On the departing tone. *Journal of Chinese Linguistics* 14(1): 90–113.

Sagart, L. 1999. The origin of Chinese tones. In *Cross-Linguistics Studies of Tonal phenomena: Tonogenesis, Typology, and Related Topics*, ed. S. Kaji, 91–104. Tokyo: Institute for the Study of of Languages and Cultures of Asia and Africa, Tokyo University of Foreign Studies.

Shen, Ruiqing. 2013. From short-long to high-low: The evolution of Cantonese stopped tones. 从短长到高低: 广府片粤语入声的声学性质及演化路径. In *The 18th International Conference on Yue Dialects*. HKUST.

Shen, Ruiqing. 2016. Tonal Variation: A Quantitative Study of Jianyang Min Chinese (A dissertation for the degree Doctor of Philosophy). The Hong Kong University of Science and Technology.

Silva, D.J. 2006. Acoustic evidence for the emergence of tonal contrast in contemporary Korean. *Phonology* 23(02): 287–308.

Steed, William, and Rose, Phil. 2009. Same tone, different category: linguistic-tonetic variation in the areal tone acoustics of chuqu wu. In *Presented at the 10th Annual Conference of the International Speech Communication Association*, 2295–2298. Brighton, UK.

Svantesson, J.-O., and D. House. 2006. Tone production, tone perception and Kammu tonogenesis. *Phonology* 23(02): 309–333.

Thurgood, Graham. 2002. Vietnamese and tonogenesis: Revising the model and the analysis. *Diachronica* 19: 333–363.

Tsay, Jane. 1994. Phonological pitch. Doctoral dissertation, Tucson: University of Arizona.

Wang, William S-Y. 1967. Phonological Features of Tone. *International Journal of American Linguistics* 33(2): 93–105.

Wang, William S-Y. 1969. Competing changes as a cause of residue. *Language* 45(1): 9–25.

Wang, Hongjun. 王洪君. 2012. Yetan Minbei Fangyan de Zhuoruohua Shengmu—Jianlun Yuanshiyu Gouni Ruhe Jianbie he Chuli Jieyong Chengfen yiji Pingdeng Hunhe Zaocheng de Wutiaojian Fenhua 也谈闽北方言的浊弱化声母——兼论原始语构拟如何鉴别和处理借用成分以及平等混合造成的无条件分化. In Yuyanxue Luncong 语言学论丛 46: 1–44.

Wang, Caiyu. 2015. Multi-register tone systems and their evolution on the Jianghan plain (A dissertation for the degree Doctor of Philosophy). The Hong Kong University of Science and Technology.

Wang, William S-Y. and Lien, Chinfa. 1993. Bidirectional diffusion in sound change. In *Charles Jones ed. Historical Linguistics: Problems and Prospectives*, 345–400. London: Longman Group Limited.

Wang, Futang. 王福堂. 1999. Hanyu Fangyan Yuyin de Yanbian he Cengci 汉语方言语音的演变和层次. Yuwen Chubanshe语文出版社.

Wang, Futang. 王福堂. 2004. Yuanshi Minyu zhong de Qingruohua Shengmu he Xiangguande 'Dijiudiao' 原始闽语中的清弱化声母和相关的"第九调". In Zhongguo Yuwen 中国语文 2: 135–144.

Wang, Futang. 王福堂. 2005. Yuanshi Minyu Gouni Wenti de Yanjiu Gouci 原始闽语构拟问题的研究构词. *Language and Linguistics* 6(3): 473–481.

Wan, I., and J. Jaeger. 1998. Speech errors and the representation of tone in Mandarin Chinese. *Phonology*. 15 (03): 417–461.

Wu, Fang. 吴芳. 2009. Dialects Geography and Typology Research on the Nasal Endings "-n" & "-ŋ" in Min Dialect in East Guangdong Province. 粤东闽语-n、-ŋ韵尾的方言地理类型研究. Ph. D. Thesis, Jinan University, Guangzhou.

Zhu, Xiaonong. Jiao, Lei. Yim, Chi Sing and Hong, Ying. 朱晓农 & 焦磊 & 严至诚 & 洪英. 2008. 入声演化三途. [Three ways of Rusheng sound change]. *Zhongguo Yuwen* 中国语文 4: 324–338.

Xu, Yue, and Zhu, Xiaonong. 徐越 & 朱晓农. 2011. 喉塞尾入声是怎麼舒化的——孝丰个案研究 [How is the glottal stop softened? A case study of Xiaofeng rusheng]. *Zhongguo Yuwen* 中国语文 3: 263–270.

Xu, Fuqiong. 徐馥琼. 2010. A Phonological Study of Min Dialect in Eastern Guangdong. 粤东闽语语音研究. Ph.D. Thesis, Zhongshan University, Guangzhou.

Yip, Moira. 1980. *The tonal phonology of Chinese*. Cambridge, Mass: PhD.Thesis. MIT.

Yip, Moira. 1989. Contour tones. *Phonology* 6: 149–174.

Yip, Moira. 2002. *Tone*. Cambridge: Cambridge University Press.

Yue-Hashimoto, A.O. 1970. The Liang-Yue dialect materials. *Unicorn* 6: 35–51.

Yue-Hashimoto, A. O. 2001. The Historic Role of the Late Professor YR Chao's 1929 Field Materials. *Language and Linguistics*, 2: 197.

Zhang, Pingsheng. 张屏生. 1994. 潮阳话和闽南话地区部分次方言的语音比较. *Zhongguo Xueshu Niankan* 中国学术年刊 15: 311–374.

Zhang, Shengyu. 张盛裕. 1979a. Chaoyang fangyan de wenbai yidu 潮阳方言的文白异读. *Fangyan* 方言 4: 241–267.

Zhang, Shengyu. 张盛裕. 1979b. Chaoyang fangyan de chongdieshi 潮阳方言的重叠式. *Zhongguo Yuwen* 中国语文 2: 106–114.

Zhang, Shengyu. 张盛裕.1979c. Chaoyang fangyan de liandu biandiao 潮阳方言的连读变调. Fangyan 方言 2: 93–121.

Zhang, Shengyu. 张盛裕. 1980. Chaoyang fangyan de liandu biandiao er 潮阳方言的连读变调(二). *Fangyan* 方言 2: 123–136.

Zhang, Shengyu. 张盛裕. 1981. Chaoyang fangyan de yuyin xitong 潮阳方言的语音系统. *Fangyan* 方言 1: 27–39.

Zhang, Jingfen. 张静芬. 2013. Minnan Fnagyan de Lishi Bijiao ji Yuyin Gouni 闽南方言的历史比较及语音构拟. Master degree thesis. Peking University.

Zhan, Bohui. 詹伯慧. 1959. Chaozhou Fangyan 潮州方言. In Zhongguo yuwen zazhishe 中国语文杂志社 ed., Fangyan he Putonghua Congkan 方言和普通话丛刊 2: 39–120. Beijing: Zhonghua shuju 中华书局.

Zhengzhang, Shangfang. 郑张尚芳. 1994郑张尚芳. 汉语声调平仄分域上声去声的起源,《语言研究》增刊.

Zhu, Xiaonong. Liu, Zemin. Xu, Fuqiong. 朱晓农 & 刘泽民 & 徐馥琼. 2009. 自发新生 内爆音:来自赣语、闽语、哈尼语、吴语的一手材料. [Implosives developed from natural sound change: New findings from Gan, Min, Hani, and Wu]. *Fangyan* 方言 1: 10–17.

Zhu, Xiaonong, and Hong, Ying. 朱晓农 & 洪英. 2009. 潮州话入声的阴低阳高 [The Phonetic Nature of the Entering Tones in Chaozhou Dialect]. *Bulletin of Chinese Linguistics* 4 (1): 115–128.

Zhu, Xiaonong, and Hong, Ying. 朱晓农 & 洪英. 2010. Implosives came from voiceless stops: a case study of Chaozhou Min. *Chinese Journal of Phonetics* 中国语音学报 2: 103–107.

Zhu, Xiaonong and Yi, Li. 朱晓农 & 衣莉. 2011. 两折调的故事. [A story of double circumflex tone]. 语言研究集刊, 8: 129–141.

Zhu, Xiaonong. Shi Defu, and Wei, Mingying. 朱晓农 & 石德富 & 韦名应. 2012. 鱼梁苗语六平调和三域六度标调制. 民族语文, 4: 3–12.

Zhu, Xiaonong. 朱晓农. 1999. Shanghai Tonetics. ANU dissertation, Published by Lincom Europ.

Zhu, Xiaonong. 朱晓农. 2005. 上海声调实验录 *An Experimental Study of Shanghai Tones*. 上海教育出版社 Shanghai: Shanghai Educational Press.

Zhu, Xiaonong. 朱晓农. 2007. Zheng zaoqi shangsheng dai jiasheng [Falsetto: The origin of the Rising Tone]. *Zhongguo Yuwen* 2: 160–168.

Zhu, Xiaonong. 朱晓农. 2009. 声调起因于发声 [Phonation as the phonetic cause of tonogenesis]. Yuyan Yanjiu Jikan 语言研究集刊 6: 1–29.

Zhu, Xiaonong. 朱晓农. 2012. Multiregisters and four levels: a new tonal model. *Journal of Chinese Linguistics* 40(1): 1–17.

Zhu, Xiaonong. 朱晓农. 2012b. 降调的种类[A classification of falling tones]. 语言研究, (02): 1–16.

Zhu, Xiaonong. 朱晓农. 2014. 声调类型学大要[An outline of tone typology]. 方言 [Dialects]. 3: 193–205.

Chapter 3
Tonal Patterns Within the Chaoshan Area

Abstract This chapter presents 14 tonal patterns identified in Chaoshan dialects, namely Pattern A through N. According to the phonetic realizations of MC (Middle Chinese) tones and the evolutionary route of tones, eleven tonal patterns (A through K) identified can be further grouped into three main types: (1) Type one: Shanjie type, including Pattern A, Pattern B and Pattern C; (2) Type two: Huipu type, including Pattern D, Pattern E, Pattern F, Pattern G and Pattern H; (3) Type three: Chaoyang type, including Pattern I, Pattern J and Pattern K.

Keyword Tonal patterns · Tono-types · Subgrouping · Phonetic realizations

Mutual intelligibility among Chaoshan dialects is high, but there are still a few differences in their phonological systems, which are reflected in the phonetic realizations of certain finals and tones. In this chapter, I present 14 tonal patterns identified in Chaoshan dialects.

We investigate 65 localities (including districts 区 and towns 镇) in the Chaoshan area (see Appendix B). The materials used in this book are all firsthand acoustic data collected mainly from the field investisgations by the author. Checked tones in most of these 65 sites are consistent except Yun'ao and Dahao dialects (see Chap. 6), so for the sake of simplicity, I set aside checked tones in this chapter. The patterns of checked tones in the Chaoshan area can be found in Chap. 6.

Data from each dialect site is processed using the same criteria. By referring to the universal tonal inventories, tono-types of each tonal system can be decided. According to the occurrence frequency of each tono-type, the tonal pattern is presented according to the sequence of tono-types, namely "falling-level-low-rising-concave-high", where "low" stands for "the pure low tone" and "high" stands for tones in upper register.

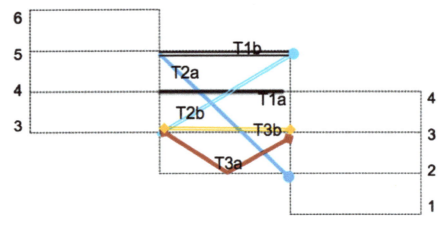

Fig. 3.1 Pattern A under MRFL

Table 3.1 Tones transcribed under MRFL, Pattern A	Present category	MC tones	Tono-type	Tonal value
	T1a	Yinping	Middle-level	44
	T1b	Yangping	High-level	55
	T2a	Yinshang	Falling	52/42
	T2b	Yangshang, Yinshang, Yangqu	Rising	35
	T3a	Yinqu	The pure low tone	22/323/23
	T3b	Yangqu	Low-level	33

3.1 Pattern A: Falling-Level-Level-Level-Low-Rising

Pattern A has six unchecked tones. Three level tones co-exist in this pattern, that is high-level, middle-level and low-level, and they are from MC Yangping, Yinping and Yangqu tones, respectively. The falling tone corresponds with MC Yinshang tone. The rising tone originates from MC Yangshang tone and some syllables from Yinshang and Yangqu. The pure low tone of this pattern corresponds with MC Yinqu tonal category. The notation of tone categories in this book includes numbers 1, 2, 3, 4 indicating the MC tone origins, and small letters "a" and "b" for subcategories originally conditioned by phonation registers of syllables, traditionally termed as Yin and Yang. The schematic figure of Pattern A under MRFL is presented in Fig. 3.1 and tones are transcribed using MRFL model in Table 3.1.

3.1 Pattern A: Falling-Level-Level-Level-Low-Rising 37

Pattern A is the main pattern of dialects in Jieyang City. Chao'an County in Chaozhou City and Chenghai District in Shantou City also present this pattern. Thirty dialect points in our database display this pattern, and their frequency curves are shown as follows in Fig. 3.2.[1]

The reason for us to identify T3b as a low-level tone is twofold. Firstly, the auditory impression for T3b is level, not falling. Secondly, T3b in Pattern A is parallel with other level tones in the system; for example, T3b parallels with T1a and their pitch contours are identical. These two aspects are different from Pattern B, in which T3b is a low falling tone. For some speakers, level tones have the trend of declining at the end of the syllables, such as XJL in Fubin Town of Chaozhou City (the 21th graph in Fig. 3.2). This is not an unusual phenomenon since it has been pointed out by Laver (1994: 467–469) that tones systematically labeled "level" are seldom strictly level. They may display a certain amount of movement, though substantially less than the so-called rises and falls.

In this case, level tones of Pattern A in some Chaoshan informants are phonetically falling but perceptually level. Of course, level tones in other patterns demonstrated in the following sections may also have this kind of effect. This phenomenon also suggests the lack of correspondence between acoustic properties and auditory impression.

Since only one falling tone appears in Pattern A, it is this falling contour that distinguishes T2a from other tones. The pitch height of this falling tone is somewhat instable with the starting point either at the value of 5 or 4. The instability of T2a's pitch height does not affect its differentiation from other non-falling tones. Speaker within this pattern exhibits his or her own preference for the realization of T2a. This suggests a space of free variations for T2a in this pattern.

T3a in this pattern has a non-modal phonation type, namely creaky voice. For this reason, even though the pitch lines for T3a and T3b are close to each other, they are not the same, like the case in Didu Town (the 7th graph in Fig. 3.2). Another potential reason for this similarity between the pitch curve of T3a and T3b is that the creaky voice in T3a may affect the pitch measurement of T3a.

3.2 Pattern B: Falling-Falling-Level-Level-Low-Rising

Pattern B has six unchecked tones. Two level tones and two falling tones co-exist in this pattern, namely high-level, middle-level, high-falling and low-falling, and they are mainly from MC Yangping, Yinping, Yinshang and Yangqu tones, respectively. The rising tone originates from MC Yangshang tone. The pure low tone comes from MC Yinqu tone.

The difference between Patterns A and B lies in the representation of MC Yangqu tone. Pattern A has three level tones, which is the same as the tonal system of

---

[1]The title of each tonal picture includes the following informations: the name of the informant, street or town of the district, city name.

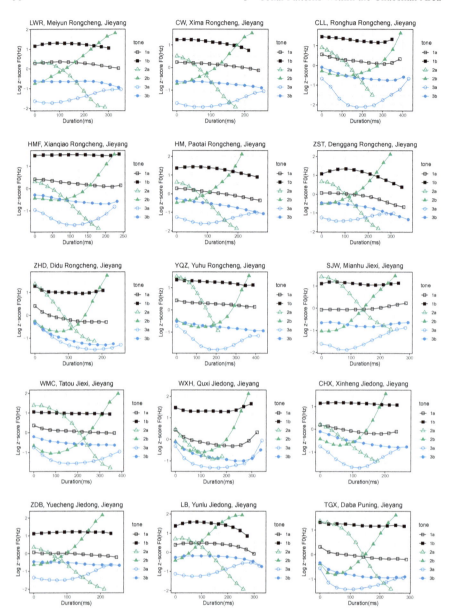

Fig. 3.2 The frequency curves of 30 dialect sites of Pattern A

3.2 Pattern B: Falling-Falling-Level-Level-Low-Rising

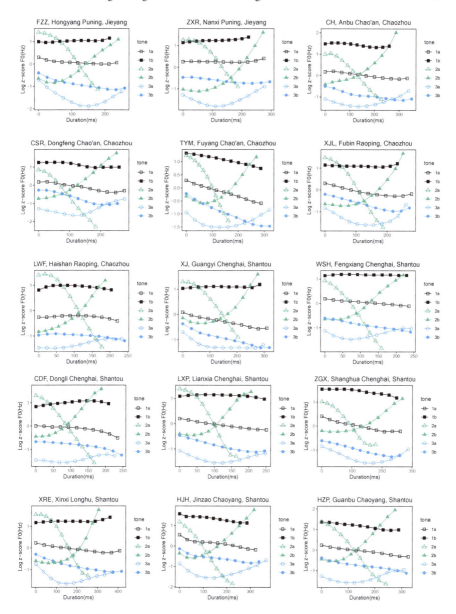

Fig. 3.2 (continued)

Cantonese. The low level-tone in Pattern A becomes low falling in Pattern B. The schematic figure of Pattern B under MRFL is presented in Fig. 3.3 and tones are transcribed in Table 3.2.

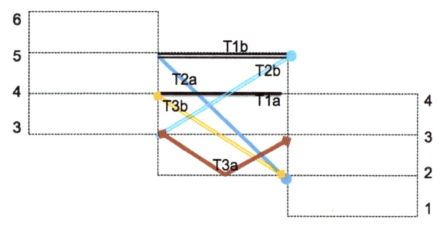

Fig. 3.3 Pattern B under MRFL

Table 3.2 Tones transcribed under MRFL, Pattern B

Present category	MC tones	Tono-type	Tonal value
T1a	Yinping	Middle-level	44
T1b	Yangping	High-level	55
T2a	Yinshang	High falling	52
T2b	Yangshang, Yinshang, Yangqu	Rising	35
T3a	Yinqu	The pure low tone	22/323/23
T3b	Yangqu	Low-falling	42

Pattern B occurs mostly in the urban area of Shantou and Chaozhou City, as well as Raoping County of Chaozhou. The frequency curves of six dialect points in our database are demonstrated in Fig. 3.4.

Just as in Pattern A, T3a in Pattern B is often accompanied by creaky voice, being the pure low tone in this pattern. What is different from Pattern A is the realization of T2a. The starting point of T2a never drops below the pitch value of T1a/44/ in our database. As there are two falling tones coexisting in Pattern B, these two falling tones are quite distinct from each other in height, with T2a starting from the pitch value of 5, namely above the tonal value of T1a, and T3b starting from the pitch value of 4 or 3, always below the tonal value of T1a. It is interesting that T1b is more like a high slight falling to in informant MWP's tonal system (4th graph in Fig. 3.4), which is the same with T1b in Houzhai dialect of Nan'ao county in Shantou city. Two informants of Jingzhou dialects (informant MWP and MBD) all display this tendency to produce T1b as a high slight falling tone.

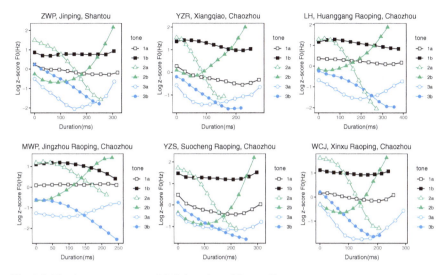

Fig. 3.4 The frequency curves of 6 dialect sites of Pattern B

3.3 Pattern C: Falling-Level-Level-Low-Rising-Rising

Pattern C has six unchecked tones. The schematic figure of Pattern C under MRFL is presented in Fig. 3.5 and tonal values are transcribed in Table 3.3.

The dialects that display Pattern C mainly show up in the remote areas of Puning and Chaozhou City. The frequency curves of Pattern C are demonstrated in the following graphs (Fig. 3.6).

The difference between Pattern C and Pattern A is that T1a is a high slight rising tone in Pattern C. Therefore, Pattern C has two rising tones with T1a a high rising tone and T2b a low rising tone. The distinction of two rising tones lies in the starting pitch point.

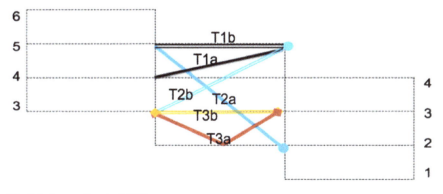

Fig. 3.5 Pattern C under MRFL

Table 3.3 Tones transcribed under MRFL, Pattern C

Present category	MC tones	Tono-type	Tonal value
T1a	Yinping	High slight rising	45
T1b	Yangping	High-level	55
T2a	Yinshang	Falling	52/42
T2b	Yangshang, Yinshang, Yangqu	Rising	35
T3a	Yinqu	The pure low tone	323/32
T3b	Yangqu	Low level	33

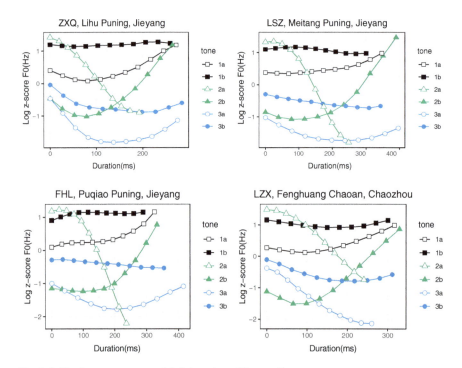

Fig. 3.6 The frequency curves of 4 dialect sites of Pattern C

3.4 Pattern D: Falling-Falling-Level-Low-Rising-Rising

Pattern D has six unchecked tones. According to Zhu (2012), what matters for the pure low tone is the lowest pitch height, regardless of any types of pitch contour. However, in Pattern C, the pure low tone has a fixed contour, being the lowest falling tone /32/. This suggests that the pure low tone may have two kinds of phonetic representation.

3.4 Pattern D: Falling-Falling-Level-Low-Rising-Rising

One is without fixed contours, and the other always takes the same contour. When the second scenario occurs, it may indicate that some kind of evolution is taking place (this will be discussed at more length in Chap. 4). The schematic figure of Pattern D under MRFL is presented in Fig. 3.7 and tones are transcribed in Table 3.4.

This pattern only occurs in Liusha District of Puning in our database. The frequency curves of this tonal pattern are presented below:

The most notable feature of Pattern C and Pattern D is that they have two rising tones, which is seldom seen in other Chaoshan dialects. Considering that two rising tones co-occurring in one tonal system is rare in Chaoshan dialects, we postulate that the tonal system of Eastern Street reflects the earlier stage in this area (see Chap. 4 for more details). In Eastern Street of Liusha District, T1a is a low-level tone, not a rising one. Therefore, the tonal system in Eastern Street is similar to Pattern B, but its pure low tone is the same as that in Pattern D, which is the lowest falling tone /32/. Xishe Village of Zhanlong Town (占陇镇西社乡) has the same tonal pattern

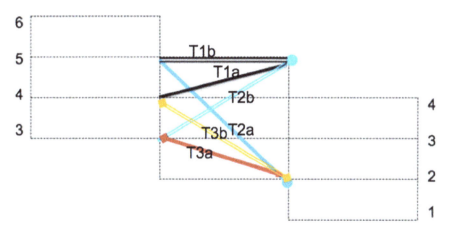

Fig. 3.7 Pattern D under MRFL

Table 3.4 Tones transcribed under MRFL, Pattern D

Present category	MC tones	Tono-type	Tonal value
T1a	Yinping	Slight rising	45
T1b	Yangping	High-level	55
T2a	Yinshang	High-falling	52
T2b	Yangshang, Yinshang, Yangqu	High-rising	25/35
T3a	Yinqu	The pure low tone	32
T3b	Yangqu	Low-falling	42

as that in Eastern Street of Liusha District. Below are the frequency curves of these dialects mentioned above (Figs. 3.8 and 3.9).

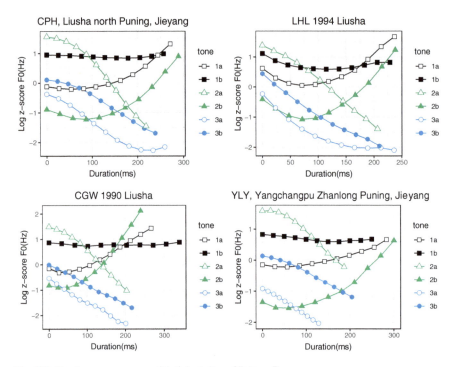

Fig. 3.8 The frequency curves of 4 dialect sites of Pattern D

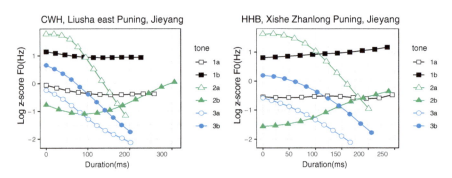

Fig. 3.9 The frequency curves of dialects in Eastern Street of Liusha District and Xishe Village of Zhanlong Town

3.5 Pattern E: Falling-Falling-Level-Low-Rising

Pattern E only has five unchecked tones and it has two sub-patterns according to the process of tonal merger. The schematic figure of Pattern E under MRFL is presented in Figs. 3.10 and 3.11 and tones are transcribed in Tables 3.5 and 3.6.

The frequency curves of Pattern E in Huilai County are presented in Fig. 3.12.

In Pattern E1, T3b merges with T3a, and in Patter E2, T3b merges with T2b. Pattern E is the main tonal pattern in Huilai County except some eastern towns, such as Jinghai Twon, which still possesses six unchecked tones. We can depict the evolutionary route of tones in Huilai County if we suppose that the dialect of the eastern towns is the most conservative one (see Chap. 4 for more details). Pattern E1

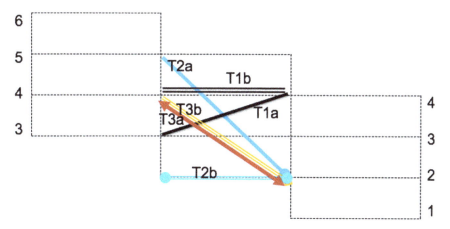

Fig. 3.10 Pattern E1 under MRFL

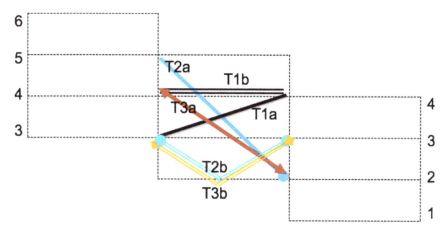

Fig. 3.11 Pattern E2 under MRFL

Table 3.5 Tones transcribed under MRFL, Pattern E1

Present category	MC tones	Tono-type	Tonal value
T1a	Yinping	Slight rising	34
T1b	Yangping	Middle-level	44
T2a	Yinshang	High-falling	52
T2b	Yinshang, Yangshang, Yangqu	The pure low tone	23
T3a/T3b	Yinqu/yangqu	Low-falling	42

Table 3.6 Tones transcribed under MRFL, Pattern E2

Present category	MC tones	Tono-type	Tonal value
T1a	Yinping	Slight rising	34
T1b	Yangping	Middle-level	44
T2a	Yinshang	High-falling	52
T2b/T3b	Yinshang, Yangshang, Yangqu	The pure low tone	323
T3a	Yinqu	Low-falling	42

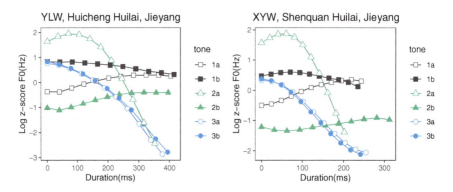

Fig. 3.12 The frequency curves of 2 dialect sites of Pattern E1

occurs in the central part of Huilai County, while Pattern E2 appears in the western part, namely Kuitan Town (Fig. 3.13).

3.6 Pattern F: Falling-Level-Level-Low-Rising

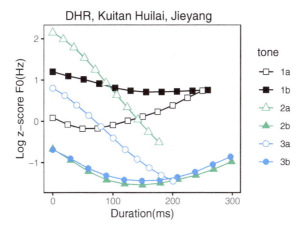

Fig. 3.13 The frequency curves of 1 dialect site of Pattern E2

3.6 Pattern F: Falling-Level-Level-Low-Rising

The younger generations in the central part of Huilai County have different tonal systems compared to their older counterparts shown in Fig. 3.12. T2a in the younger speakers's tonal system has changed from high falling to high level. The schematic figure of Pattern F under MRFL is presented in Fig. 3.14 and tones are transcribed in Table 3.7.

The frequency curves of younger speakers in central Huilai County are presented in Fig. 3.15.

T2a in some informants has a further development, in which T2a changed from high level to high slight rising, like the first graph and the fourth graph in Fig. 3.15.

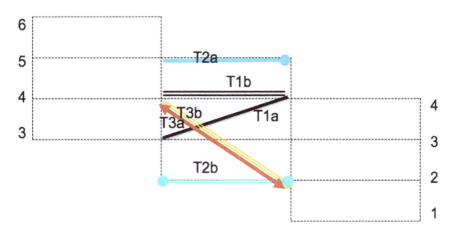

Fig. 3.14 Pattern F under MRFL

Table 3.7 Tones transcribed under MRFL, Pattern F for younger generations

Present category	MC tones	Tono-type	Tonal value
T1a	Yinping	Slight rising	34
T1b	Yangping	Middle-level	44
T2a	Yinshang	High-level/High slight rising	55/45
T2b	Yinshang, Yangshang, Yangqu	The pure low tone	323/32
T3a/T3b	Yinqu, Yangqu	Low-falling	42

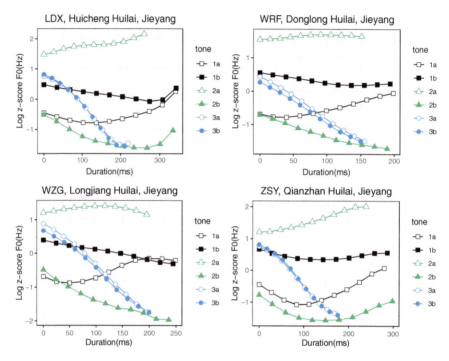

Fig. 3.15 The frequency curves of younger speakers in central Huilai County

This is an ongoing change. Some speakers have the two phonetic variations of T2a at the same time. That is to say the two phonetic representations (high level and high slight rising) of T2a co-exist within a single speaker's tonal system (see Sect. 4.8 for more details).

3.7 Pattern G: Falling-Falling-Level-Level-Low-High

The older speakers in Jinghai Town of Huilai (the eastern part of Huilai) still retain the special phonation type of fortis voice, resulting in T2a having the highest pitch height in their tonal system. We should set up the upper register for their system under

3.7 Pattern G: Falling-Falling-Level-Level-Low-High

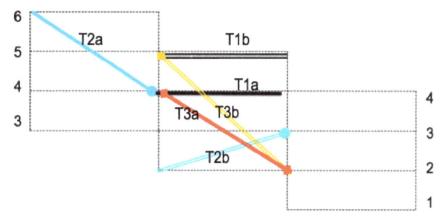

Fig. 3.16 Pattern G under MRFL

Table 3.8 Tones transcribed under MRFL, Pattern G for the older generation

Present category	MC tones	Tono-type	Tonal value
T1a	Yinping	Middle-level	44
T1b	Yangping	High-level	55
T2a	Yinshang	Register upper	64
T2b	Yinshang, Yangshang, Yangqu	Pure low tone	323/23
T3a	Yinqu	Low-falling	42
T3b	Yangqu	High-falling	52

MRFL. By "high" we mean the upper register. The schematic figure of Pattern F for the older generation under MRFL is presented in Fig. 3.16 and tones are transcribed in Table 3.8.

The frequency curves of Pattern G are demonstrated in Fig. 3.17.

As can be seen from Fig. 3.17, the pitch height of T2a is significantly higher than that of other tones. This tonal pattern only exists in the older speakers of Jinghai town.

3.8 Pattern H: Falling-Falling-Level-Level-Level-Low

The younger generations in Jinghai and Xian'an towns have lost the special phonation (fortis voice) that is preserved in the older speakers' tonal system. T2a has changed to high level in Register Modal in their system. The schematic figure of Pattern H for younger generations under MRFL is presented in Fig. 3.18 and tones are transcribed in Table 3.9.

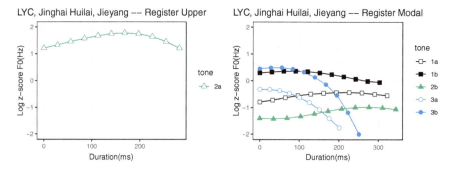

Fig. 3.17 The frequency curves of Jinghai Town, older speakers, Pattern G

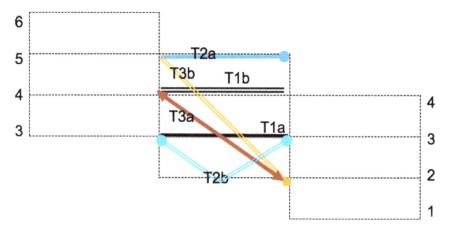

Fig. 3.18 Pattern H under MRFL

Table 3.9 Tones transcribed under MRFL, Pattern H for younger generations

Present category	MC tones	Tono-type	Tonal value
T1a	Yinping	Low-level	33
T1b	Yangping	Middle-level	44
T2a	Yinshang	High-level	55
T2b	Yinshang, Yangshang, Yangqu	The pure low tone	323
T3a	Yinqu	Low-falling	42
T3b	Yangqu	High-falling	52

3.8 Pattern H: Falling-Falling-Level-Level-Level-Low 51

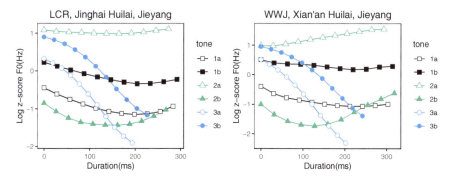

Fig. 3.19 The frequency curves of 2 dialect sites of Pattern H

The frequency curves of Pattern H of the younger generations in Jinghai and Xian'an towns are demonstrated in Fig. 3.19.

It is notable that three level tones co-exist in Pattern H. The historical origins of these level tones are different from that of Pattern A which also possesses three level tones. Some informant's phonetic representation of T2a has changed form high level to high slight rising, like the case in Xian'an town (the second graph of Fig. 3.19). Rising tone is absent from this pattern.

3.9 Pattern I: Falling-Falling-Falling-Level-Low

T2b and T3b have merged in Pattern I, so this pattern only has five unchecked tones. The schematic figure of Pattern I under MRFL is presented in Fig. 3.20 and tones are transcribed in Table 3.10.

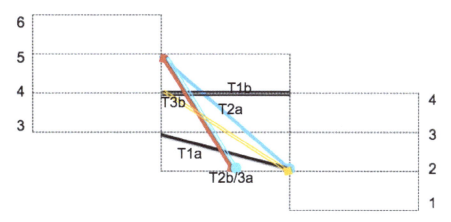

Fig. 3.20 Pattern I under MRFL

Table 3.10 Tones transcribed under MRFL, Pattern I

Present category	MC tones	Tono-type	Tonal value
T1a	Yinping	The pure low tone	32
T1b	Yangping	Level	44 or 33
T2a	Yinshang	Deferred-high-falling	552
T2b/T3a	Yinshang, Yangshang, Yangqu, Yinqu	Mid-short high-falling	52
T3b	Yangqu	Low-falling	42

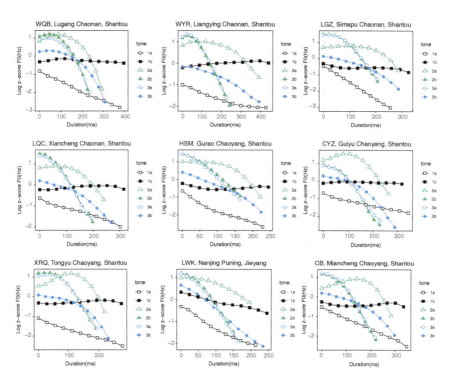

Fig. 3.21 The frequency curves of 9 dialect sites of Pattern I

The pure low tone has a fixed contour—the lowest falling {32}—just like the case in Liusha dialect (see Pattern D in Sect. 3.4). Therefore, strictly speaking, this pattern has four falling tones, which is rarely seen in the world of tonal languages. The phenomenon that four falling tones co-exist in one single dialect turns out to be quite prevalent in the Chaoyang area; it is nothing special at all. Older speakers in Chaoyang District and Chaonan District share this common feature. Hong et al. (2013) have discussed the phonetic features of the four falling tones in Gurao dialect with abundant phonetic details. They discover that length plays a pivotal role in distinguishing the four falling tones. We will further delve into the phonetic characteristics of the four-falling-tone system and their evolution with first acoustic data from a wider range

3.9 Pattern I: Falling-Falling-Falling-Level-Low

Fig. 3.22 The frequency curves of tones in Hongchang Town

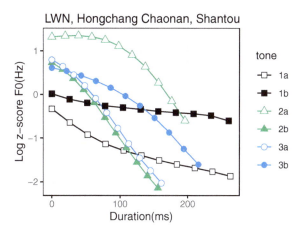

of dialectical varieties in the Chaoyang area (refer to Chap. 5 for more details) (Fig. 3.21).

The older generations (informants older than 35 years old at the time of recording will be defined as older generation here) in Chaonan and Chaoyang districts display this tonal pattern and they are quite consistent across different towns. Miancheng, the administration center of Chaoyang District, however, has a further development compared with other towns. The frequency curves of the older speakers' tonal systems are shown in Fig. 3.21.

Only one level tone exists in Pattern I, and it varies with informants. It can be realized either as middle level or as low level. In Hongchang Town of Chaonan District, the tonal system also displays this pattern. However, T2b/T3a is not a mid-short **high falling**, but a mid-short **low falling**, just as the frequency curves shown in Fig. 3.22.

The tonal system of informant LWN shown in Fig. 3.22 demonstrates that the distinction of T2b/3a and T3b may lies in the duration. 66 tokens of T2b/3a and 34 tokens are used in the significance test (Anova test). The result shows that data of length and the slope[2] are all significantly different, and the p-values are all smaller than < 2e−16.

In Shanpu Village (杉埔村) of Zhanlong Town, T2b/T3a is a low falling tone as well, but its T1a is a low level tone. Thus, its tonal pattern is "falling-falling-falling-level-level", which is a new tonal pattern compared with Pattern I (Fig. 3.23).

---

[2]I use the eight pitch points by omitting the first two points and the last two points to calutate the slove value.

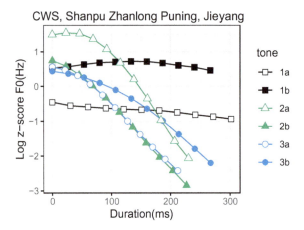

Fig. 3.23 The frequency curves of tones in Shanpu Village of Zhanlong Town

3.10 Pattern J: Falling-Falling-Level-Level-Low

In some towns of Chaonan and Chaoyang districts, T2a in the tonal system of the younger generations has changed from high-falling to high-level (or middle-level), constituting another tonal pattern, namely Pattern J. Meanwhile, the older speakers in Miancheng Town of Changyang District also display this pattern. The schematic figure of Pattern J under MRFL is presented in Fig. 3.24 and tones are transcribed in Table 3.11.

The frequency curves of Pattern J are shown in Fig. 3.25.

It is notable that some informant prefect to pronounce T1b as a rising tone, such as informant CYZ (Liangying), CXY (Xiashan), ZYL (Gurao) and XZH (Tongyu). This change is still on-going among younger speakers in these above towns. However,

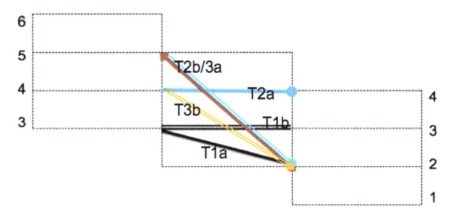

Fig. 3.24 Pattern J under MRFL

3.10 Pattern J: Falling-Falling-Level-Level-Low

Table 3.11 Tones transcribed under MRFL, Pattern J

Present category	MC tones	Tono-type	Tonal value
T1a	Yinping	The pure low tone	32
T1b	Yangping	Low-level	33
T2a	Yinshang	High or Middle-level	55 or 44
T2b/T3a	Yinshang, Yangshang, Yangqu, Yinqu	High-falling	52
T3b	Yangqu	Low-falling	42

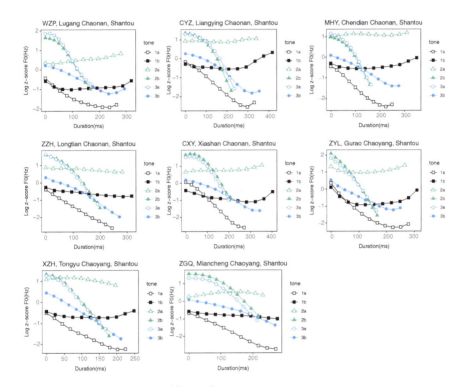

Fig. 3.25 The frequency curves of Pattern J

this change has been completed in all the younger speakers we investigated in Guiyu Town. That is to say there is a strong tendency for T1b to change to rising contour from level contour.

T2a in Younger speakers's tonal system in Haojiang District has further developments compared with younger speakers in other towns. In Haojiang dialect, T2a has changed from high level to high rising. Tonal developments in this area are disscussed in detail in Chap. 5. Here are the younger speakers' tonal frequency curves in Guiyu Town and Haojiang distrcit (Fig. 3.26). Their tonal pattern is identical with Pattern E, but the corresponding rules with MC tones are not the same.

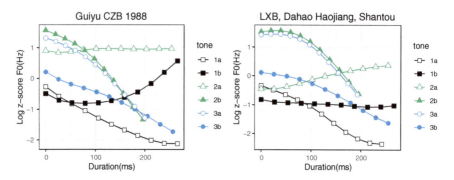

Fig. 3.26 The frequency curves of the younger generations' tonal system in Guiyu and Dahao

The older speakers in Haimen Town also display Pattern J, but the corresponding rules between the phonetic representations and MC tones are not the same. In pattern J, T2b merged with T3a, while in Haimen dialect, T2b merged with T1a. The frequency curves of the older speakers' tonal system in Haimen and their tonal value under MRFL are demonstrated in Fig. 3.27 and Table 3.12.

Fig. 3.27 The frequency curves of Haimen Town, older speaker

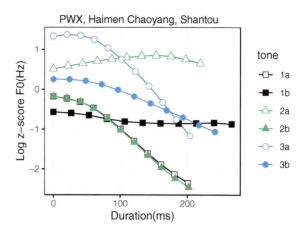

Table 3.12 Haimen tones transcribed under MRFL

Present category	MC tones	Tono-type	Tonal value
T1a/T2b	Yinping, Yinshang, Yangshang, Yangqu	The pure low tone (The lowest falling)	32
T1b	Yangping	Low-level	33
T2a	Yinshang	Middle-level	44
T3a	Yinqu	High-falling	52
T3b	Yangqu	Low-falling	42

3.11 Pattern K: Falling-Falling-Level-Level-Rising

Pattern K is the tonal pattern of the younger generations in Chaoyang district. From the perspective of evolution, Pattern K is the final stage of the tonal development in the Chaoyang area. It has three tonal changes compared with the older generation's tonal system:

(1) T1a changes from the lowest falling tone /32/ to low falling /42/;
(2) T2a changes from middle-level /44/ to high slight-rising {45}
(3) T3b changes from low falling /42/ to middle-level /44/.

These three tonal changes are proved to have constituted a pull-chain shift, and details can be referred to in Sect. 5.3.

The schematic figure of Pattern K under MRFL is presented in Fig. 3.28 and tones are transcribed in Table 3.13.

The frequency curves of pattern K are presented in Fig. 3.29.

The younger speakers' tonal system in Haimen also displays Pattern K, but the direction of tonal merger is not the same as that in Miancheng dialect. Just as noted in Sect. 3.10, the two tones that merge together are T2b and T1a. T1a/2b changes from the pure low tone to low falling tone in the younger speaker's system. The frequency

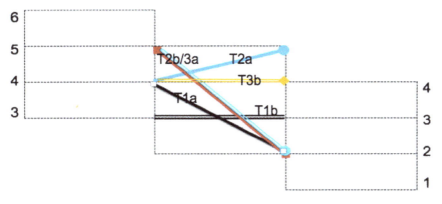

Fig. 3.28 Pattern K under MRFL

Table 3.13 Tones transcribed under MRFL, Pattern K

Present category	MC tones	Tono-type	Tonal value
T1a	Yinping	Low-falling	42
T1b	Yangping	Low-level	33
T2a	Yinshang	High slight-rising	45
T2b/T3a	Yinshang, Yangshang, Yinqu, Yangqu	High-falling	52
T3b	3b	Middle-level	44/43

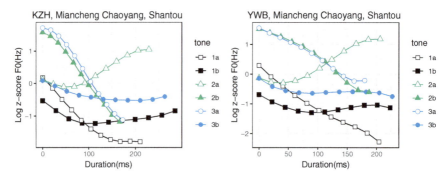

Fig. 3.29 The frequency curves of Pattern K

Fig. 3.30 The frequency curves of Haimen Town, younger speakers

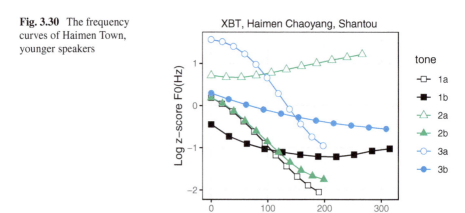

curves of the younger generations' tonal pattern of Haimen dialect are shown below (Fig. 3.30):

3.12 Three Other Patterns

The tonal patterns of certain towns are different from those of nearby towns and those differences need more investigation. Here are some examples.

(1) Pattern L: Falling-falling-falling-level-level-rising

Xilu 西胪 Town in Chaoyang District has a tonal system different from those of nearby towns, such as Guanbu Town (Pattern A) and Miancheng Town (Pattern K). Xilu dialect has six unchecked tones. The Xilu tones transcribed under MRFL are shown in Table 3.14 and the schematic figure of Pattern L under MRFL is presented in Fig. 3.31.

3.12 Three Other Patterns

Table 3.14 Xilu tones transcribed under MRFL

Present category	MC tones	Tono-type	Tonal value
T1a	Yinping	Low-level	33
T1b	Yangping	Middle-level	44
T2a	Yinshang	High-falling	52
T2b	Yinshang, Yangshang, Yangqu	High-rising/low-risng	35/24
T3a	Yinqu	Mid-short low-falling	42
T3b	Yangqu	Low-falling	42

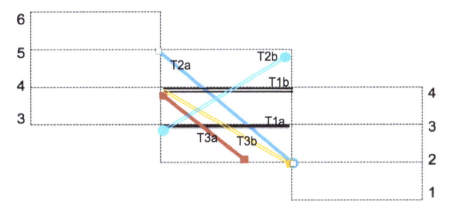

Fig. 3.31 Pattern L under MRFL

The frequency curves of four Xilu informants are shown in Fig. 3.32.

The differences between T3a and T3b of Xilu dialect lie in the length and the slope. The results of Anova test on the differences of these two tones's length and slope are all significant for all the four informants.

Younger speakers from Xilu dialect have changed their T2a from high falling contour to high level contour. Figure 3.33 demonstrates the pitch curves of three younger speakers.

(2) Pattern M: Falling-falling-falling-level-low-rising

Houzhai Town in Nan'ao County displays pattern M. Houzhai tones are transcribed under MRFL in Table 3.15 and the schematic figure of Pattern M under MRFL is presented in Fig. 3.34.

The frequency curves of Houzhai tones are demonstrated in Fig. 3.35.

What is interesting is that Houzhai dialect has two slight falling tones; one is high slight falling, and the other is low slight falling. The phenomenon that two slight falling tones co-exist in one tonal system is quite scarce in the Chaoshan area. So Houzhai dialect has a very important typological significance in this regard.

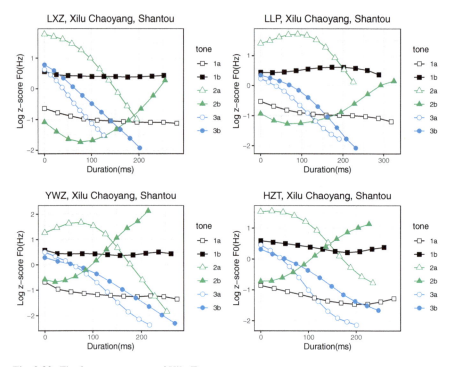

Fig. 3.32 The frequency curves of Xilu Town

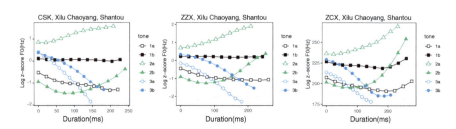

Fig. 3.33 Younger speakers's tonal system in Xilu dialect

(3) Pattern N: Falling-level-level-low-rising

Pattern N only occurs in Yun'ao, Shen'ao and Qing'ao towns of Nan'ao County. The corresponding rules and tones transcribed under MRFL are presented in Table 3.16 and the schematic figure of Pattern N under MRFL is presented in Fig. 3.36.

The frequency curves of these three towns are demonstrated in Fig. 3.37.
There are two prominent features of this pattern: first, the method of tonal merger, in which T2b merges into T3b; second, the tonal value of the MC tones in the

3.12 Three Other Patterns

Table 3.15 Houzhai tones transcribed under MRFL

Present category	MC tones	Tono-type	Tonal value
T1a	Yinping	High-level	55
T1b	Yangping	High slight-falling	54
T2a	Yinshang	High-falling	52
T2b	Yinshang, Yangshang, Yangqu	High-rising	35
T3a	Yinqu	Pure low tone	323
T3b	Yangqu	Low slight-falling	43

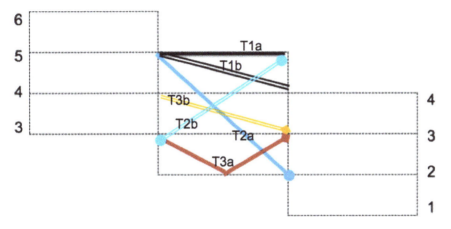

Fig. 3.34 Pattern M under MRFL

synchronic system, especially the value of T1b. These two aspects are the same with most Southern Min dialects in Fujian Province. This is not surprising. In the ancient past, Yun'ao, Shen'ao and Qing'ao all belonged to Fujian Province until the year of 1914, which can explain the similarities between Pattern N and the tonal patterns of Fujian Southern Min dialect (Committee for Nan'ao Chorography 2000: 717).

It is notable that T2a of Pattern N is significantly shorter than the other unchecked tones. Figure 3.38 plots the density curve of 23 Yun'ao speakers' total tokens' relative duration for illustrative purpose. There are 2822 tokens in total. Obviously, the relative durations of eight tones can undoubtedly be grouped into three patterns. The length distinctions between checked and unchecked tones are prevalent in most Southern Chinese dialect. What is unexpected is that T2a is significantly shorter than the other unchecked tones, making the tri-length distinction possible. However, referring to the contour of T2a, it is not uncommon. Slope may be a plausible candidate that is responsible for the different realization of duration. According to Rose (1981)

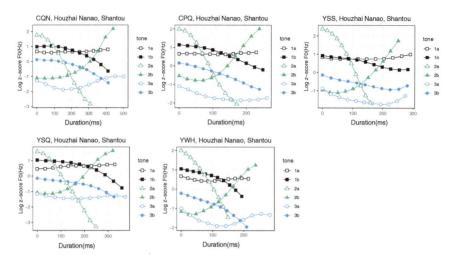

Fig. 3.35 The frequency curves of Houzhai Town

Table 3.16 Tones transcribed under MRFL, Patter N

Present category	MC tones	Tono-type	Tonal value
T1a	Yinping	Middle-level	44
T1b	Yangping	High rising	35/24
T2a	Yinshang	High-falling	52
T3a	Yinqu	Pure low tone	323/32/22
T3b/T2b	Yinshang, Yangshang, Yangqu	Low-level	33

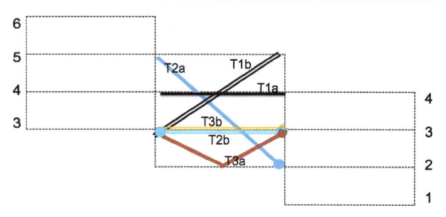

Fig. 3.36 Pattern N under MRFL

3.12 Three Other Patterns

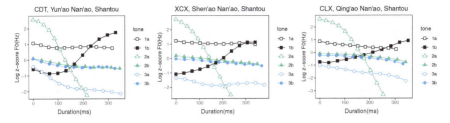

Fig. 3.37 The frequency curves of Pattern N

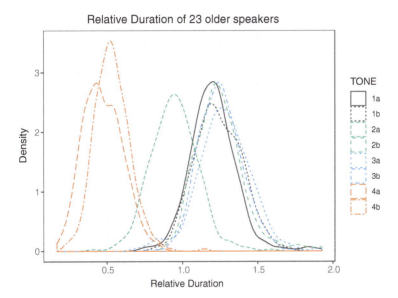

Fig. 3.38 The tri-length distinction of Yun'ao dialect

and Zhu (2005), in the tonal system of Wu dialects, it is very common that the falling contour is the shortest tone and rising contour is the longest one. Assuming there is a target at the concluding portion of the falling tone, plain falling with steeper falling movement reaches this target point faster, resulting in shorter duration of T2a than other unchecked tones.

3.13 Three Main Types: The Dialectical Classification of Chaoshan Chinese

According to the phonetic realizations of MC tones and the evolutionary route of tones, eleven tonal patterns (A through K) identified above can be grouped into three main types:

(1) Type one: Shanjie type, including Pattern A, Pattern B and Pattern C.
(2) Type two: Huipu type, including Pattern D, Pattern E, Pattern F, Pattern G and Pattern H.
(3) Type three: Chaoyang type, including Pattern I, Pattern J and Pattern K.

There are three major distinctive tonal patterns identified in this book, Shanjie type, Huipu type and Chaoyang type, respectively. The dialect locations of these three types are contiguous. In Pan and Zheng (2009), by taking the initial and final systems into account, the authors divide Chaoshan dialects into two sub-groups, namely Shantou sub-group (identical to Shanjie type here) and Chaopu sub-group (including Huipu type and Chaoyang type here). Figure 3.39 demonstrates the classification of Chaoshan dialects.

Pan and Zheng (2009)'s data include dialects from Shanwei city which are set aside in our book. Our research supports Pan and Zheng (2009)'s classification, but provides a refinement of Chaopu subgroup by dividing it into Huipu type and Chaoyang type.

The geographic distributions (or town) of these three types are shown in Fig. 3.40. In this book, around 78 towns (streets) or districts are investigated. Only those towns (streets) or districts that we have investigated are flagged.

Table 3.17 further shows the towns or districts belonging to each type and pattern.

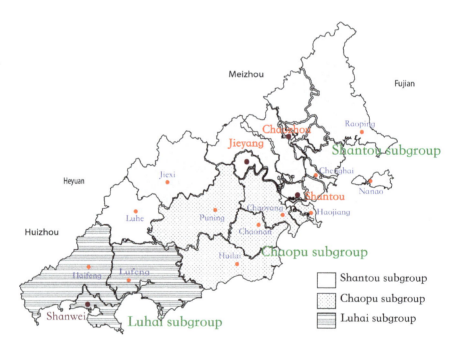

Fig. 3.39 The geographic distributions of the three tone types

3.13 Three Main Types: The Dialectical Classification of Chaoshan Chinese

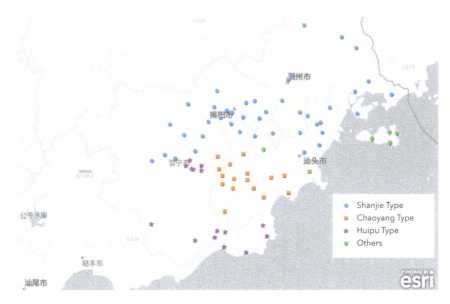

Fig. 3.40 The geographic distributions of the three tonal types

Shanjie type is the main type in the Chaoshan area, occurring in the downtown areas of Shantou, Jieyang and Chaozhou Cities. There are remarkable tonal uniformities among the three tonal patterns within Shanjie type. For example, four MC tones, Yangping, Yinshang, Yangshang and Yinqu, have the same phonetic realizations among the three tonal patterns (Pattern A to C) as shown in Table 3.18.

The different manifestations of MC Yinping and Yangqu can be explained by the variation of tones. Pattern A with three level tones is the starting point for Patterns B and C. Low level in Pattern A becomes low falling in Pattern B, and middle level in Pattern A becomes high slight rising in Pattern C. The reason behind this hypothesis is twofold: First of all, pattern A is the most prevalent pattern among Shanjie type. Secondly, it needs more effort to produce and perceive three level tones, so it is reasonable for us to postulate that the stage of three level tones is the initial stage in Shanjie type.

The most significant characteristic of Chaoyang type is that T2b and T3a have merged. Patterns I, J and K reflect the age differences in the Chaoyang area. Chaoyang type is the main type in Chaoyang and Chaonan districts, which we call the Chaoyang area.

Regarding Huipu type, different patterns within this type can be linked together by setting the starting point at Pattern G (the tonal system of the older speakers in Jinghai Town). The differences among Pattern D (such as Liusha dialect in Puning), E (Huicheng dialect as an example) and H (the tonal system of the younger speakers of Jinghai dialect) are due to the tonal changes motivated by the loss of the fortis voice; see Chap. 4 for more details. Huipu type mainly appears in Huilai County and Liusha District of Puning City.

Table 3.17 Districts and towns belonging to each pattern

Type	Pattern	Dialect points
First: Shanjie type	A: falling-level-level-level-low-rising	(1) Jieyang City: Meiyun Street (梅云街道), Xianqiao Street (仙桥街道), Ronghua Street (榕华街道), Sima Street (西马街道), Quxi Street (曲溪街道), Lancheng (蓝城区), Yuhu Town (渔湖镇), Didu Town (地都镇), Paotai Town (炮台镇), Dengang Town (登岗镇), Yunlu Town (云路镇), Yuecheng Town (月城镇), Xinheng Town (新亨镇), Mianhu Town (棉湖镇), Tatou Town (塔头镇), Nanxi Town (南溪镇), Hongyang Town (洪阳镇), Daba Town (大坝镇); (2) Shantou City: Xinxi Town (新溪镇), Guangyi Street (澄海广益街道), Fengxiang Street (凤翔街道), Shanghua Town (上华镇), Lianxia Town (莲下镇), Dongli Town (东里镇), Jinzao Town (金灶镇), Guanbu Town (关埠镇); (3) Chaozhou City: Anbu Town (庵埠镇), Dongfeng Town (东凤镇), Fuyang Town (浮洋镇), Haishan Town (海山镇), Fubin Town (浮滨镇);
	B: falling-falling-level-level-low-rising	(1) Shantou City: Jinping District (金平区); (2) Chaozhou City: Xiangqiao District (湘桥区), Jingzhou Town (井洲镇), Suocheng Town (所城镇), Huanggang Town (黄冈镇), Xinxu Town (新圩镇);
	C: falling-level-level-low-rising-rising	(1) Jieyang City: Lihu Town (里湖镇), Meitang Town (梅塘镇), Puqiao Distrct (普侨区); (2) Chaozhou City: Fenghuang Town (凤凰镇);
	D: falling-falling-level-low-rising-rising	Puning City in Jieyang City: Liusha North Street (流沙北街道), Chiwei Street (池尾街道), Liaoyuan Street (燎原街道), Yanchangpu Village in Zhanlong Town (占陇镇的延长埔村); Liusha East Street (流沙东街道), Xishe Village in Zhanlong Town (占陇镇的西社乡)
Second: Huipu type	E: falling-falling-level-low-rising	Older speakers in the central part of Huilai County in Jieyang City: Qianzhan Town (前詹镇), Shenquan Town (神泉镇), Huahu Town (华湖镇), Huicheng Town (惠城镇), Donglong Town (东陇镇), Longjiang Town (隆江镇), Kuitan Town (葵潭镇);

(continued)

3.13 Three Main Types: The Dialectical Classification of Chaoshan Chinese

Table 3.17 (continued)

Type	Pattern	Dialect points
	F: falling-level-level-low-rising	Younger speakers in the central part of Huilai County in Jieyang City: Qianzhan Town (前詹镇), Shenquan Town (神泉镇), Huahu Town (华湖镇), Huicheng Town (惠城镇), Donglong Town (东陇镇), Longjiang Town (隆江镇), Kuitan Town (葵潭镇);
	G: falling-falling-level-low-high	Older speakers in the eastern part of Huilai County in Jieyang City: Jinghai Town (靖海镇), Xian'an Town (仙庵镇);
	H: falling-falling-level-level-low	Younger speakers in Eastern part of Huilai County in Jieyang City: Jinghai Town (靖海镇), Xian'an Town (仙庵镇);
Third: Chaoyang type	I: falling-falling-falling-level-low	Older speakers[a] in (1) Shantou City: Xiashan Street (峡山街道), Lugang Town (胪岗镇), Liangying Town (两英镇), Longtian Town (陇田镇), Xiancheng Town (仙城镇), Chendian Town (陈店镇), Simapu Town (司马埔镇), Guiyu Town (贵屿镇), Gurao Town (谷饶镇), Tongyu Town (铜盂镇); (2) Puning City in Jieyang City: Nanjing Town (南径镇), Shanpu Village in Zhanlong Town (占陇镇的杉埔村);
	J: falling-falling-level-level-low	(1) Younger speakers in ① Shantou City: Xiashan Street (峡山街道), Lugang Town (胪岗镇), Liangying Town (两英镇), Longtian Town (陇田镇), Xiancheng Town (仙城镇), Chendian Town (陈店镇), Simapu Town (司马埔镇), Guiyu Town (贵屿镇), Gurao Town (谷饶镇), Tongyu Town (铜盂镇); ② Puning City in Jieyang City: Nanjing Town (南径镇), Shanpu Village in Zhanlong Town (占陇镇的杉埔村); (2) Older speakers in Jinpu Street (金浦街道), Miancheng Town (棉城镇), Haojiang District (濠江区);
	K: falling-falling-level-level-rising	Younger speakers in Jinpu Street (金浦街道), Miancheng Town (棉城镇), Haojiang District (达濠区); Haimen Town (海门)

[a]The age differences in type three are very complicated; so one dialect point may contain more than one tonal pattern

Table 3.18 The phonetic realizations of four MC tones in type one

MC tones	Present category	Phonetic realizations
Yangping	T1b	High-level, 55
Yinshang	T2a	High-falling, 52
Yangshang	T2b	High-rising, 25
Yinqu	T3a	Pure low tone, 323

It is generally acknowledged in Chinese dialectology that the sub-grouping boundaries often correspond with administrative boundaries (Zhou and You 1986: 52). However, in the Chaoshan area, even one single town may have more than one tonal pattern depending on the surrounding dialects. For example, Zhanlong (占陇) Town in Puning has demonstrated two tonal types, namely Huipu type and Chaoyang type.

3.14 The Tono-Types of MC Tones Within the Chaoshan Area

After describing all the above tonal patterns, we can further summarize the tono-types of each MC tone (except checked tones) from the perspective of typology. Table 3.19 shows corresponding rules between MC tones and their modern tono-types. One can refer to Appendix G for more detail about the tono-types of each tonal pattern.

Interestingly, except the dialects in Nan'ao County and the younger generations' tonal system in Guiyu Town, Yangping tone in the other sites is always realized as a level tone. And the phonetic manifestations of T2a in most dialects are high falling. Coming back to the question raised in Sect. 2.3.2, which tonal contour is more prevalent, level contour or falling contour? We still cannot answer this question by only using Chaoshan dialects investigated so far, since there are at least one falling tone and one level tone co-existing in each dialect. However, the rising tone and the pure low tone are not obligated in a tonal system, as shown by Pattern I and Pattern J.

Moreover, the process of the tonal merger varies with dialects in the Chaoshan area. To put it in a nutshell, there are at least four types of tonal merger in the Chaoshan area:

Table 3.19 The corresponding rules between tono-types and MC tone categories

MC tones	Present categories	Tono-types	Representative dialects
Yinping	T1a	(1) Middle level /44/	Rongcheng District, Jinping District, Xiangqiao District, etc.
		(2) High slight rising /45/	Liusha District, Fenghuang Town, etc.

(continued)

3.14 The Tono-Types of MC Tones Within the Chaoshan Area 69

Table 3.19 (continued)

MC tones	Present categories	Tono-types	Representative dialects
		(3) Low slight rising /34/	Huicheng Town, Kuitan Town, etc.
		(4) The pure low tone (the lowest falling) /32/	Lugang Town, Guiyu Town, etc.
		(5) Low falling /42/	Miancheng Town, Haimen Town, etc.
		(6) High level /55/	Houzhai Town
Yangping	T1b	(1) High level /55/	Rongcheng District, Jinping District, Xiangqiao District, Liusha District, etc.
		(2) Middle level /44/	Jinghai Town, Huicheng Town, etc.
		(3) Low level /33/	Lugang Town, etc
		(4) High rising /35/	Younger speakers in Guiyu Town, Yun'ao Town, etc.
		(5) High slight falling /54/	Houzhai Town
Yinshang[a]	T2a	(1) High falling /52/	Rongcheng District, Jinping District, Xiangqiao District, Liusha District, etc.
		(2) Deferred high falling /552/	Older speakers in Lugang Town, etc
		(3) High or middle level /55/ or /44/	Younger speakers in Lugang Town, Huicheng Town, etc.
		(4) High slight rising /45/	Younger speakers in Miancheng Town, etc.
		(5) High rising /35/	Younger speakers in Dahao District, etc.
		(6) Upper register high falling /64/	Older speakers in Jinghai Town
Yangshang	T2b	(1) High rising /35/	Rongcheng District, Jinping District, Xiangqiao District, Liusha District, etc.
		(2) Pure low /23/	Jinghai Town, Huicheng Town, etc.
		(3) Mid-short high falling /52/	Lugang Town, etc.
		(4) High falling /52/	Miancheng Town, etc.
		(5) Pure low (the lowest falling) /32/	Haimen Town
		(6) Low level /33/	Yun'ao, Shen'ao, and Qing'ao Town
		(7) Mid-short low falling /42/	Hongchang Town

(continued)

Table 3.19 (continued)

MC tones	Present categories	Tono-types	Representative dialects
Yinqu	T3a	(1) Pure low /323/	Rongcheng District, Jinping District, Xiangqiao District, etc.
		(2) The lowest falling /32/	Liusha District
		(3) Mid-short high falling /52/	Lugang Town, etc.
		(4) High falling /52/	Miancheng Town, etc.
		(5) Mid-short low falling /42/	Hongchang Town, Xilu Town
		(6) Low falling /42/	Jinghai Town, Xian'an Town
Yangqu	T3b	(1) Low level /33/	Rongcheng District, Yun'ao Town, etc.
		(2) Low falling /42/	Jinping District, Xiangqiao District, Liusha District, Lugang Town, Xilu Town, etc.
		(3) High falling /52/	Jinghai Town, Xian'an Town
		(4) Middle level /44/	Miancheng Town, etc.

[a] Some Cizhuo Initials (次浊声母) of the Yinshang tone have merged with the Yangshang tone, and some Yangqu tones also merged with the Yangshang tone. At present, we just deal with the main corresponding rules between MC tones and their modern categories, such as most of the Yinshang tones correspond with the present T2a.

(1) T3a = T3b in the central part of Huilai County;
(2) T2b = T3a in the Chaoyang area;
(3) T1a = T2b in Haimen dialect;
(4) T2b = T3b in Kuitan dialect of western Huilai County, and Yun'ao, Qing'ao, Shen'ao dialects in Nan'ao County.

References

Committee for Nan'ao Chorography. 南澳县地方志编纂委员会 (2000)《南澳县志》,中华书局, 北京。
Hong, Ying. Lam, Man Fong and Zhu, Xiaonong. 洪英 & 林文芳 & 朱晓农. 2013. Gurao Fangyan de Sige Jiangdiao 谷饶方言的四个降调. In *Festschrift in Honor of Professor William S-Y. Wang on his 80th Birthday*, ed. Shifeng, Penggang. 219–233. HongKong: City University Press.
Laver, J. 1994. *Principles of Phonetics*. Cambridge: Cambridge University Press.
Pan, Jiayi and Zheng, shouzhi. 潘家懿 & 郑守治. 2009. 粤东闽语的内部差异与方言片划分的再认识.语文研究, 03: 55–59.
Rose, Phil. 1981. An acoustical based phonetic description of the syllable in the Zhenhai dialect. Cambridge: University of Cambridge. (Doctoral dissertation).

References

Zhou, Zhenhe and You, Rujie. 周振鹤、游汝杰. 1986. 方言与中国文化. Fangyan yu zhongguo wenhua. 上海人民出版社.

Zhu, Xiaonong. 朱晓农. 2005. 上海声调实验录An Experimental Study of Shanghai Tones. 上海教育出版社 Shanghai: Shanghai Educational Press.

Zhu, Xiaonong. 朱晓农. 2012. 降调的种类[A classification of falling tones]. 语言研究, (02): 1–16.

Chapter 4
The Tonal Chain Shifts in the Huipu Area

Abstract This chapter deals with the tone evolutions in the Huipu area. Two tonal chain shifts are proposed to account for the diversified tonal patterns within this area. The V-shaped shift involving the downward shift of falling tones and the upward shift of rising tones, can explain the tonal development from Jinghai dialect to Liusha dialect. The downward chain shift of level tones is hypothesized to explain the age-related differences of Jinghai dialect. At the same time, tonal merger will serve as an obstacle to interrupt these tonal shifts, such as the case in central Huilai County where falling tone's downward shift is blocked by the merger of T3a and T3b.

Keywords V-shaped · Chain shift · Age-related differences · Geographic differences · Tonal merger

Chapter 4 through Chap. 6 are devoted to a detailed consideration of three case studies on tone evolution in the Chaoshan area. This chapter first deals with the great tonal chain shifts in Huilai and Liusha dialects.

The chain shift evolutions of consonants and vowels have long been a topic of heated debate in the literature (Grimm 1819; Jespersen 1949; Xu 1991; Labov 1994; Zhu 2005; Zhu and Cun 2006; Zhu and Jiao 2006). The first and second Germanic sound shifts are the best-known examples in the consonant domain. In vowel systems, the proto-type is the English Great Vowel Shift (Jespersen 1949: 231–247; Labov 1994: 145–154). Research on chain shift has focused mainly on consonants and vowels. Only a few acoustic studies have been carried out involving tones (Hirayama 1998; Zhu et al. 2008; Zhu and Yan 2009; Xu and Zhu 2011). In other words, the study on chain shifts concerned with tone and phonation is still in its infancy.

Moreover, we still know little about the way tonal changes occurred. In this chapter, based on firsthand acoustic data from twelve Southern Min varieties in Huilai County and Liusha District (hereafter, "the Huipu area"), we have identified two main tonal chain shifts, as well as the motive behind these changes. These two tonal chain shifts can account for the diversified tonal patterns (patterns D, E, F, G and H) in this area. The primary assumption of this chapter is that the various dialects within one area have the same proto-language. The synchronic differences of these dialects reflect the different stages of diachronic change from this proto-language.

The direction of natural tonal evolutions can be obtained from the synchronic variations within and among different speakers as well as different regional dialects (Labov 1975; Ohala 1987).

4.1 General Introduction to the Huipu Area

Armed with this evolutionary perspective, we now come to a discussion of the tonal development in the Huipu area. Huilai County is located in the southeastern part of Guangdong province, which borders Puning City and Chaonan District to the north and Lufeng City to the west, with the South China Sea to the southeast. The geographic distributions of the Huipu area are shown in Fig. 4.1.

As demonstrated in Chap. 3, five tonal patterns have been identified in the Huipu area. The tonal values of these patterns under MRFL are transcribed below in Table 4.1. These five patterns demonstrate strong correlation of tonal evolution.

Based on firsthand acoustic data from the 12 dialect sites shown in Fig. 4.1, we define the tonal patters in the Huipu area and spot their consecutive changes with perspective of evolution. Two kinds of chain shift are identified. One is the V-shaped chain shift that is consisted of the downward shift of falling tones and the upward shift of rising tones; the other is the downward shift of level tones. The V-shaped chain shift can explain the differences between Jinghai and Liusha dialects. Tonal

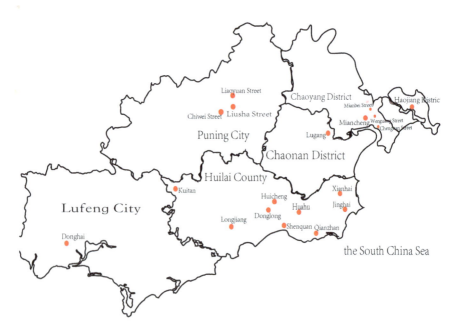

Fig. 4.1 The geographic distribution of Huipu dialects

4.1 General Introduction to the Huipu Area

Table 4.1 Various tonal patterns within the Huipu area

Patterns	Dialects	T1a	T1b	T2a	T2b	T3a	T3b
Pattern G	Older speakers in Jinghai Town	44	55	64	23	42	52
Pattern E1	Older speakers in Central Huilai County	34	44	52	22	42	42 (=T3a)
Pattern E2	Kuitan Town	34	44	52	323	42	323 (=T2b)
Pattern D	Liusha District	45	55	52	35	32	42
Pattern H	Younger speakers in Jinghai and Xian'an Town	33	44	55	323	42	52
Pattern F	Younger speakers in Central Huilai County	34	44	55	22	42	42 (=T3a)

merger will interrupt the V-shaped chain shift, resulting in different tonal patterns, such as Huicheng dialect. The downward shift of level tones can further explain age-related differences of Jinghai dialect.

For the sake of simplicity, we do not discuss checked tones for they are quite consistent in the Huipu area, with T4a at a lower pitch height and T4b at a higher pitch height. Please refer to Appendix D for detailed information of each informant presented in this chapter.

4.2 The Special Phonation in T2a

The tonal changes in the Huipu area can be explained by setting the starting point at the tonal system of the older speakers in Jinghai Town. The reasons why we regard the older speakers' tonal system in Jinghai as the starting point are two folds: first, the special fortis voice is only preserved in the older generations, while it is lost in the younger generations; and second, the synchronic variations of T2a among the older speakers in Jinghai reveal that T2a has a tendency to lose this special phonation, which may trigger subsequent tonal changes in the synchronic system. As illustrated in Fig. 4.2, T2a has various variations among different older Jinghai informants.

The pitch height of T2a is strikingly higher than that of the other unchecked tones. The average pitch range for the other five unchecked tones is 60–140 Hz; however, the average frequency range for T2a is 160–200 Hz. The bottom end of T2a is higher than the peak value of the other tones. This difference indicates that T2a may have some special phonation.

Laver (1994: 197) asserts that the top of the fundamental frequency range of falsetto is markedly higher than that of modal voiced phonation. Therefore, is it falsetto in this case? Hollien and Michel (1968: 602) report that the average pitch-range for male falsetto is 275–634 Hz, as against their estimate of 94–287 Hz for ordinary voiced phonation. The pitch value of three informants' T2a is far from

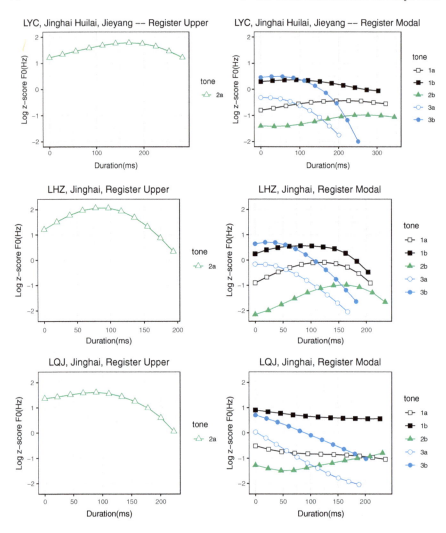

Fig. 4.2 Tonal systems of three older informants in Jinghai Town

this range, so it may not be appropriate to regard T2a as having falsetto phonation. According to Zhu (2010: 104–105), the fortis voice can result in higher pitch as well and it is frequently seen in Chinese dialects, like Wu and Xiang dialects. In addition, if we take the auditory impression of T2a into account, regarding T2a as possessing a fortis voice is a more plausible solution. Although fortis voice cannot independently define Register Upper, in the case of evolution, that is to say, when falsetto is weak or has already disappeared, strong fortis voice can still define Register Upper.

Comparing T2a and the high-level tone (T1b) in the synchronic system, we see that informant LYC produced T2a consistently higher than T1b, while the other

4.2 The Special Phonation in T2a

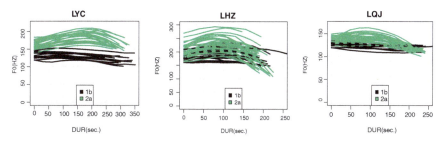

Fig. 4.3 Comparison of T2a and T1b of Jinghai older speakers

two informants (LHZ and LQJ) showed some overlap between T2a and T1b as demonstrated in Fig. 4.3.

Therefore, we set the tonal system of informant LYC as the initial tonal system because he steadily produced T2a at the highest pitch range with the fortis voice. On the contrary, the production of the fortis voice in T2a in the other two older speakers is not stable. They presented more variations of T2a, like deferred high falling {552} in informant LHZ (Fig. 4.2).

The above differences show that the fortis T2a is not stable and changing. Judging from the variants of T2a found among different older speakers, it is likely that T2a has a tendency to become a high-deferred falling tone {552}, and subsequently a high falling tone {52}. If T2a loses the fortis phonation and turns into a high falling tone {52}, it will become a homophone for T3b, which originally is a high falling tone. If these homophones are avoided, there will be other subsequent changes. This hypothesis has been testified in the central and western towns of Huilai County, as well as in Liusha District of Puning county-level City.

The diachronic developments in the central and western Huilai County as well as Liusha Distrcit are discussed in the following sections. We propose a V-shaped chain shift to account for the tonal development from Jinghai to Liusha. Howerver, tonal merger will block this chain shift, which has been spotted in the central and western Huilai County.

4.3 The Downward Chain Shift of Falling Tones

If T2a becomes a high falling tone in Register Modal, it will create pressure on T3b, the formal high falling tone. T3b has two copping methods: one is merging with T2a and maintaining itself as a high falling tone {52}; the other is to become a low falling tone {42}, causing pressure to the original low falling tone, namely T3a, in the system. What is happening in Huilai County is the second scenario.

What should we expect for how T3a may respond to the change of T3b? Likewise, there are two possibilities: one is for T3a to merge with T3b; the other is for T3a to become the lowest falling tone, creating pressure on the formal pure low tone. The

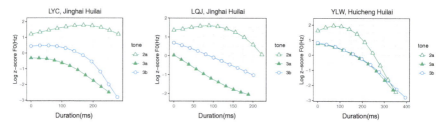

Fig. 4.4 Downward shift of falling tones, from Jinghai (first two pictures) to Huicheng (the third picture)

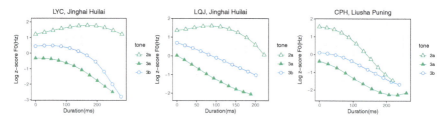

Fig. 4.5 Downward shift of falling tones, from Jinghai (first two pictures) to Liusha (the third picture)

first scenario happens in the central towns of Huilai county (Fig. 4.4) and the second scenario happens in Liusha District of Puning City (Fig. 4.5).

The downward chain shift of falling tones is a typical push chain, which involves three tonal categories, namely T2a, T3b and T3a. In scenario one, the downward shift is interrupted by the merger of T3a and T3b. However, in scenario two, when T3a becomes the lowest falling tone pushed by T3b, another chain shift will be initiated.

(1) Scenario One: T3b = T3a, From Jinghai to Huicheng (central town).
(2) Scenario Two: T3b ≠ T3a, From Jinghai to Liusha.

4.4 The Upward Chain Shift of Rising Tones

If T3a becomes the lowest falling tone, which is one of the phonetic manifestations of the pure low tone, it will create evolutionary pressure on the original pure low tone by pushing it to evolve to the low rising tone. T2b among different Liusha speakers displays various variations, including the lowest rising tone {23}, low rising tone {24} and high rising tone {35}. These variations may suggest that T2b is undergoing a change from the pure low tone to the rising tone.

When T3a becomes a pure low tone, it will create a "crowding" effect, and cause T2b {23} to move toward the rising tone {35}. This upward movement of T2b further pushes T1a to a higher position. These processes constitute the upward chain shift

4.4 The Upward Chain Shift of Rising Tones

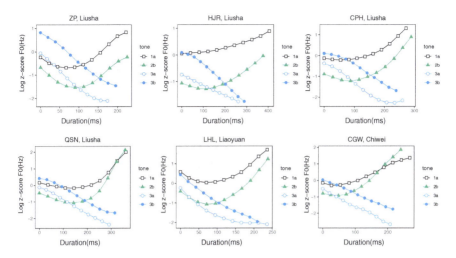

Fig. 4.6 The upward chain shift

of rising tones, which involves T3a, T2b and T1a. The pitch curves of T3a, T2b and T1a of Liusha dialect are shown in Fig. 4.6.

The tonal value of rising tones (T1a and T2b), can be determined by referring to the value of T3b {42} and T3a {32}. The evolutionary routes of T1a and T2b can be extrapolated based on synchronic variations among different speakers as illustrated below:

$$T2b: First stage : 323/23 \text{ in ZP}$$
$$\rightarrow \text{Second stage} : \{24\} \text{ in HJR}$$
$$\rightarrow \text{Third stage} : \{25\} \text{ in CPH}; \{35\} \text{in CGW}; /\{325\} \text{ in LHL and QSN}.$$
$$T1a : \{34\} \text{ in ZP} \rightarrow \{45\} \text{ in other informants}.$$

According to Zhu (2012), one single tonal system has one and only one pure low tone, for its tonal target is the lowest pitch regardless of any tonal contours. However, in the case of Liusha dialect, T3a as a pure low tone has a fixed tonal value, the lowest falling tone {32}, indicating its original contour—the low falling {42}. At first sight, the tonal system of informant ZP has two pure low tones, T3a {32} and T2b {323}, respectively. From the perspective of evolution, we can tell that a tonal system like informant ZP's will not be stable and will have subsequent changes as have happened with the other informants. Two pure low tones co-existing in one tonal system is just a transitional stage.

4.5 V-Shaped Tonal Shift

Base on the downward shift of falling tones and the upward shift of rising tones, we propose a V-shaped chain shift to account for the tonal development from Jinghai to Liusha dialects.

4.5.1 From Jinghai to Liusha

The tonal changes from Jinghai to Liusha involve two tonal chain shifts: the downward movement of falling tones and the upward movement of rising tones. They constitute a V-shaped tonal shift, which can explain the differences between the tonal systems of Jinghai and Liusha dialects. The average frequency curves of multiple informants from Jinghai and Liusha dialects are shown in Fig. 4.7.

The diachronic evolutionary route of tones can be determined by observing the synchronic variations in different speakers within one single dialect or among different dialects. Table 4.2 shows the different tonal values of Jinghai and Liusha dialects.

If we take the tonal system of Jinghai as the starting point, the changes of each tone from Jinghai to Liusha are shown below:

T2a: {64} → {552} → {52};
T3b: {52} → {42};
T3a: {42} → {32};
T2b: {23} → {24}/{25}/{35}.
T1a: {44}/{34}/ → {45};
T1b: unchanged.

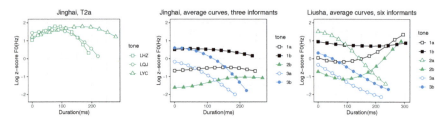

Fig. 4.7 The tonal systems of Jinghai (the first two pictures) and Liusha (the third picture)

Table 4.2 Tonal values of Jinghai and Liusha dialects transcribed under MRFL

	T2a	T3b	T3a	T2b	T1a	T1b
Jinghai	64	52	42	323/23	44	55
Liusha	52	42	32	24/25/35	45	55

4.5 V-Shaped Tonal Shift

The reasons why we assert that T1a is a low slight rising tone when T2b becomes a low rising tone are twofold: firstly, some informants still maintain the earlier stage of these tonal changes, such as ZP in Fig. 4.6, whose T2b is {323} and T1a is {34}; Secondly, in the central part of Huilai County, the tonal value of T1a is {34} too, suggesting that T1a in this area is undergoing a dynamic development of changing to low slight rising from middle level.

In Eastern Street of Liusha District, T1a is still a middle level tone (see Fig. 4.8) as that in Jinghai. The tonal system in Eastern Street is similar to pattern B, but its pure low tone is the same as that in pattern D, which is the lowest falling tone. Considering that two rising tones co-occurring in one tonal system is rare, we postulate that the tonal system of Eastern Street reflects the earlier stage of Liusha dialects.

Figure 4.9 shows the geographic distributions of different tono-types of T1a in the Huipu area.

The V-shaped tonal shift involves five tones (T2a, T3b, T3a, T2b and T1a), and the changes of each tone are summarized in Fig. 4.10. These processes are interrelated and can justifiably be identified as a push chain according to the sequence of these changes. The upper T2a first became a high falling tone, pushing T3b towards a low falling tone in order to avoid merger with T2a, and so forth. The assumption of the push chain is that gradual movement of sounds is necessary. Otherwise, there would exist the possibility of immediate merger after the initial step and the push chain would not arise.

This V-shaped tonal chain shift results from the diachronic change of Liusha tones, whose original tonal pattern as we suppose is like that in Jinghai. Just as pointed out in Labov (2001: 421), the changes that have the most profound effect and represent the main stream of linguistic evolution are not isolated shifts of single elements, but movements of one or more elements in a continuous direction. The V-shaped chain shift represents the main evolutionary route of tones from Jinghai to Liusha, which involves five tonal categories. The loss of fortis voice plays a significant role in

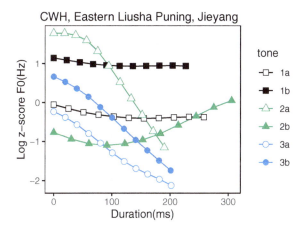

Fig. 4.8 The tonal system of Eastern Liusha Street

Fig. 4.9 The tono-types of T1a in the Huipu area

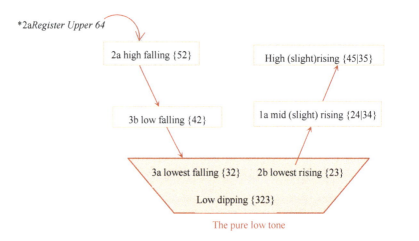

Fig. 4.10 The V-shaped tonal shift

initiating this shift by creating evolutionary pressure on the original high falling tone and pushing the revelant tones to change in an anticlockwise direction as shown in Fig. 4.10. Simply put, this V-shaped chain shift preserves the capacity of the tonemic system to make distinctions (Fig. 4.11).

4.5.2 The Significant Role of the Pure Low Tone

The downward shift of falling tones and upward shift of rising tones are connected by the pure low tone, which is the buffer area that allows different contours to co-exist with the same tonal target—the lowest pitch height. The lowest falling contour, the lowest rising contour and the low dipping contour are all phonetic manifestations of the pure low tone.

Zhu et al. (2012) discuss the typology of the dipping tone and further point out its possible paths of evolution. The dipping tone can become low falling, low rising, etc., indicating the close relations among these tono-types. The establishment of the pure low tone is of great typological significance. Its various pitch contours actually compose a phonetic continuum. These different contours (323/23/32/22) featuring with the lowest pitch height have the similar phonetic characteristics.

Theoretically, when the pure low tone is pushed by the falling tones, multiple solutions are possible, such as (1) exploiting special phonations like creaky, or (2) merging with the lowest falling tone, or (3) changing to the low rising tone to ease the tension from falling tones. What happens in Liusha dialect is exactly the third solution by changing to the low rising tone.

What is important from the perspective of evolution is that the pure low tone can evolve with a fixed contour that can alleviate the systematic pressure from other contours. For example, in the case of Huipu dialects, the evolutionary pressure comes from the falling tones, so the formal pure low tone takes the lowest rising tone {23} as its phonetic manifestation and further changes to low rising {24}. The pure low tone incorporates different contours and acts as a buffer region for the continuous change of contours in the lower pitch range. It serves as a transitional channel for the evolution of different tono-types.

4.5.3 More Chain Shift Evolutions of Tone in Chinese Dialects

The tonal V-shaped chain shift is not uncommon in Chinese dialects. In 1998, Hirayama Hisao (平山久雄) reported a tonal chain shift in Dezhou, Shandong Province. He claims in Hirayama (1998) that the tone sandhi forms of neutral tones reflect the earlier stage of citation tones of Dezhou dialect as shown in Table 4.3.

Table 4.3 Tonal values of Dezhou dialect

Position	T1b	T3a/T3b/T2b	T1a	T2a
Tone sandhi forms of neutral tones	55[a]	42	21	213
Citation tones	42	21	213	55

[a]Tones here are transcribed using the five-point scale model, just the same way used in the original paper.

It is assumed that the tonal values of the sandhi forms are the early forms for the citation tones. When T1b changes from 55 to 42, it will push T3a to change from 42 to 21, and then T1a from 21 to 213. T2a circles back to the high-level tone. Therefore, the chain shift in Dezhou dialect is circular. What is sure is that this is a V-shaped shift involving both falling tones and rising tones. However, it is a pity that we cannot delve into this chain shift because of the lack of phonetic data.

Recently, more tonal chain shifts have been identified in Tai language (Zhu et al. 2015) and Hakka dialects (Zhu and Li 2016). Different from the anticlockwise tonal shift in the Huipu area, the tonal chian shift in Tai language occurred in a clockwise direction. Moreover, tonal chain shifts with the direction of both anticlockwise and clockwise are spotted at the same time in Hakka dialects.

4.6 Non-natural Merger of Tones Due to Language Contact

We have discussed the V-shaped chain shift happens in the Huipu area. The assumption of our discussion is that the need to maintain contrast is the motivation behind this chain shift. However, tonal merger will interrupt this chain shift. This kind of tonal merger has been spotted in the central and western towns of Huilai County. This interruption happens in the downward movement of falling tones (Fig. 4.11).

As shown in Sect. 4.3, the process of the downward chain shift starts from the change of T2a. The sequence of this chain shift is T2a pushing T3b, and T3b further pushing T3a. If T3a stays unchanged, it is natural for T3b to merge with T3a for they have similar contour. This is what happens in central towns of Huilai county. Yet in a western town, Kuitan town, the direction of tonal merger is T3b merging into T2b. This is peculiar. With the pressure from T2a, T3b overpasses T3a whose pitch contour and pitch height are closer to it, and merges with T2b.

This unnatural tonal merger may be due to language contact. Kuitan borders Lufeng City, whose phonetic system is more similar to that of the Zhangzhou dialect in Fujian Province. One of the notable features of Lufeng (Donghai Town) tones is that T3b and T2b have merged (Pan and Zheng 2009; Xu 2010).

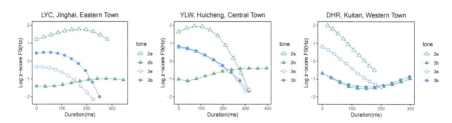

Fig. 4.11 Tonal merger in central (second picture) and western (third picture) towns of Huilai county

4.6 Non-natural Merger of Tones Due to Language Contact   85

Accordingly, the strategy of tonal merger adopted in Kuitan Town is more likely an interaction of internal evolutionary force and external language contact. The pressure from T2a on T3b is the internal force to impel T3b to change. If T3a stays unchanged, it is probably for T3b to merge with T3a. However, the external environment provides an additional choice for T3b's evolution, namely the direction of merging with T2b. Therefore, we prefer to take the view that the essential motive for the evolution of T3b in Kuitan town is internal linguistic factor; however, the method of tonal merger adopted in Kuitan town is confined to external factors.

In addition, the phenomenon that "voiced shangsheng merges into voiced qusheng" (浊上归去) is very common among Chinese dialects, including southern Min dialect in Fujian Province. It means that the direction of the merger of T2b and T3b is T2b moves into the position of T3b according to their historical origins. However, the Kuitan case provides us with another direction of the tonal merger of T2b and T3b. In Kuitan, T3b merges into T2b.

To put it in a nutshell, this case further sheds light on the evolution of languages. Language contact as an external factor may have potential impact on language evolution, so it cannot be set aside. Extensive treatments of the effects of contact on language change are available in Trudgill (1986), Kerswill (1993) and Williams and Kerswill (1999). However, it should be noted that language contact is not the fundamental factor; the essential element that triggers language change is still the internal evolutionary factor. I believe that phonetic motivation is the most fundamental factor in determining the direction of sound change. In the Huipu case, for example, the initial force of tonal changes is the loss of fortis phonation. Therefore, when considering the mechanism that underlies language change, we must combine both internal and external factors together.

4.7 The Downward Chain Shift of Level Tones

As is shown in the above sections, the evolution of T2a has triggered a series of chain shifts. The younger speakers of Jinghai have taken another strategy in which T2a has changed to a high-level tone, leading to a tonal pattern (Pattern H) different from that of the older speakers (Pattern G) as shown in Fig. 4.12.

The evolutionary route of T2a is shown below:

① upper register high falling {64}

→ ② deferred high falling {552}

→ ③ high level {55}

The determination of the second stage is based on the following two reasons: first is the inter-speaker variation: the older speaker (LQJ) has this variant {552} in his synchronic system; second is the intra-speaker variation: the younger speaker (SZX)

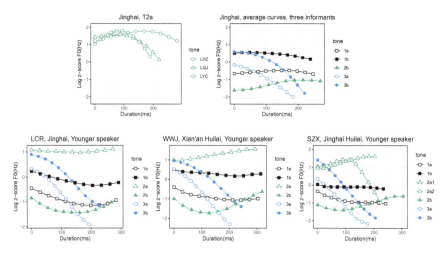

Fig. 4.12 Age-related differences in Jinghai Town

has two variations, namely {552} and {55}, in his system at the same time. This also suggests that the variations at community level manifests within individual level. The two variations (T2a1 {552} and T2a2 {55}) of T2a in SZX's tonal system are plotted in Fig. 4.13.

T2a's turning into a high-level tone will activate another tonal chain shift—the downward shift of level tones. If we take the pitch height of T3b {52} as the baseline, in the older generations, the starting point of T1b is the same as that of T3b {52}, while in the younger speakers, the starting point of T1b is lower than T3b {52} and is identical with that of T3a {42}. These different relationships are plotted in Fig. 4.14. This means that along with T2a's becoming a high-level tone, the former high-level tone (T1b) becomes a middle level tone, and the former middle level tone (T1a) becomes a low-level tone. These changes are demonstrated in Table 4.4.

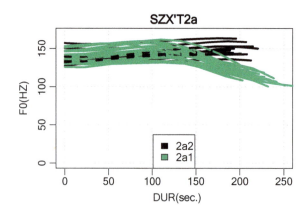

Fig. 4.13 The two variations of T2a of informant SZX

4.7 The Downward Chain Shift of Level Tones

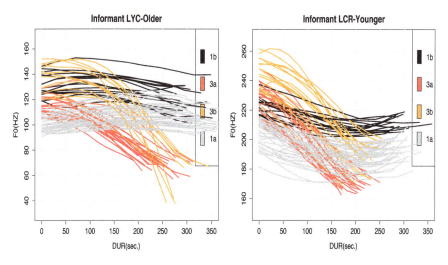

Fig. 4.14 The changes of T1b and T1a from older to younger speakers in Jinghai

Table 4.4 Downward tonal shift of level tones

Speakers	T2a	T1b	T1a	T3b	T3a	T2b
Older	**64**	**55**	**44**	52	42	23/323
Younger	**55**	**44**	**33**	52	42	23/323

From the older speakers to younger speakers, the tonal changes are summarized as below:

T2a: {64} → {552} → {55}.
T1b: {55} → {44}.
T1a: {44} → {33}.

4.8 The Further Development of T2a in Central Huilai County

Age-related differences also exist in central Huilai County, and the discrepancy rests on the phonetic manifestation of T2a. Figure 4.15 plots the frequency curves of eight informants from the central part of Huilai County. The tono-type of T2a in the older speakers' system is high falling /52/, while in their younger counterparts' system, the tono-type of T2a changes to high level /55/ or high slight rising /45/ (Fig. 4.15).

T2a in older speakers' tonal system is a high falling tone, while in the younger generations' system; it becomes a high-level tone. Moreover, some younger speakers produce T2a as a high slight rising tone. The potential evolutionary route of T2a in central Huilai County is summarized here:

(1) T2a is a high falling tone, older speakers

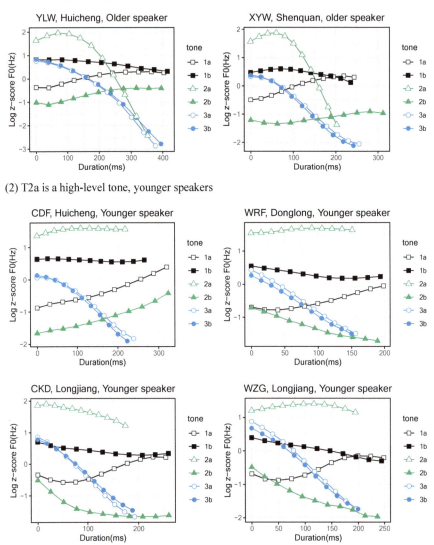

(2) T2a is a high-level tone, younger speakers

Fig. 4.15 Age-related differences in central Huilai County

① high falling /52/ → ② high level /55/ → ③ high slight rising /45/.

These three variations may sometimes co-exist in a single speaker's tonal system. One of the younger speakers in central Huahu Town consistently produces the first two variants of T2a during our investigations. Figure 4.16 plots his average frequency curves.

4.8 The Further Development of T2a in Central Huilai County

(3) T2a is a high slight rising tone, younger speakers

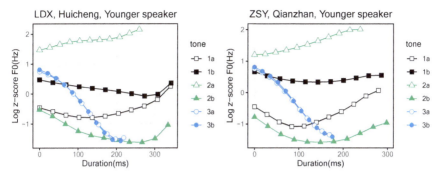

Fig. 4.15 (continued)

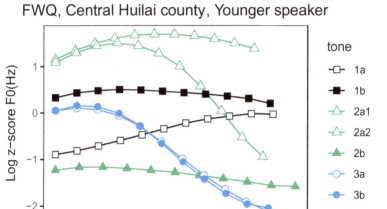

Fig. 4.16 Two variations co-existing in one single tonal system

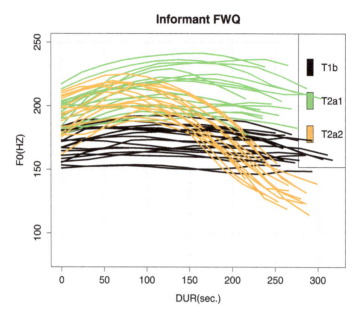

Fig. 4.17 The frequency curves of T2a's two variations

Taking T1b {44} as the baseline, the frequency distributions of two variants of T2a are shown in Fig. 4.17.

The two variations stand for different stages in T2a's change, which is a typical lexicon diffusion process. From an evolutionary point of view, it is of great importance that we spot different variations within one single system for it indicates the way of language change—through diffusion across lexicons (Wang 1969).

The evolutionary path of T2a is similar to what is happening in the Chaoyang area (discussed at more length in Chap. 5), suggesting the close relationship between the Huipu and Chaoyang areas. As noted in Chap. 3, T2a in most of the Chaoshan dialects manifests as high falling contour; however, in the Huipu and Chaoyang areas, they all have the innovation of T2a's changing to a high-level tone and subsequently a high slight rising and even high rising tone. This shared innovation is strong evidence that these two dialectical areas should be grouped together first, just as seen in the classification in Pan and Zheng (2009).

4.9 Summary

In this chapter, we have identified three tonal chain shifts that can account for the diversified tonal patterns in the Huipu area. At the same time, tonal merger will serve as an obstacle to interrupt these tonal shifts, such as the case in central Huilai County where falling tone's downward shift is blocked by the merger of T3a and T3b.

4.9 Summary

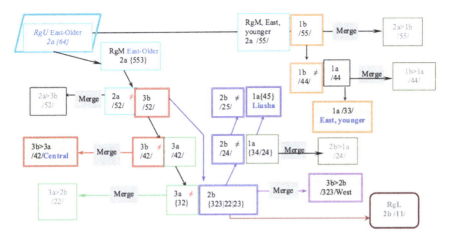

Fig. 4.18 The possible evolutionary routes triggered by the loss of fortis phonation in T2a

Theoretically, motivated by the loss of fortis phonation in T2a, the plausible routes of the subsequent changes are multiple. We have only discussed those that have been spotted in the Huipu area in the above sections. For the sake of completeness, Fig. 4.18 shows all the possible evolutionary results we can deduce.

What is worth noting is that the underlying assumption in Fig. 4.18 suggests that the mechanism behind tonal merger in the Huipu area is the similarity of pitch contours. This similarity provides a plausible solution for tackling the tonal developments of other Chinese dialects, especially Northern dialects. Cao (1998) explicitly asserts that the closeness of "tonal values" is the solo determinant factor for tonal merger in the case of Sui'an dialect. What he means by "tonal values" is actually tonal contour in his latter description. Nevertheless, the utility of this mechanism needs further verification from more dialects or languages.

Last but not least, the V-shaped tonal chain shift is of great typological significance. First of all, it reflects the diachronic development of Liusha tones from the original Jinghai type. Secondly, it sheds light on the evolution of tones by providing an anticlockwise tonal shift with detailed phonetic data. The tonal chain shifts proposed in this chapter can further serve as a reference for the prediction of tonal changes in other dialects or languages.

References

Cao, Zhiyun. 1998. Hanyu Fangyan Shengdiao Yanbian de Liangzhong Leixing 汉语方言声调演变的两种类型. *Yuyan Yanjiu* 语言研究. 1: 89–99.

Grimm, Jacob. 1819. Deutsche Grammatik (German Grammar). English version in Lehmann, Winfred P., eds. 1967. *A Reader in Nineteenth Century Historical Indo-European Linguistics*, 46–60. Bloomington: Indiana University Press.

Hirayama Hisao. 平山久雄. 1998. Cong Shengdiao Diaozhi Yanbianshi de Guandian Lun Shandong Fangyan de Qiangshengqian Biandaio. 从声调调值演变史的观点论山东方言的轻声前变调. Fangyan 方言1: 7–13.

Hollien, H., and J. Michel. 1968. Vocal fry as a phonational register. *Journal of Speech and Hearing Research.* 11: 600–604.

Jespersen, Otto. 1949. *A Modern English Grammar on Historical Principles: Part I—Sounds and Spelling.* Copenhagen: E. Munksgaard.

Kerwill, Paul. 1993. Rural dialect speakers in an urban speech community: The role of dialect contact in defining a sociolinguistic concept. *International Journal of Applied Linguistic* 3(1): 33–56.

Labov, W. 1972/1975. On the use of the present to explain the past. In *Proceedngs of the 11th International Congress of Linguist,* ed. L. Heilmann, 825–851. Bologna: Il Mulino.

Labov, W. 1972/1994. Principles of linguistic change: internal factors. Oxford & Cambridge, Mass.: Blackwell.

Labov, W., 1972/2001. *Principles of Linguistic Change.* Social Factors: Wiley.

Laver, J. 1994. *Principles of Phonetics.* Cambridge: Cambridge University Press.

Ohala, J.J. 1987. Sound change is drawn from a pool of synchronic variation. *Presented at the Symposium on The causes of Language Change, Do We Know Them Yet?* Norway: University of Troms.

Pan, Jiayi and Zheng, shouzhi. 潘家懿 & 郑守治. 2009. 粤东闽语的内部差异与方言片划分的再认识.语文研究, 03: 55–59.

Trudgill, Peter. 1986. *Dialects in Contact.* Oxford and New York: Blackwell.

Wang, William S-Y. 1969. Competing changes as a cause of residue. *Language* 45(1): 9–25.

Williams, Ann, and Paul Kerswill. 1999. Dialect leveling: Continuity vs. change in Milton Keynes, Reading and Hull. In *Urban Voice,* ed. P. Foulkes and G. Docherty, 141–162. London: Arnold.

Xu, Yue and Zhu, Xiaonong. 徐越 & 朱晓农. 2011. 喉塞尾入声是怎麼舒化的——孝丰个案研究 [How is the glottal stop softened? A case study of Xiaofeng rusheng]. *Zhongguo Yuwen* 中国语文 3: 263–270.

Xu, Fuqiong. 徐馥琼. 2010. A Phonological Study of Min Dialect in Eastern Guangdong. 粤东闽语语音研究. Ph.D. Thesis, Zhongshan University, Guangzhou.

Xu, Tongqiang 徐通锵. 1991. Bainian lai Ningbo Yinxi de Yanbian. 百年来宁波音系的演变. Yuyanxue Luncong 语言学论丛 16: 1-48.

Zhu, Xiaonong and Cun, Xi. 朱晓农 & 寸熙. 2006. 清浊音变圈: 兼论吴、闽语内爆音非出于侗台底层,《民族語文》3: 3–13.

Zhu, Xiaonong. Jiao, Lei. Yim, Chi Sing and Hong, Ying. 朱晓农 & 焦磊 & 严至诚 & 洪英. 2008. 入声演化三途. [Three ways of Rusheng sound change]. *Zhongguo Yuwen* 中国语文 4: 324–338.

Zhu, Xiaonong and Jiao, Nina. 朱晓农 & 焦妮娜. 2006. 晋城方言中的卷舌边近音[]——兼论"儿"音的变迁,《南开语言学刊》1: 33–39.

Zhu, Xiaonong. Lin, Qing and Pachaiya 朱晓农 & 林晴 & 趴差桠. 2015. 泰语声调的类型和顺时针链移. 民族语文. 4: 1–18.

Zhu, Xiaonong and Yan, Zhicheng. 朱晓农 & 严至诚. 2009. 入声唯闭韵尾的共时变异和历时演化: 香港粤语个案研究,《南方语言学》1: 34–44.

Zhu, Xiaonong. Shi, Defu and Wei, Mingying. 朱晓农 & 石德富 & 韦名应. 2012. 鱼梁苗语六平调和三域六度标调制. 民族语文, 4: 3–12.

Zhu, Xiaonong and Li, Fei. 朱晓农 & 李菲. 2016. 梅州客方言的双向声调大链移. [Bi-directional tonal shifts of Hakkas dialect]. 语文研究, 4: 1–8.

Zhu, Xiaonong. 朱晓农. 2005. 上海声调实验录 An Experimental Study of Shanghai Tones. 上海教育出版社 Shanghai: Shanghai Educational Press.

Zhu, Xiaonong. 朱晓农. 2010. 语音学. Phonetics: An Introduction. Beijing: Commercial Press.

Zhu, Xiaonong. 朱晓农. 2012. 降调的种类 [A classification of falling tones]. 语言研究, (02): 1–16.

Chapter 5
Tonal Changes in the Chaoyang Area

Abstract This chapter deals with the tonal development in the Chaoyang area, with a special focus on the change of T2a. The age-related differences and geographical variations can be accounted for by two tonal chain shifts: one is the groove chain shift of Yinshang (T2a), in which T2a has changed from a high convex falling tone to a high level tone (or middle level tone), and subsequently a rising tone; the other is the pull chain shift involving Yinping (T1a), Yinshang (T2a) and Yangqu (T3b), whose initiator is T2a. The direction of this pull chain shift is determined by the tonal variations of different speakers. The features of four falling tones are discussed on the basis of the firsthand acoustic data of 23 older speakers in the suburban area. We argue that slope is the main distinct feature of the two high falling tones, with length an important supplementary feature. The evolution trend of the four-falling-tone system in the Chaoyang area is towards the system with diversified pitch contours.

Keywords Groove chain shift · Pull chain shift · Slope · Age-related differences · Geographic differences

Cross-dialectical tonal comparisons have yielded several insights into the evolution of tones, like the case in the Huipu area. Chapter 4 depicts the evolution of tones in Huipu dialects and proposes two main tonal chain shifts (V-shaped tonal chain shift and the downward shift of level tones) to account for the diversified tonal patterns within this area. This chapter further deals with tonal development in the Chaoyang area, with a special focus on the change of T2a. Geographical variations as well as age-related differences will be observed for the inference of tonal changes in this area.

5.1 General Introduction to the Chaoyang Area

The Chaoyang area consists of three administrative districts in Shantou City, namely Haojiang, Chaoyang and Chaonan Districts. From the 1950s, most towns in these three districts were united in Chaoyang County. The official establishment of these three districts was announced in 2003.

Geographically speaking, Chaoyang and Haojiang Districts are the central areas and Chaonan District is a suburban area in terms of economic development and distance from Central Shantou City. Usually, linguistic variations found in the central area are deemed to be an indicator of future sound change, while variations found in the suburban area are thought to be more conservative forms (Labov 1972: 1–42, 1994: 43–72; Bailey et al. 1991).

The situation in the Chaoyang District is complicated. The two northern towns, Jinzao and Guanbu, display the same tonal patterns as the nearby Shanjie Type as shown in Chap. 3. These two towns border Rongcheng District of Jieyang City. Xilu Town has a tonal pattern different from the other towns as demonstrated in Sect. 3.12. Xilu is located in the transitional region between Shanjie Type and Chaoyang Type. The unique tonal system of Xilu may be due to its complicated geographic location and dialectical environment. For the sake of simplicity, these three northern towns, namely Jinzao, Guanbu and Xilu, will not be discussed in this chapter. Haimen town has similar initial and final systems with those dialects in other Chaoyang towns. In terms of the tonal pattern, it displays the same pattern too; however, with regard to the process of tonal merger, a difference emerges. T2b merged with T1a in Haimen, not T3a as that happened in other towns. Figure 5.1 below shows these tonal patterns in the Chaoyang area. The pitch curves are average data from multiple informants, with four informants from Haimen dialect and Xilu dialect, two informants from Guanbu dialect and one from Jinzao dialect.

In addition, Gurao, Guiyu and Tongyu towns in the western part of the Chaoyang District, are more closely related to other Chaonan towns in terms of linguistic

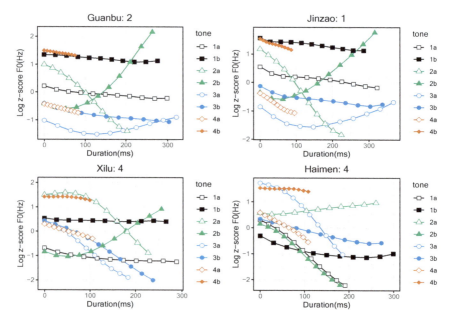

Fig. 5.1 Four tonal patterns distinctive from most Chaoyang dialects in the Chaoyang area

5.1 General Introduction to the Chaoyang Area

Fig. 5.2 Geographic distributions of towns and four tono-types in the Chaoyang area

system. Consequently, to be more specific, three western Chaoyang towns as well as towns in the Chaonan District will be regarded as the representatives of the suburban Chaoyang area, while Miancheng town in the Chaoyang District and Dahao Street in the Haojiang District will be viewed as the central Chaoyang area. The geographic distributions of towns in the Chaoyang area are shown in Fig. 5.2. The places signaled by red dots are the towns we have investigated.

In terms of informants, we recorded 98 informants (including the three northern towns and Haimen town) from the Chaoyang area. The distinction between older speakers and younger speakers lies in the production of T2a. Older speakers in the suburban Chaoyang area produce T2a as a high convex falling tone, while younger speakers produce T2a as a high-level tone. Older speakers in the central Chaoyang area produce T2a as a high-level tone, while younger speakers produce T2a as a high (slight) rising tone. Please refer to Appendix E (Chaoyang type dialect) for more details.

5.2 Changes in the Production of T2a in the Chaoyang Area

Our pool of data differs from those of previous studies in that it contains firsthand acoustic materials from a wider geographic area and covers variations from different age groups. Variations observed among the younger speakers are usually linked to sound change in a latter stage, and similarly, variations found in the central area (economically more developed region) are often thought to represent sound change in a latter stage of development. Following this line of reasoning, the change of T2a in the Chaoyang area can be inferred from age variations and geographic variations.

Maintaining the contrast of four falling tones is relatively rare, so it was very startling when scholars first reported that there were four falling tones co-existing in Gurao dialect (Jin and Shi 2010). Hong et al. (2013) further delve into this phenomenon and argue that length and phonation are key factors in the contrast of these four falling tones of Gurao dialect (which is spoken in the suburban Chaoyang area). Younger speakers no longer maintain the contrast of four falling tones. Their T2a has changed to a high-level tone. Therefore, in the following section, we intend to probes the dynamic evolution of T2a in the perspective of synchronic variations, particularly the age-related differences and the regional differences.

5.2.1 Age-Related Differences Parallel with Geographic Variations

In our recent investigations, younger speakers in the suburban Chaoyang area, including Gurao town, only have three falling tones in their tonal system. Figure 5.3 plots an example of age-related differences based on normalized data from Lugang dialect in Chaonan District.

In the system of the older speakers in the suburban Chaoyang area, four falling tones are densely distributed in the tonal space and only one level tone occurs among

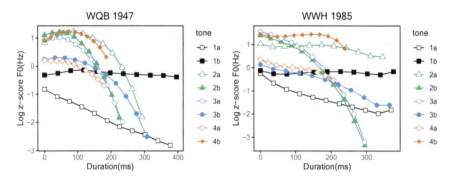

Fig. 5.3 Age-related different tonal systems in Lugang dialect, suburban Chaoyang area

5.2 Changes in the Production of T2a in the Chaoyang Area

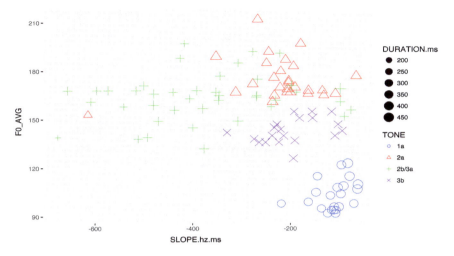

Fig. 5.4 Tonal acoustic space of four falling tones, older speakers

five unchecked tones. T1b is the only non-falling tone. The four falling tones in the older speakers' tonal system are T1a, T2a, T2b/T3a and T3b. Under the model of "Tonal Acoustic Space" (Shen 2016), average pitch, slope and duration are sufficient for the contrast of them. The acoustic space of the four falling tones produced by Lugang older speakers (Informant WQB 1947) is shown in Fig. 5.4.

The contrast of four falling tones produced by other older speakers in the suburban Chaoyang area is demonstrated in Fig. 5.5 for illustrative purposes. For instance, length is not explicitly exploited by informant WHS (the first graph) compared with the notable difference of duration produced by other speakers.

There are multiple phonetic cues to distinguish these four falling tones.

(1) Average pitch height: Average pitch height is sufficient to separate T1a and T3b. T1a occupies the lower pitch range while T3b is in the middle part. T2a occupies the highest part of the pitch range, while T2b/3a is slightly lower. These two tones' ranges of height overlap greatly.

(2) Duration: Hong et al. (2013) for the first time put the emphasis on the length dimension to differentiate T2a and T2b/3a. It has long been acknowledged that many languages utilize contrastive length as a phonological property of either or both consonants and vowels (Laver 1994: 436). However, regarding the tonal distinction, length is seldom regarded as a distinctive feature until in the model of MRFL (Zhu 2010). The examples of contrastive length in tones are also rare. Therefore, the length difference of tones in the Chaoyang area has important typological significance.

(3) Pitch contour (slope): With regard to the contour, T2b/T3a is a high plain falling tone, and T2a is a high convex falling tone. The higher pitch height of T2a may result from its apparent convex trajectory.

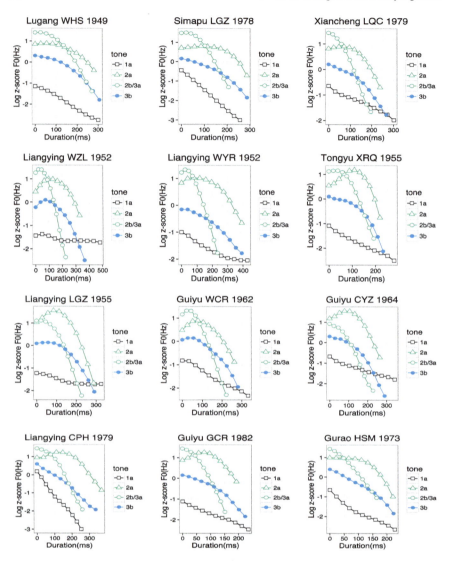

Fig. 5.5 The contrast of four falling tones in the group of older speakers in the suburban Chaoyang are

We use Anova calculated in R-studio to see whether 23 older speakers in urban Chaoyang dialect display significant differences between T2a and T2b/3a in terms of duration and slope. The result is shown in Table 5.1.

In Table 5.1, NS means non-significant, while * denotes statistical significance and *** means high statistical significance just as the significance codes imply. Statistical results show that slopes between T2a and T2b/3a produced by 23 older speakers all have significant difference, while 22 speakers display significant difference in terms

5.2 Changes in the Production of T2a in the Chaoyang Area

Table 5.1 Anova test on duration and slope between T2a and T2b/3a produced by 23 older speakers in urban Chaoyang

Informants	Duration	Slope	Interaction between duration and slope	Informants	Duration	Slope	Interaction between duration and slope
WQB	*** p = 5.41e−14	*** p = 3.09e−05	*** p = 1.25e−07	WHS	NS p = 0.143	*** p = 1.34e−12	*** p = 6.22e−13
WXS	*** p < 2e−16	*** p = 3.53e−05	*** p = 1.11e−13	WZL	*** p < 2e−16	*** p < 2e−16	*** p < 2e−16
LGZ-Liangying	*** p = 1.56e−13	*** p = 1.23e−08	*** p = 6.81e−16	WXQ	*** p < 2e−16	*** p < 2e−16	*** p < 2e−16
LGZ-Simapu	*** p < 2e−16	*** p < 2e−16	*** p < 2e−16	LQC	*** p = 1.78e−13	*** p < 2e−16	*** p < 2e−16
ZHJ	*** p < 2e−16	*** p = 9.19e−14	*** p < 2e−16	ZWJ	*** p = 5.25e−15	*** p = 4.71e−15	*** p < 2e−16
HSM	*** p < 2e−16	*** p < 2e−16	*** p < 2e−16	WSB	*** p = 0.000175	*** p = 8.5e−09	*** p = 7.07e−11
CPL	*** p < 2e−16	*** p < 2e−16	*** p < 2e−16	XRQ	*** p = 2.51e−08	*** p < 2e−16	*** p < 2e−16
WCR	*** p = 3.42e−07	*** p < 2e−16	*** p < 2e−16	CYZ	*** p = 9.57e−14	*** p = 1.23e−11	*** p = 1.96e−15
GHL	*** p < 2e−16	*** p = 6.72e−12	*** p < 2e−16	GCR	*** p = 7.72e−10	*** p < 2e−16	*** p < 2e−16
WLY	*** p < 2e−16	*** p < 2e−16	*** p < 2e−16	WYR	*** p < 2e−16	*** p < 2e−16	*** p < 2e−16
CPH	*** p < 2e−16	*** p < 2e−16	*** p < 2e−16	HSQ	*** p < 2e−16	*** p < 2e−16	*** p < 2e−16 lePara>
CYM	*** p < 2e−16	*** p < 2e−16	*** p < 2e−16				

(Significance level: 0.05; Significance codes: 0 '***' 0.001 '**' 0.01 '*' 0.05 '.' 0.1 ' ' 1)

of duration (except informat WHS). At the same time, the interactions between duration and slope all show significant difference among 23 older speakers. That means that slope is the most pivotal facter in distinguishing T2a and T2b/3a, while duration is an accompanying facter.

Normalized data in Fig. 5.3 clearly show that T2a has changed from a high convex falling tone to a high-level tone with decreasing age. Figure 5.6 plots the tonal acoustic

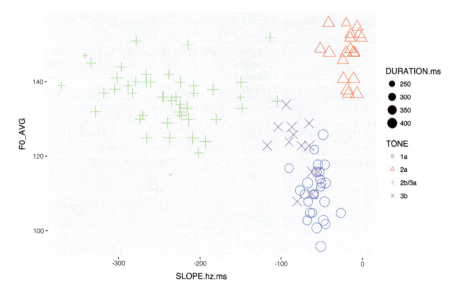

Fig. 5.6 Slope being the primary cue to the distinction of T2a and T2b/3a in younger speakers

space of the relevant four tones in the system of one younger speaker (Informant WWH 1987).

The pitch trajectories of these four tones produced by other younger speakers are shown in Fig. 5.7.

In the suburban Chaoyang area, slope has a tendency to increase with the decrease of age. The average slopes of T2a produced by 17 informants are plotted in a scatter diagram to show this tendency and the result is demonstrated in Fig. 5.8. In fitting a curve to the data, the best fit proved to be that for a quadratic equation ($R^2 = 0.612$), indicating that the relationship between slope and year of birth is non-linear (cf. the R^2 of 0.5966 for a linear regression).

The age effect shown in Fig. 5.8 suggests a change in apparent time; and also provides support for the claim that generational differences mirror diachronic developments in a language (Labov 1972: 1–42, 1994: 43–72; Bailey et al. 1991; among others). Slope becomes the primary cue for the distinction of T2a and T2b/3a in the group of younger speakers. As slope has been increasingly informative in distinguishing between these two tones, length may have become less informative for their distinction. The above speculation is confirmed by the fact that length of T2b/3a in younger speakers overlaps greatly with other unchecked tones compared with that in the system of older speakers as demonstrated in Fig. 5.9.

The density curves of seven tones illustrate the distribution of relative durations from 23 older speakers (4880 tokens) and 19 younger speakers (3989 tokens). At the same time, Anova test is conducted in R studio to see how 19 younger speakers distinguish T2a and T2b/3a in terms of duration and slope and the result is demonstrated in Table 5.2.

5.2 Changes in the Production of T2a in the Chaoyang Area

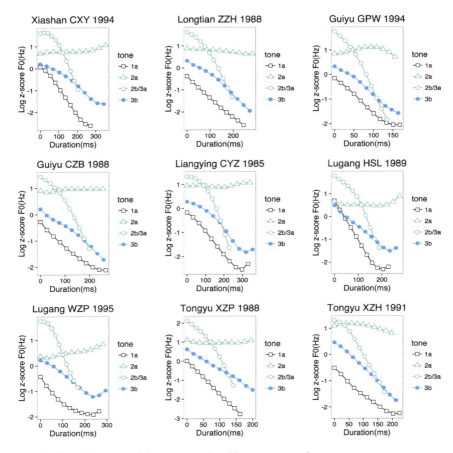

Fig. 5.7 The pitch curves of four tones produced by younger speakers

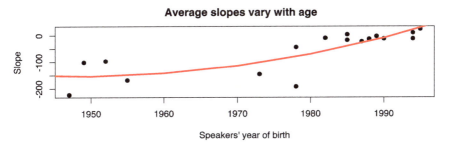

Fig. 5.8 Scatter plot of slopes that vary with age in Chaonan District

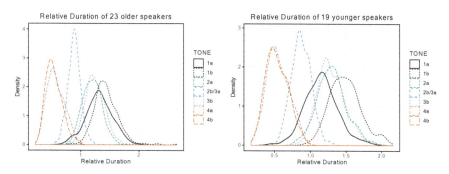

Fig. 5.9 Relative duration of seven tones produced by 23 older speakers and 19 younger speakers

Table 5.2 Anova test on duration and slope between T2a and T2b/3a produced by 19 younger speakers in urban Chaoyang

Informants	Duration	Slope	Interaction between duration and slope	Informants	Duration	Slope	Interaction between duration and slope
WWH	*** p = 1.95e–08	*** p < 2e–16	*** p < 2e–16	WZP	*** p < 2e–16	*** p < 2e–16	*** p < 2e–16
ZZH	*** p < 2e–16	*** p < 2e–16	*** p < 2e–16	XZP	*** p < 2e–16	*** p < 2e–16	*** p < 2e–16
LZJ	*** p = 9.85e–10	*** p < 2e–16	*** p < 2e–16	XZH	*** p = 5.61e–06	*** p < 2e–16	*** p < 2e–16
CZHB	*** p < 2e–16	*** p = 5.75e–15	*** p < 2e–16	CZB	*** p < 2e–16	*** p < 2e–16	*** p < 2e–16
GZY	*** p < 2e–16	*** p < 2e–16	*** p < 2e–16	GPW	*** p = 7.21e–10	*** p < 2e–16	*** p < 2e–16
HSL	*** p < 2e–16	*** p < 2e–16	*** p < 2e–16	WWL	*** p < 2e–16	*** p < 2e–16	*** p < 2e–16
WWX	*** p < 2e–16	*** p < 2e–16	*** p < 2e–16	CYZ	*** p < 2e–16	*** p < 2e–16	*** p < 2e–16
LZQ	*** p < 2e–16	*** p < 2e–16	*** p < 2e–16	CXY	*** p < 2e–16	*** p < 2e–16	*** p < 2e–16
LMN	*** p < 2e–16	*** p < 2e–16	*** p < 2e–16	CSJ	*** p < 2e–16	*** p < 2e–16	*** p < 2e–16
MYH	*** p < 2e–16	*** p < 2e–16	*** p < 2e–16				

(Significance level: 0.05; Significance codes: 0 '***' 0.001 '**' 0.01 '*' 0.05 '.' 0.1 ' ' 1)

5.2 Changes in the Production of T2a in the Chaoyang Area

Statistical results in table 5.2 reveal that 19 younger speakers all show significant difference in terms of duration, slope and the interations between duration and slope. It means that younger speakers still preserve the tri-length distinction; the checked tone is the shortest one and T2b/3a is the middle short tone. It is very common that different contours of tones result in different lenghth of tones. Rose (1981) and Zhu (2005: 215–216) have reported that the falling tone is the shortest tone in Wu dialect and while rising tone is the longest one. Although the younger speakers do not suspend the length distinction between T2a and T2b/3a, they tend to minimize such differences. Slope has taken the role of marking the distinction of T2a and T2b/3a. After all, the perception of different slopes is more straightforward.

To sum up, length is an important cue functioning at the phoneme level to separate T2a from T2b/3a for older speakers, while younger speakers do not rely on the length to distinguish T2a and T2b/3a. Slope is a more primary cue for the contrast of T2a and T2b/3a in the younger speakers' system.

With regard to the tonal systems in the central Chaoyang area, Miancheng dialect shows three tonal patterns according to different age groups. Our sample of data has five speakers who are above the age of 65 in Miancheng Town; and three of them's tonal systems still preserve the same pattern as that of the older speakers in Lugang dialect (suburban area). In the system of the other older Miancheng speakers, T2a has changed to a middle-level tone, which can be deemed as a latter development compared with the high convex falling contour in suburban Chaonan District. Moreover, T2a in younger generations from Miancheng dialect has undergone subsequent change. The age-based tonal differences of Miancheng dialect are demonstrated in Fig. 5.10.

Clear acoustic differences among generations provide evidence for diachronic sound change in the tonal systems of the Chaoyang area. Based on the age variations in the suburban and central part of the Chaoyang area, the direction of T2a's change can be determined. Three tentative stages of this change are summarized below:

① High convex falling > ② High level / middle level > ③ Rising

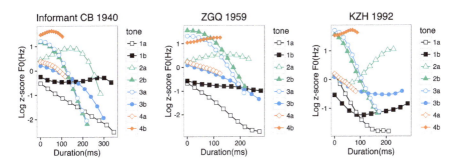

Fig. 5.10 Age-related tonal difference in Miancheng dialect

If the tendency of sound change observed along the dimension of age variation is parallel with that inferred from the geographic variation, then the degree of plausibility of the sound change in question is undoubtedly high. The change of T2a belongs to this type, in which the differences among age groups have analogs in differences among geographic varieties.

Simply put, inferences of tonal change from geographical variations and age variations are parallel and analogous in the Chaoyang area.

5.2.2 A Perceptual Experiment on T2a of Lugang Dialect

As can be seen from Sect. 5.2.1, T2a has changed to a high-level tone in the tonal system of younger speakers. How will younger speakers respond to the two high falling tones (T2a and T2b/3a) produced by their older counterparts? An identification test is designed to answer the following question: Will younger speakers categorize T2a produced by older speakers into the category of T2b/3a of their own systems?

As a pilot study, only two younger speakers (informants WWH and WWX) participated in this perceptual experiment. They are native Lugang speakers. We will recruit more informants to join in our perception experiment in the future. To avoid the unnaturalness of the synthesized sounds, we used the natural sound produced by informant WQB from Lugang dialect. Six groups of stimuli produced by WQB were chosen for this experiment. Syllables in each group are segmentally identical but different in tone. The order of syllables in each group was randomized and played six times by OpenSesame. Stimuli of each group are shown in Table 5.3.

The above six groups were conducted separately. The experiment for each group was repeated twice. The participants listened to the syllables within each group and were required to decide which one he or she was hearing by pressing the corresponding number as shown in Fig. 5.11.

Two participants were first familiarized with the experiments by the introduction of the author and then several exercises were performed before the experiment. Two participants consistently attributed T1a, T1b, T2b/3a, T3b and T4a produced by older speakers to their corresponding numbers; however, with regard to T2a, the results

Table 5.3 Stimuli for the perceptual experiment on T2a

Groups	T1a	T1b	T2a	T2b/3a	T3b	T4a
1: ku	龟	/	久	舅	旧	骨
2: si	诗	时	死	四	视	薛
3: taŋ	东	/	党	重	洞	/
4: ti	低	池	抵	弟	地	滴
5: to	刀	逃	短	在	袋	桌
6: tu	猪	橱	赌	著	箸	/

5.2 Changes in the Production of T2a in the Chaoyang Area

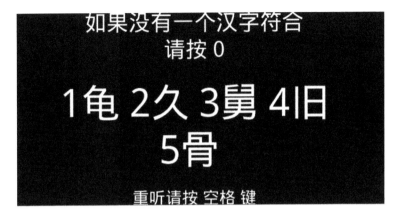

Fig. 5.11 Demo: Identification test

Table 5.4 Identification results of T2a for each group

Group	WWH			WWX	
	T2a	T2b	T3b	T2a	T2b
1: ku 久舅	0	6	0	6	0
	2	4	0	3	3
2: si 死	6	0	0	6	0
	6	0	0	6	0
3: taŋ 党	6	0	0	6	0
	6	0	0	6	0
4: ti 抵弟	0	4	2	0	6
	1	5	0	0	6
5: to 短	6	0	0	6	0
	6	0	0	6	0
6: tu 赌	6	0	0	6	0
	6	0	0	6	0

are quite interesting. Results of the two sections for each group are shown in Table 5.4.

In the groups of "si", "taŋ", "to" and "tu", two participants both chose correctly. Younger speakers WWH and WWX do not show preference in regarding T2a produced by older speakers as T2b/3a except in the group of "ku" and "ti". However, in the group of "ku" and "ti", two participants both made mistakes by assigning some of the T2a tokens as T2b/3a. By communicating with informants, the reason for "ti 抵" to be recognized as "弟" and "ku久" to be recognized as "舅" may be due to the relatively high frequency use of these kinship terms.[1]

---

[1] Such insights are inspired by the conversations with the informants.

It is not surprising that the younger speakers do not categorize T2a produced by older speakers into their T2b/3a since the change of T2a does not cause any trouble for communication within the whole community. From our communication with the local younger speakers, we can see that they generally believe that they share the same tonal system with the older speakers. Therefore, there should exist certain similarities between T2a produced by the older speakers and those produced by the younger speakers. The higher pitch height may be a plausible candidate. T2a in the older speakers' system is a high convex falling tone. The pitch curve of T2a usually has an apparent bulge in the middle part, or there is an apparent level portion before the pitch curve goes down. Examples are shown in Fig. 5.12, and the horizontal lines and arrows mark the bulge or level portion of the syllables.

The bulge or the level portion in the front or middle part of the T2a syllables helps the younger speakers to correctly identify them as T2a in the experiment. The longer

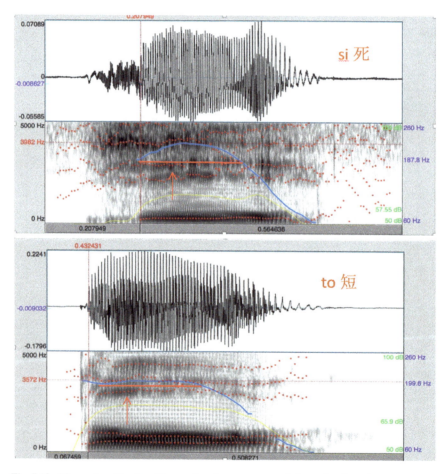

Fig. 5.12 T2a produced by the older speakers has an apparent bulge or level portion

the bulge or the level portion is, the higher T2a's overall pitch height is. Therefore, on the basis of the perception of the salient bulge or level portion, the younger speakers can identify the T2a stimuli as the highest one in the system and assign them to the correct category. This result also suggests that some cues, like high pitch, provide more information about the perceptual identity of a tone. That T2a has this kind of bulge or level portion is very prevalent among the older speakers in Chaonan District. This can be seen from Fig. 5.5. The experimental result also confirms that the convex contour or the higher pitch height of T2a makes it very distinct from its T2b/3a counterparts.

In a nutshell, by conducting this perceptual experiment, we seek to understand how the younger speakers respond to T2a produced by the older speakers. Younger speakers can partially recognize T2a in this experiment. This result indicates that T2a produced by the older generations is similar to that produced by their younger counterparts. This similarity is probably the higher pitch height. The perception of the higher pitch is achieved by the salient bulge or level portion in the front part of the T2a syllables.

5.2.3 Listener as an Initiator in Tonal Changes

As demonstrated above, listeners take an active role in tonal evolutions. They are capable of distinguishing tones with subtle differences, but at the same time, they can ignore some notable features.

In the Lugang case, the final falling part of T2a in the production of older speakers is absent in the production of younger speakers. Younger speakers probably regard this final falling glide as a result of returning to the speaker's original pronunciation state (an inert middle level position, requiring the least articulatory effort), and not a linguistic target. The perceptual result in Sect. 5.2.2 can partially serve as an evidence for our suggestion that younger speakers regard the high-level portion as the sole target of T2a. Therefore, when younger listeners turn into speakers, they will, at their most careful, pronounce T2a as a high-level tone.

The mechanism underlying this change is called "hyper-correction" in Ohala (1981). Implementing the rules when they are not called for is "hyper-correction". The younger speaker applies the rule of eliminating the non-target portion at the end of the syllable, thus restoring the form that he or she thinks he or she has heard. However, this rule is not called for in the perception of T2a produced by older speakers. This is because the falling part is actually part of the older speaker's intention and is a linguistic target at which older speakers aim.

T2a syllables are perceived as a high-level contour plus a naturally falling part at the end, and when listeners turn into speakers, they will carefully avoid this falling at the concluding part of the syllables. Consequently, the new tonal representation of T2a emerges. That is to say, a tonal change has occurred among the younger speakers. At first, this kind of change may involve only one younger listener-speaker, and then spread among the whole younger community as we observe at present. It seems that

Table 5.5 Tonal values of Miancheng dialect under MRFL

Speakers	T2a	T3b	T1a	T1b	T2b/3a
Older	44	42	32	33	53
Younger	45	44	42	33	53

reducing the number of falling tones from four to three will ease the perception of falling tones.

To sum up, this section provides phonetic evidence for T2a's change. The social and perceptual factors of this change are closely examined to give a plausible explanation for this change. The multiple variations within and across speakers and dialects suggest that this is a change in progress.

5.3 The Chain Shift of Tones in Miancheng Dialect

If we compare the tonal systems of the older speakers and the younger speakers in Miancheng dialect, a tonal chain shift can be identified.

5.3.1 *Tones Involved in the Chain Shift*

Table 5.5 gives the tonal differences of unchecked tones from different age groups of Miancheng dialect. If we take the system of the older generations as the earlier stage of Miancheng dialect, its change to the latter stage presented by the younger generation can be accounted for by a series of changes that involve three tonal categories, namely T2a, T3b and T1a.

The tonal acoustic space of Miancheng tones produced by one older speaker and one younger speaker are demonstrated in Fig. 5.13.

5.3.2 *A Pull Chain or a Push Chain?*

The changes of T2a, T3b and T1a constitute a chain shift and can be summarized as follows: 32 → 42 → 44 → 45. What kind of chain shift is it, a pull chain or a push chain? Essentially, before answering this question, we need to find out where the chain starts. If /44/ changes to /45/ first, opening up a space at the position of /44/ which /42/ then moves to fill, and the place of /42/ in turn is filled by /32/, then the chain shift is a pull shift.

On the contrary, if /32/ invades the territory of /42/, creating a pressure on /42/ and causing /42/ to move toward /44/ before the two sounds merge into one, and so forth,

5.3 The Chain Shift of Tones in Miancheng Dialect

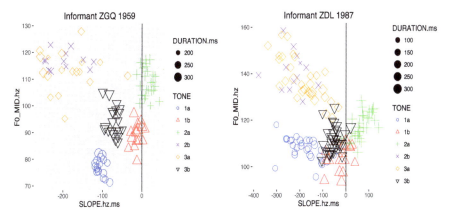

Fig. 5.13 Tonal acoustic space of Miancheng dialect produced by one older speaker (left) and one younger speaker (right)

then it is a push chain shift. Which scenario is the most plausible? The answer lies in the observation of the tonal variations within Miancheng dialect. Figure 5.14 plots the normalized frequency curves of T1a, T2a and T3b with T1b /33/ and T2a/2b /52/ as a reference.

Acoustic data from 12 younger speakers imply that T2a changes first, because all the informants investigated have accomplished the change of /44/ to /45/. Moreover, some speakers even produce T2a as a high rising tone /35/, a further development of /45/. Tonal variations among different speakers do not support the claim that T1a changes first from /32/ to /42/, because some informants still keep T1a unchanged as /32/, such as informant ZDP shown in the eleventh graph in Fig. 5.14. This means that the tonal chain shift for ZDP is in progress synchronically.

It should be noted that the change of T3b from /42/ to /44/ is not a sudden change, but a continuous process along the dimension of slope. This is reflected in the different phonetic realizations of T3b among different speakers. For instance, T3b in informants ZZX, ZDL, ZDP and YYP is a low slight falling tone /43/, which is a transitional type in the change of a low falling tone /42/ becoming a middle level tone /44/.

Consequently, based on the tonal variations among Miancheng speakers, it is more plausible that the chain shift of "32 → 42 → 44 → 45" is a pull chain triggered by the change of T2a. T2a changes to /45/ first, and T3b changes to /44/ and then /32/ to /42/ in a stepwise fashion. This pull chain shift happens in the clockwise direction as specified in Fig. 5.15, which is different from the situation in the Huipu area (Sect. 4.5).

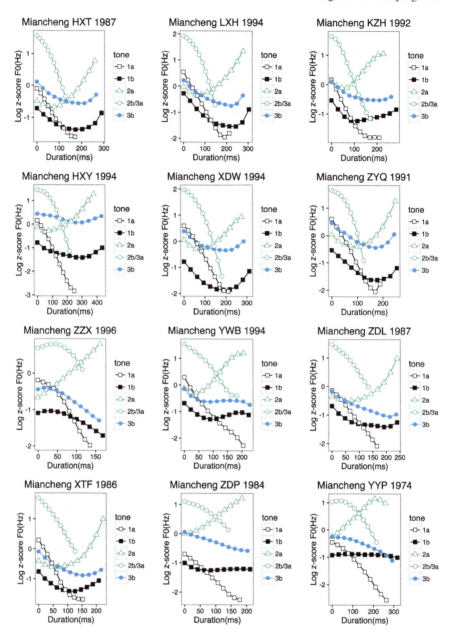

Fig. 5.14 Frequency trajectories of four tones produced by 12 Miancheng speakers

5.4 Tonal Changes in Haimen Dialect   111

Fig. 5.15 The pull chain shift of Miancheng tones

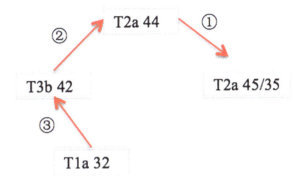

5.4 Tonal Changes in Haimen Dialect

Haimen dialect shares the same tonal pattern with Miancheng dialect, but the tones involved in the tonal merger are not the same. In Miancheng dialect, just as other Chaoyang dialects, T2b merges with T3a, while in Haimen dialect, T2b merges with T1a. Haimen dialect is the only dialect that we find within the Chaoshan area to have this kind of tonal merger. Considering its initial and final systems, we still regard it as a sub-dialect of the Chaoyang type as specified in Sect.3.13. Figure 5.16 plots the pitch curves of seven tones from one older speaker and one younger speaker respectively.

Haimen dialect also presents the age-related differences, which is the same with that in Miancheng dialect. The different tonal patterns of different age groups are summarized in Table 5.6.

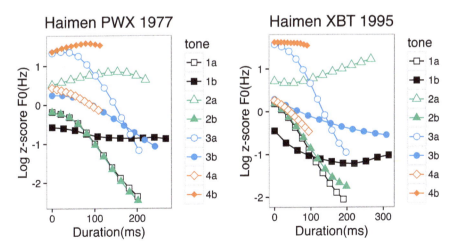

Fig. 5.16 Pitch curves of seven tones of Haimen dialect

Table 5.6 Tonal values of Haimen dialect under MRFL

Age groups	T2a	T3b	T1a/T2b	T3a	T1b	T4a	T4b
Olders	44	42	32	53	33	43	55
Youngers	45	44/43	42	53	33	43	55

The changes of T2a, T3b and T1a/2b demonstrate a pull chain shift that also happens in Miancheng dialect. T2a changes from /44/ to /45/, creating a gap in the position of /44/. Then T3b moves to fill the gap by changing from /42/ to /44/. After the change of T3b, a new gap emerges, so the process of pulling continues. T1a/2b becomes /42/ to fill the gap left by T3b. This pull chain shift can account for the distinct tonal patterns produced by different age groups.

5.5 Tonal Changes in Dahao Dialect

The pull chain shift that has happened in Miancheng and Haimen dialects can further shed light on the development of Dahao tones. In Dahao dialect, T2a has become a high slight rising tone /45/, leaving a gap at /44/. However, T3b in Dahao dialect is still maintained as a low falling tone /42/ as shown in Fig. 5.17. Tones of Dahao dialect do not demonstrate a pull chain shift, although the initial pulling force resulting from the change of T2a is present.

With reference to the tonal development in Miancheng and Haimen dialect, one may expect that the next step for Dahao dialect is the change of T3b into a middle level tone /44/. Indeed, tonal variations among multiple Dahao speakers lend support to this speculation. Moreover, some informants show the similarity between T1a and T3b. What can be inferred from the Dahao tonal variations? It is the tendency of T1a changing into a low falling tone /42/. However, this will create a "crowding" effect in the place of the low falling tone /42/, and thus trigger subsequent changes before any two tones merge.

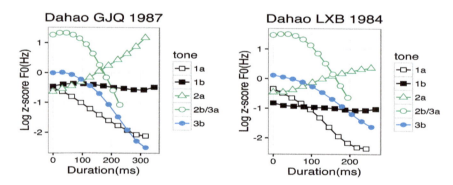

Fig. 5.17 T3b remains as low falling tone /42/ in Dahao dialect

5.5 Tonal Changes in Dahao Dialect

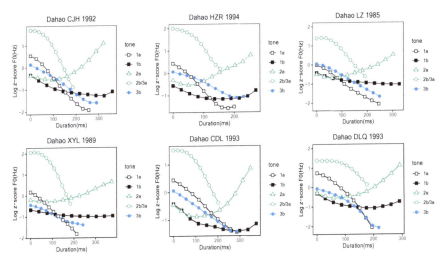

Fig. 5.18 T1a is close to T3b in Dahao dialect

The existence of synchronic tonal variations can imply the dynamic tone evolution. Different from Fig. 5.17, in which T1a is still the lowest falling tone /32/ in these two informants' system, T1a in the other six informants' system has gradually moved into the territory of the low falling tone /42/, as shown in Fig. 5.18. If we compare the situation in Dahao dialect with that in Miancheng dialect, we can see that T1a in Dahao dialect shows a stronger feature of changing than does T3b.

The distributions of frequency trajectories of T1a and T3b from the above six Dahao speakers are shown in Fig. 5.19.

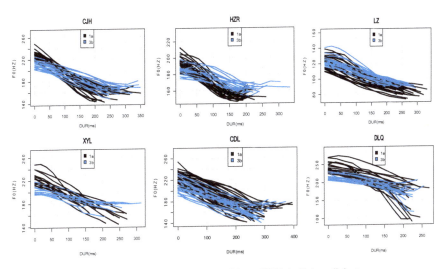

Fig. 5.19 The distributions of frequency curves of 1a and T3b in Dahao dialect

T1a and T3b are quite close to each other no matter in terms of their pitch height or pitch contour. Continuation in the direction of T1a's raising its starting pitch point will open the door for the merging of T1a and T3b.

Different speakers may have different strategies in employing phonetic cues to separate T1a and T3b. Whatever means they take, five speakers all produce significant differences between T1a and T3b. Three characteristics can be considered to be different between T1a and T3b, namely length, height and slope. Statistical analysis can help us determine whether a phonetic cue is significantly different or just random error. The statistical results are provided in Table 5.7.

Interestingly, slope turns out to be the most salient cue in distinguishing T1a and T3b for five out of six informants in our sample (the exception is LZ). Under the model of MRFL, it is difficult to assign a proper tono-type to T1a and T3b respectively, because they crowd together in the position of the low falling tone /42/. We often encounter this kind of tricky issue when dealing with tonal systems that are in a process of change. Therefore, one stance we can take is to treat the overlap of T1a and T3b as a transitional stage in a certain tonal change.

If we adopt a functional perspective that sound merger will cause more effort in communication, it seems that the distinctions between T1a and T3b will become more distinct in the future tonal change. Two possible options are available for T1a and T3b to further move away from each other. One is for T3b to move to fill the position left by T1a and become the lowest falling tone /32/. The alternative one is for T3b to change to the middle level tone /44/ left open by T2a. If the second one wins out, and denotes the future change in Dahao dialect, then T3b's becoming a middle level tone /44/ is both pulled and pushed. In our later investigation, some informants have already shown the change specified in the second scenario. Figure 5.20 plots the four speakers that have changed T3b from low falling tone to the middle level tone or middle slight falling tone.

5.6 Tonal Changes in Guiyu Dialect

Before our study, tones of Guiyu dialect have never been reported. The age-related differences in Guiyu dialect not only lie in the phonetic manifestations of T2a, but also rest on the phonetic representations of T1b. Younger speakers in Guiyu share an innovation in which T1b is changing from a low-level tone /33/ to a rising tone /35/.

The change of T2a into a high-level tone is quite prevalent among the younger speakers in the suburban Chaoyang area. However, the innovation of T1b's changing to a rising tone was only spotted in Guiyu dialect among all the towns investigated in the Chaoyang area. The differences based on the different age groups of Guiyu dialect are demonstrated in Fig. 5.21.

The younger speakers of Guiyu dialect take one more step forward in the process of tonal change compared with other younger speakers in other towns. In addition to the falling and level contour, this change further adds a new tonal contour, namely rising contour, to the tonal system. As is shown in Fig. 5.22, slopes in the system of

5.6 Tonal Changes in Guiyu Dialect

Table 5.7 Statistical results of phonetic cues in distinguishing T1a and T3b

Informants Phonetic cues	CJH	HZR	LZ	XYL	CDL	DLQ
Length	* p = 0.0175	** p = 0.00153	* p = 0.0102	NS p = 0.0935	NS p = 0.969	NS p = 0.742
Average pitch height	NS p = 0.869	* p = 0.0159	*** p = 2.12e–06	* p = 0.0231	** p = 0.00176	* p = 0.0176
Slope	*** p = 7.97e–06	*** p = 4.59e–11	NS p = 0.274	*** p = 0.000449	*** p = 2.31e–08	*** p = 0.000959

(Significance level: 0.05; Significance codes: 0 '***' 0.001 '**' 0.01 '*' 0.05 '.' 0.1 ' ' 1)

116 5 Tonal Changes in the Chaoyang Area

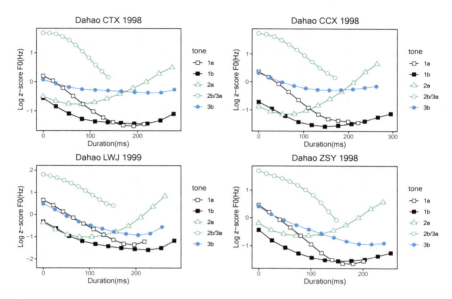

Fig. 5.20 The distributions of frequency curves of 1a and T3b in Dahao dialect

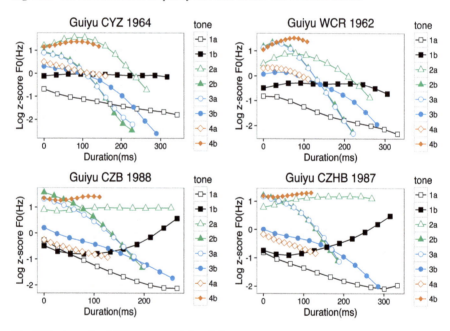

Fig. 5.21 Age-related differences of Guiyu dialect

5.6 Tonal Changes in Guiyu Dialect

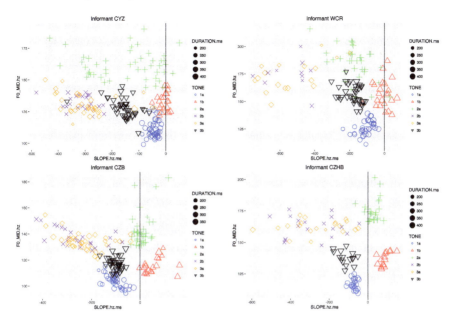

Fig. 5.22 Tonal acoustic space of Guiyu dialect

the younger speakers span both negative and positive values. However, slopes of the older speakers' system are crammed into the negative side.

5.7 The Motive Behind the Tonal Changes in the Chaoyang Area

Compared with the Shanjie and Huipu areas, the Chaoyang area demonstrates more varieties and variations. Having presented the tonal variation and changes in the Chaoyang area, we want to raise another question: Is there a general mechanism underlying these changes? My proposed answer is yes, and it is the same mechanism that accounts for a good deal of historical change: simplification.

By "simplification" here, I mean that the efforts needed to distinguish different tones are reduced after the change of tones. From the tone system of the older speakers to that of the younger speakers, as well as from the suburban area to the central area of Chaoyang, a tendency of utilizing more tonal contours can be observed. The tone systems are changing towards an optimal pattern, in which the tones are well distributed in terms of their relative distance in the tonal acoustic space. In other words, diversified contours are utilized.

That means the distinctions of tones put more weight on the differences of slope. It calls for more effort to differentiate different tones with slopes being on the same negative or positive side, as well as being around zero (level contour). To determine whether a tone is a falling, a rising, or a level one is easier than to determine its height. In other words, the determination of height needs reference; consequently, it is less straightforward than the determination of slope. Therefore, the changed tonal systems are more efficient in the differentiation of tones.

As argued in Sect. 5.2.3, T2a's changing from a high convex falling tone to a high level tone may be due to the "hyper-correction" on the part of the younger listeners; and at the same time, this change will substantially reduces the effort of maintaining the contrast of four relevant tones when the younger listeners turn into speakers. The Miancheng younger speakers further change T2a to become a high slight rising tone /45/ (or high rising tone /35/) and T3b to become a middle level tone, making the acoustic distributions of tones more widely dispersed. In addition, in the Guiyu case, the younger speakers change T1b from low level /33/ to rising /35/, which is the only rising tone, making the contour of T1b salient enough to separate it from other tones.

To say a syllable is high or low relies on a certain reference, which is not a requirement for the determination of slope. That is, the contrast between falling and rising contours is perceptually more salient than the contrast between different slopes of falling or rising. Under this assumption, we can say that the newly changed tonal systems are simpler in terms of the effort needed to maintain or to perceive the contrasts.

It should also be noted that tonal changes in the Chaoyang area are far from finished and are still in progress, like the case in Dahao dialect. There exists no mechanism that mandates that the changes of Chaoyang tones must evolve to a certain uniform tonal pattern. The reason why tones in the Chaoyang area are so dynamic may lie in the difficulty of maintaining the contrast of four falling tones and the effort needed to maximize perceptual distinctiveness of contrasts. Dialects within the Chaoyang area are changing towards a tonal pattern with more contours exploited, making the contrasts among different tones easier to be produced and perceived.

The tonal evolutionary routes of these Chaoyang dialects are not the same. Moreover, the progress of the relevant evolutionary path varies from dialect to dialect, as well as from speaker to speaker. This may explain why the multiple tonal patterns and tonal variations can be spotted in this area.

5.8 Summary

This chapter is concerned primarily with the tonal changes in the Chaoyang area. In order to probe the direction of these tonal changes, variations within and across speakers as well as dialectal varieties are presented from the perspective of evolution.

Acoustic evidence shows that the production of T2a in the Chaoyang area has changed from a high convex falling tone to a high-evel tone, and subsequently a rising tone. The evolutionary tendency observed along different age groups is parallel with that revealed by different geographical variations. The older speakers in the suburban Chaoyang area maintain the contrast of four falling tones. The younger speakers in the suburban Chaoyang area and the older speakers in the central Chaoyang area actually

5.8 Summary 119

possess the same tonal pattern by changing T2a to a high-level tone. The younger speakers of Miancheng dialect (the central Chaoyang area) further change T2a to a rising tone, and this follow-up development triggers a pull chain shift consisting of T2a, T3b and T1a as discussed in Sect. 5.3.

Different from the case in Miancheng dialect, T3b in Dahao dialect is still a low falling tone, although T2a in these two dialects all manifests as rising contours. Dahao dialect displays a transitional stage in which the pitch height and slope (contour) of T1a and T3b are quite close. Haimen dialect is unique for its tonal merger of T1a and T2b; however, the developments of T1a, T2a and T3b are almost the same as those happening in Miancheng dialect. Guiyu dialect provides us with a new case in which T1b has changed from a middle level tone to a rising tone.

Slope has turned out to be a very important coefficient in maintaining the tonal contrasts in the Chaoyang area. At the same time, the tendency to employ more diversified slopes is observed in various Chaoyang dialects. In conclusion, based on the computer-assisted acoustic measurements, various tonal patterns in the Chaoyang area are presented and a systematic account with regard to tonal changes in this area is provided at the same time. Age and geographic differences are two important factors in determining the direction of tonal changes. In addition to the acoustic evidence, perceptual results can further shed light on tone evolution and facilitate a more in-depth explanation for the mechanism behind tonal changes.

References

Bailey, Guy, Tom Wikle, Jan Tillery, and Lori Sand. 1991. The apparent time construct. *Language Variation and Change* 3: 241–264.
Hong, Ying. Lam, Man Fong and Zhu, Xiaonong. 洪英 & 林文芳 & 朱晓农. 2013. Gurao Fangyan de Sige Jiangdiao 谷饶方言的四个降调. In *Festschrift in Honor of Professor William S-Y. Wang on his 80th Birthday*, ed. Shifeng, Penggang. 219–233. HongKong: City University Press.
Labov, W. 1972. *Sociolinguistic patterns*. Philadelphia: University of Pennsylvania Press.
Laver, J. 1994. *Principles of Phonetics*. Cambridge: Cambridge University Press.
Labov, W. 1972/1994. *Principles of Linguistic Change: Internal Factors*. Oxford & Cambridge, Mass.: Blackwell.
Ohala, J.J. 1981. The listener as a source of sound change. In *The Parasession on Language and Behavior*, eds. C.S. Masek, R.A. Hendrick, and M.F. Miller, 178 – 203. Chicago: Chicago Ling. Soc.
Rose, Phil. 1981. *An Acoustical Based Phonetic Description of the Syllable in the Zhenhai Dialect*. Cambridge: University of Cambridge. (Doctoral dissertation.)
Shen, Ruiqing. 2016. Tonal Variation: A Quantitative Study of Jianyang Min Chinese (A dissertation for the degree Doctor of Philosophy). The Hong Kong University of Science and Technology.
Zhu, Xiaonong. 朱晓农. 2005. 上海声调实验录 *An Experimental Study of Shanghai Tones*. 上海教育出版社 Shanghai: Shanghai Educational Press.
Zhu, Xiaonong. 朱晓农. 2010. 语音学. *Phonetics: An Introduction*. Beijing: Commercial Press.

Chapter 6
The Evolution of Checked Tones

Abstract This chapter examines the checked tones of Chaoshan dialects with an abundant of firsthand acoustic data. By comparing with Fujian Jinjiang dialect, an evolutionary path for checked tones of Chaoshan dialects is proposed. At the first stage, the pattern of checked tones of Chaoshan dialects is the same as that in Zhangquan dialect, such as Jinjiang dialect, being "Yin-high versus yang-low"; At the second stage, the pattern of checked tones is "Yin-mid-falling versus yang-mid-rising", and just like the case in Yun'ao dialect; At the third stage, the pattern of checked tones is "Yin-falling-low versus yang-rising-high", and the example is drawn from Dahao daielct. The last stage is "Yin-low versus yang-high", which can be found in most Chaoshan dialects. We argue that the historical "flip-flop" of Chaoshan checked tones is not a sudden change, but is accomplished via a process of gradual phonetic change. Being the transitional stages, Yun'ao and Dahao dialects are characterized by distinctive pitch contours, which are triggered by different phonation types. Experimental measures of acoustic cues using data from ten Yun'ao and Shen'ao speakers confirm that there are different phonation types in T4a and T4b, with creaky voice in T4a and fortis voice (the final glottal stop) in T4b, respectively.

Keywords Checked tone evolution · Flip-flop · Yin-high versus yang-low · Yin-low versus yang-high · Gradual phonetic change · Phonation types

In this section, we are concerned with the phonetic realization of checked tone (also known as Rusheng 入声 in Chinese), with a special focus on Yun'ao dialect. By demonstrating the pitch patterns of T4a and T4b among various Southern Min dialects, we identify four stages with regard to the development of checked tones. Furthermore, we delve into the phonetic features of phonation in the two checked tone syllables by comparing multiple acoustic cues. The motive behind the evolution of checked tones are also expounded in this chapter.

6.1 General Introduction

This concept of "flip-flop" was first proposed by Wang (1967) to account for the reversal of tonal values both synchronically and diachronically. Yue-Hashimoto (1986) further examines this phenomenon comprehensively. In this chapter, we discuss the phenomenon of "flip-flop" in the diachronic sense. The higher pitch height of T4b compares to that of T4a in the Chaoshan area is traditionally regarded as a result of "flip-flop", since the assumption is that the Yin tone should have originally had a higher pitch.

In most Chinese dialects, the Yin and Yang dichotomy of tones resulting from the loss of voiced initial consonants (breathy phonation) generally manifests as higher pitch height in Yin tone syllables than that in their Yang tone counterparts. The phonetic motivation behind this claim has been explored in previous phonetic studies (Hombert et al. 1978). The consensus is voicing in initials or breathy phonation will have a lowering effect on F0. Therefore, it seems quite plausible to attribute the reversal of the tonal values of checked tones to "flip-flop".

Although the phenomenon of Yin tone having a lower pitch value than Yang tone has long been a heated topic in phonetic studies (Zhu et al. 2008; Zhu and Hong 2009; Hong 2009), the mechanism behind this "flip-flop" is still unclear. Our understanding of "flip-flop" in the Chaoshan area seems not to have advanced much. We still have no idea how this "flip-flop" happens. To which category of tonal change, sudden change or gradual change, does it belong?

Yun'ao dialect can further shed light on this question and expand our understanding of "flip-flop", and at the same time, of checked tone evolutions in the Chaoshan area. We find that the development of checked tones in Chaoshan dialects is not a sudden "flip-flop" change, but a gradual phonetic change that leads to a "flip-flop" result in comparison to the initial stage.

6.2 Different Stages in the Development of Checked Tones

We have identified four different stages in the development of checked tones by reference to the pitch relations between T4a and T4b in different dialects. The initial stage is demonstrated by the Quanzhou type (Fujian Min dialect), in which the pitch height of T4a is higher than that of T4b as shown in Fig. 6.1. At the same time, the rising contour of T4b is very apparent. As can be seen from the previous chapters, the value of T4b is higher than that of T4a in most Chaoshan dialects. Some Fujian Southern Min dialects (like the case here) still maintain the original contrast, in which the pitch value of T4a is higher than that of T4b.

The second stage is complicated because the difference between T4a and T4b does not rely merely on the pitch height but also on the pitch contour. Yun'ao dialect is distinguishable from other Chaoshan dialects in that it shows more similarity with

6.2 Different Stages in the Development of Checked Tones 123

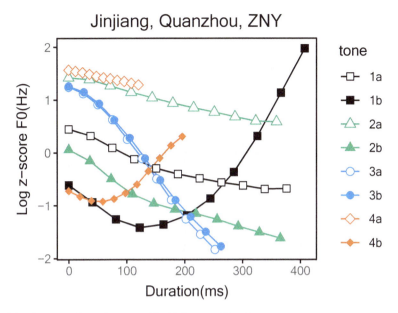

Fig. 6.1 First stage, Quanzhou type: Yin-high versus Yang-low

Fujian Southern Min dialects. It displays an intermediate stage, where T4a and T4b have similar pitch onset values but different tonal contours (Fig. 6.2).

The third stage occurs in Dahao dialect, with both pitch height and pitch contour having notable differences in T4a and T4b (Fig. 6.3).

The fourth stage is the Chaozhou type, in which the relationship of pitch height between T4a and T4b is reversed compared with the Quanzhou type. The pitch height of T4b in this type is higher than that of T4a (Fig. 6.4).

If we just take Quanzhou and Chaozhou type into account, we may think this is a sudden "flip-flop" change, in which T4a and T4b exchange their pitch heights. This is the view held in previous studies since data from Yun'ao and Dahao dialects are absent. However, by referring to the Yun'ao and Dahao types, we are able to claim that the change of T4a and T4b in the Chaozhou type occurs in a gradual fashion.

Twenty-three informants from Yun'ao, Shenao and Qing'ao towns were investigated to show the gradual process of this change. There are subtle differences between the relations of T4a and T4b and they can be divided into three groups:

(1) Group one: The pitch curves of T4a and T4b cross (13 informants) (Fig. 6.5)
(2) Group two: The starting points of T4a and T4b are the same (8 informants) (Fig. 6.6)
(3) Group three: The pitch height of T4b is slightly higher than that of T4a (2 informants) (Fig. 6.7)

Gender, age, occupation and education level have no relation with the distributions of these different pitch patterns between T4a and T4b. The instability of the pitch

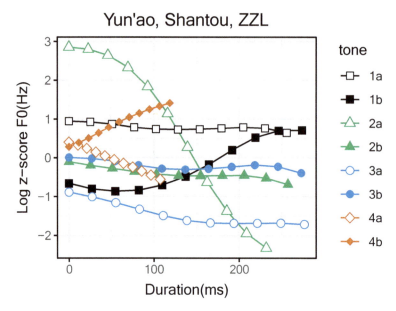

Fig. 6.2 Second stage, Yun'ao type: Yin-falling and Yang-rising

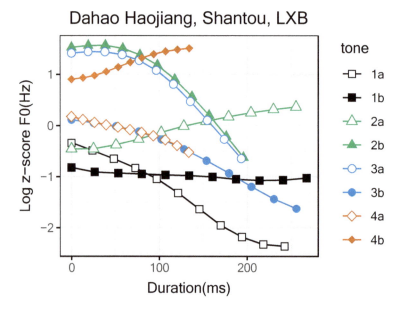

Fig. 6.3 Third stage, Dahao type: Yin-low-falling and Yang-high-rising

6.2 Different Stages in the Development of Checked Tones

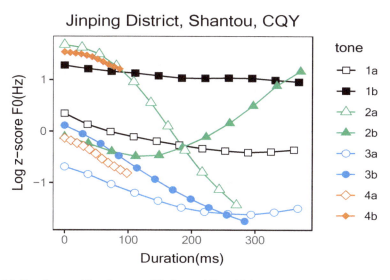

Fig. 6.4 Fourth stage, Chaozhou type: Yin-low and Yang-high

relationship of T4a and T4b within Yun'ao type dialects indicates that checked tones are experiencing some kind of dynamic changes; this is seen in the changing of T4b to the higher pitch level and of T4a to the lower pitch part. The degree to which T4b is above T4a is speaker-specific in Yun'ao type dialects.

The Dahao case is relatively simpler; eleven speakers in our sample display the same pattern, with the pitch height of T4b being higher than T4a, and meanwhile, their contours are significant different too. The frequency trajectories of Dahao dialect are shown in Fig. 6.8.

The change from the Quanzhou type to the Chaozhou type in terms of pitch height is what we call "flip-flop", with the Quanzhou type ("Yin-high versus Yang-low") being the original stage and the Chaozhou type ("Yin-low versus Yang high") the final result. The transitions of T4b from low to high and T4a from high to low are gradual. The Yun'ao and Dahao types represent the intermediate stages and further prove that "flip-flop" is occurring gradually by means of cumulative phonetic increments. Different speakers of the transitional dialects may show different paths of evolution as shown above.

Tonal variations across communities can be used for inference about sound change. From this point of view, synchronically, four different types of pitch relationships between T4a and T4b in different dialects reflect the diachronic change of checked tones. In this regard, I propose that there are at least four stages of change in the case of checked tones based on the pool of synchronic variations among different communities (Ohala 1987):

① Quanzhou type → ② Yun'ao type → ③ Dahao type → ④ Chaozhou type

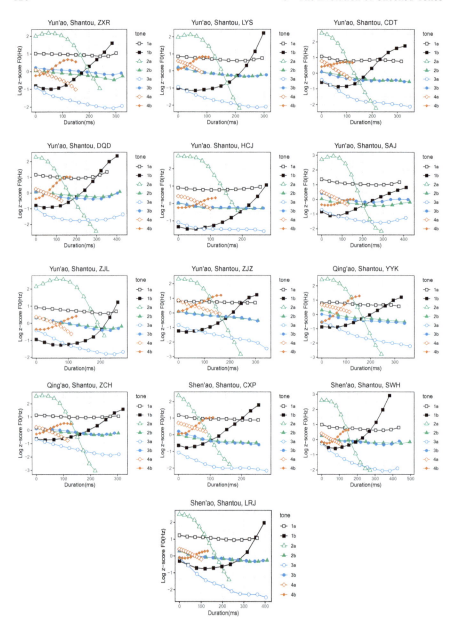

Fig. 6.5 The pitch curves of T4a and T4b cross

6.2 Different Stages in the Development of Checked Tones

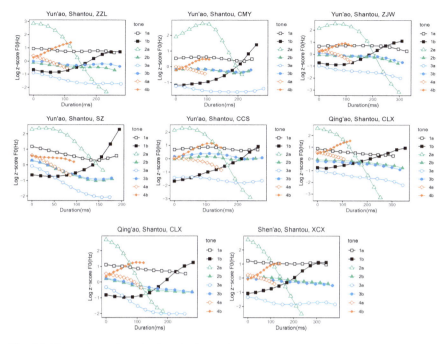

Fig. 6.6 The starting points of T4a and T4b are the same

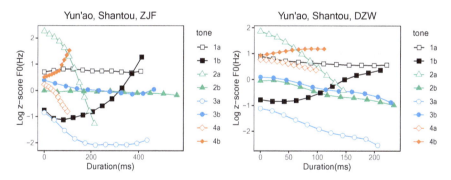

Fig. 6.7 The pitch height of T4b is slightly higher than that of T4a

What we do here is to sequence and connect the tonal systems of geographical related dialects to form reasonable process of tonal evolution. Although the historical developments in different dialects cannot be traced in any written sources, the above tentative scenario for the development of checked tones can be suggested to mirror the historical "flip-flop" change.

Distributions of the average frequency and the slope, which represent pitch height and pitch contour respectively, are plotted here to illustrate their different roles in distinguishing T4a and T4b in these four types of dialects. Average frequency is the

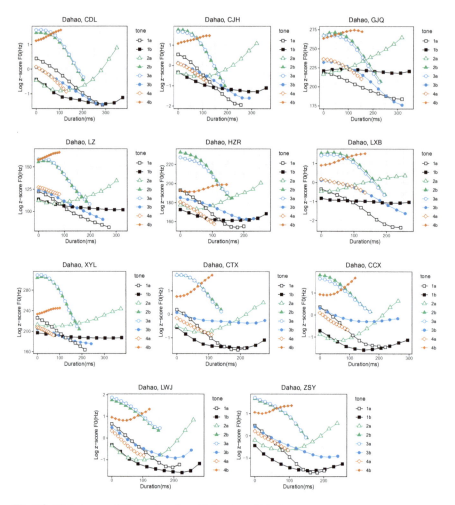

Fig. 6.8 Pitch curves of 11 speakers from Dahao type dialects

arithmetic mean of the third pitch point to the eighth point. Slopes are obtained using the formulation "Slope" in Excel. The first two points and the last two points of each syllable are excluded in our calculation of "Slope" too.

Plotting multiple speakers' distributions of average frequency and slope shows the gradual process of the "flip-flop" in T4a and T4b.

(1) At the first stage ("Yin-high versus Yang low"), both the pitch height and the slope play a role in distinguishing T4a and T4b as shown in Fig. 6.9.
(2) At the second stage, the most important feature separating T4a and T4b is pitch contour (slope). In terms of average pitch height, T4a and T4b overlap greatly, a fact that is obvious in the following graph of two speakers of Yun'ao dialect (Fig. 6.10).

6.2 Different Stages in the Development of Checked Tones

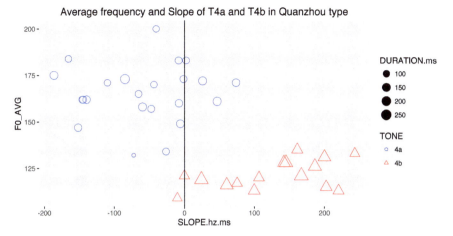

Fig. 6.9 Average frequency and slope of T4a and T4b in Quanzhou type dialects

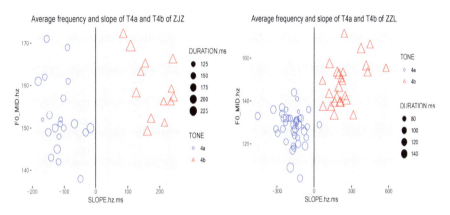

Fig. 6.10 Average frequency and slope of T4a and T4b in Yun'ao type dialects

(3) At the third stage, apart from the dimension of pitch contour, pitch height also shows considerable disparities between T4a and T4b. Figure 6.11 below plots the distributions of these two parameters as observed in Dahao dialect.
(4) At the final stage, pitch height plays a key role in distinguishing T4a and T4b, while slopes have negative as well as positive values in both T4a and T4b as shown in Fig. 6.12.

As can be seen, contour is a very pivotal in differentiating T4a and T4b at the first three stages. However, at the last stage, namely in Chaozhou type dialects, the distributions of slope span both positive and negative values. That means contour is not a primary cue for T4a and T4b in Chaozhou type dialects, since their pitch heights are sufficient to separate them. Simply put, contours do not necessarily have to be different in this case.

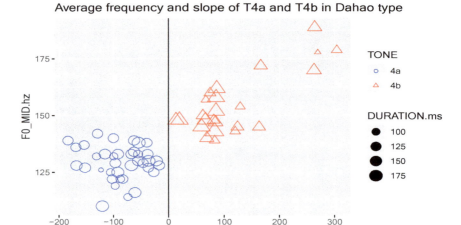

Fig. 6.11 Average frequency and slope of T4a and T4b in Dahao type dialects

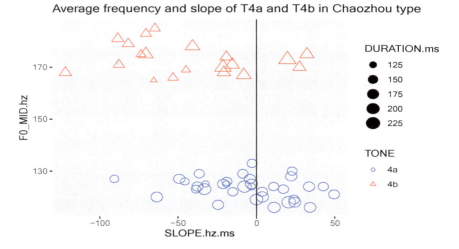

Fig. 6.12 Average frequency and slope of T4a and T4b in Chaozhou type dialects

It is supposed that longer duration is needed for listeners to perceive tonal contour (Zhu 2005: 200). Working with this assumption, we can expect that the absolute duration of checked tones in Yun'ao and Dahao type dialects should be longer than that in their Chaozhou counterparts. Figure 6.13 plots the absolute durations of checked tones in these three types of dialects.

Data of the Chaozhou type are drawn from 21 speakers with 497 tokens of T4a and 325 of T4b. Twenty-three Yun'ao speakers provide 485 tokens of T4a and 340 of T4b. One hundred forty-one tokens of T4a and 110 of T4b produced by seven speakers of

6.2 Different Stages in the Development of Checked Tones

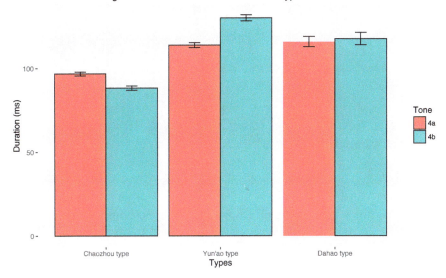

Fig. 6.13 Absolute durations of checked tones in three types of dialects

Dahao dialect are calculated here. Just as expected, the absolute durations in Yun'ao (114 ms for T4a and 130 ms for T4b) and Dahao (116 ms for T4a and 110 ms for T4b) are obviously longer than those in Chaozhou (97 ms for T4a and 88 ms for T4b). Our finding supports the conjecture that it requires longer duration to perceive contour.

However, it is still unclear whether longer duration in Yun'ao and Dahao dialects is a motivation for short tones to have distinctive contours, or it is just a method to satisfy the duration requirement for perception of contours. Our preference is for the second possibility.

This typical tonal reversal change of "Yin-high versus Yang-low" to "Yin-low versus Yang-high" is not unique to the Chaoshan area. Zeng (2013) investigates 17 dialects in Quanzhou and Xiamen Cities, and finds that 11 out of 17 dialects still preserve the pattern of "Yin-high versus Yang-low", while 6 dialects present the mode of "Yin-low versus Yang-high". The details of checked tone evolutions in Quanzhou and Xiamen dialects await further investigation.

What the phonetic motivations are behind these changes is a question worthy of being explored. The most plausible solution to this question may lie in the different phonation types of T4a and T4b.

6.3 Different Phonation Types of Checked Tones

Taking Yun'ao type dialects as an example, we will delve into the mechanism behind the evolutions of checked tones in this section. Distinct phonations related to T4a and T4b are the possible candidates to trigger the change of checked tones.

6.3.1 Two Basic Forms of Checked Tone Syllables in Chaoshan Dialect

There are two basic forms of checked tone syllables in Chaoshan dialects. One preserves the non-audible or unreleased coda stops [−p, −t, −k], whereas the other has a glottal stop [−ʔ] as a coda. Their durations are short compared with those of unchecked tones. It is claimed in previous studies (Chao et al. 1948: 170; Iwara Rei 岩田礼 1984, 1992) that checked tone syllables have the characteristics of "jinhou" 紧喉 (glottalization or laryngealization) regardless of what types of coda they possess.

Chao et al. (1948: 170)[1] for the first time suggested that most of the checked tones with codas [−p, −t, −k] in dialects that preserve checked tone syllables, like Cantonese, to a certain degree possess a glottal stop ending (here the "glottal stop" refers to glottalization or laryngealization). Following this line of reasoning, the stop codas in Chaoshan dialects should be transcribed as [−ʔk], [−ʔt] and [[−ʔp]. Iwata Rei (1984, 1992) conducted another remarkable study on the phonetic nature of checked tones by investigating checked tones in Cantonese, Southern Min and Taigu Jin dialects using fiberscopy and electromyography, he proved that laryngealization is a notable feature accompany the pronunciation of [−p, −t, −k], thus supporting Prof. Chao's claim.

Moreover, Iwata asserted that this larygealization is actually a kind of phonation. In the Chao'an and Chaozhou cases, previous research has revealed that the so-called "glottal stop" 喉塞尾 of checked tones are realized as creaky voice and creaky-falsetto voice in T4a and T4b, respectively (Zhu et al. 2008; Zhu and Hong 2009).

Consequently, we have two questions. The first question is how to verify the existence of phonations in checked tones. The second is what type of phonations exists in T4a and T4b. Are there any different phonations in T4a and T4b, so that they lead to different pitch heights of checked tones?

Before answering the first question, we should add some words on the phonetic feature of glottal stop ([−ʔ]) since both T4a and T4b are transcribed as glottal stops in traditional dialectology. The key to the second question lies in the different phonetic manifestations (such as pitch height and pitch contour) of T4a and T4b. In Yun'ao dialect, glottal stop in T4a is associated with lower fundamental frequency, while in

---

[1] In the Chinese translation version of Études sur la Phonologie Chinoise, transaltor Chao et al. added a footnote quoted as follows: "据译者观察, 中国有–p, –t, –k尾的方言, 例如广州, 大都同时带一点喉头塞音–ʔ的作用, 结果 "十文" (–pʔm–), "一年" (–tʔn–), "六艺" (–kʔ–) 中的各闭音并不像英文 "Chapman", "at nine" 那么直接从软腭向鼻腔爆发。" (《中国音韵学研究》).

6.3 Different Phonation Types of Checked Tones   133

T4b it is associated with raised frequency. That indicates that the so-called glottal stops in a single dialect may have different phonetic natures.

6.3.2 What is the So-Called Glottal Stop?

As a rhyme coda, the glottal stop [−ʔ] has long been a confusing notion in the investigation of Chinese dialects. According to the definition in Laver (1994: 187–188), glottal stop is a maintained, complete glottal closure. In production, there are at least two ways to cause the vocal cords to close, by dragging them vertically and by squeezing them internally. From a series of studies conducted by Esling and his colleagues (Esling et al. 2005), we know that glottal stop is not merely referring to the glottal closure but also includes the adduction of the arytenoid cartilages and ventricular folds, and so on. Moreover, the glottal stop does not represent a single articulation but rather a set of combined articulations such as glottal plus ventricular constriction. Garellek (2013) argues that glottal stops are truly glottal sounds; though the degree of glottal and supraglottal constrictions varies by token, speaker, syllable position, etc. He also points out that glottal stops are highly variable in their articulations and they can be produced with complete or incomplete closure of the glottis, and with or without ventricular incursion.

Given the different production mechanisms introduced above, it is not surprising that the glottal stop may have different phonetic manifestations in different languages.

Kong (2001) has demonstrated that there are distinctive features of glottal stop in different languages. They probably trigger lower or higher tones in accordance with different phonation types. In Ladefoged and Maddieson (1996: 75), it is stated that glottal stop may be realized either with creaky phonation on an adjacent vowel or as a complete closure without any creakiness.

Similarly, a few studies show that there are two modes of laryngealized voicing: one is creaky voice, which is associated with lower F0, and the other is harsh voice having higher F0 (Esling et al. 2005; Edmondson and Esling 2006). Harsh voice in their description is typically associated with constriction of the ventricular folds, an articulation that is also common in glottal stop.

According to Zhu (2008), glottal closure is a state of glottal stop originated from higher tension of vocal cords in vertical, with pre-glottal stops at the beginning of a syllable and glottal stops at the end of syllables. The latter one is the glottal-stop coda [−ʔ], one kind of non-modal phonation types, occurring as a variant of fortis voice, common in the checked tone syllables in Chinese dialects. Creaky voice refers to the tightening condition in vocal cords, which has been a particular phonation discovered in checked tones of Chaozhou dialects.

These two phonations occur in Yun'ao dialect too, with creaky voice in T4a and the final glottal stop in T4b. Creaky voice in Yinru syllables is associated with lowered frequency while that in Yangru syllables is linked with raising frequency. Chen (2014) hypothesize that the final phontions are different for T4a and T4b in Puxian Min, and they are linked to different pitch heights.

Table 6.1 A classification of phonations, cited from Zhu (2015)

Major type	Type	Notation	Supra-phonational	
I. Falsetto	1. Falsetto	á		L
II. Fortis	2. Pre-glottalization/implosive	ʔp/ɓ	length	M
	3. Final-glottalization/ejective	aʔ/k'		S
III. Voiceless	4. Unaspirated	p		2-way
	5. Weak Aspiration	pʻ	pitch	3-degree
	6. Aspirated	pʰ		4-level
IV. Stiff	7. Glottal Muffle	a̰		
	8. Creaky Voice	a̰		
	9. Weak Stiff	a̰		
V. Modal	10. Modal Voice	b		
VI. Breathy	11. Voiced Aspiration	bʱa		
	12. Slack Voice	b̤a		
	13. Weak Slack	pa̤		

In Zhu (2010: 92–108)'s classification of phonations, the phonation of T4a belongs to creaky voice (stiff voice) and the phonation of T4b is final-glottalization (fortis voice). According to Zhu (2008, 2011, 2015), phonation is one of the components of tone and is the supra-segmental element of the syllable. Zhu presents a lucid discussion on phonation types in a series of studies. A detailed classification of phonations is provided in Zhu (2015); it is cited here for reference in Table 6.1.

In sum, glottal stop has different linguistic meanings. Phonologically, it can be used as pre-glottalization at the beginning of the syllable, but also be used as a coda (final-glottalization) occurring at the end of the syllable. Phonetically, it belongs to stiff voice (creaky phonation) or fortis voice (final-glottalization), which may lead to different pitch heights of checked tones. Therefore, the so-called glottal stop coda used in traditional Chinese dialectology actually possesses different phonetic natures, namely different phonation types, including stiff voice and fortis voice.

6.3.3 Different Phonetic Manifestations of T4a and T4b

The graphs below show the waveform and spectrograms of T4a and T4b in Yun'ao dialect. It can be seen that the intensity of the latter part of T4a is weaker than that of the front part, while this relationship is reversed in T4b. Examples from four Yun'ao speakers (two males and two females) are provided in the following figures. Bule line denotes the pitch curve and the yellow line stands for intensity curve (Fig. 6.14).

The decrease of intensity at the end of Yinru syllables is one notable feature of the creaky voice. According to Gordon and Ladefoged (2001), the creaky phonation is

6.3 Different Phonation Types of Checked Tones

(1a) Informant DZW: 左"约" [ioʔ43]，右"药" [ioʔ45]

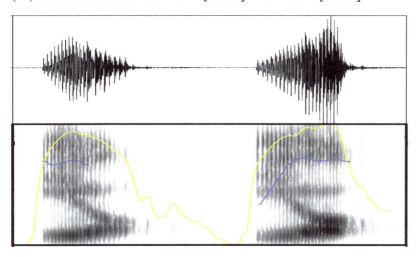

(1b) Informant DZW: 左"得" [tik43]，右"直" [tik45]

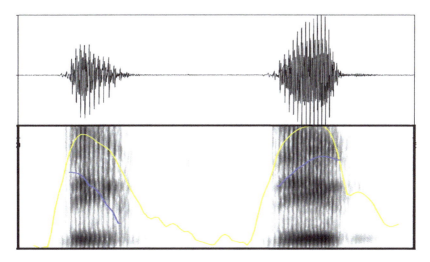

Fig. 6.14 Waveform and spectrogram of T4a and T4b from four Yun'ao speakers

characterized by the irregularity of spaced pitch periods and the decreased intensity in the waveform relative to modal phonation. Since it is hard to sustain creaky phonation through the entire duration of the phonemically creaky vowel, it tends to localize the creakiness to the latter portion of the vowel. As can be seen above, the feature of creaky phonation in Yun'ao dialect is most salient at the concluding part of the syllable. That is why it demonstrates less intensity in the latter part of the whole syllable (Fig. 6.14).

(2a) Informant ZJZ: 左"搭" [taʔ43], 右"踏" [taʔ45]

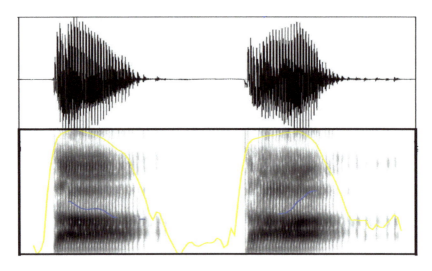

(2b) Informant ZJZ: 左"得" [tk43], 右"直" [tk45]

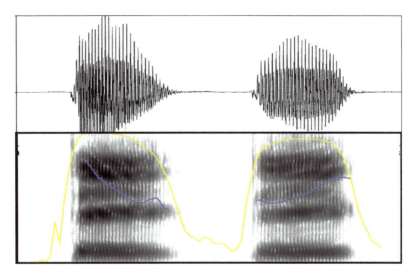

Fig. 6.14 (continued)

The creaky voiced vowel is not only characterized by decreased intensity in the waveform, but also a lowered fundamental frequency relative to the modal voiced vowel. That is to say, there are fewer pitch periods per second in the creaky voice than in the modal one. The creaky voice leads to the lower pitch height at the end of the

6.3 Different Phonation Types of Checked Tones   137

(3a) Informant ZXR: 左 "搭" [taʔ43]，右 "踏" [taʔ45]

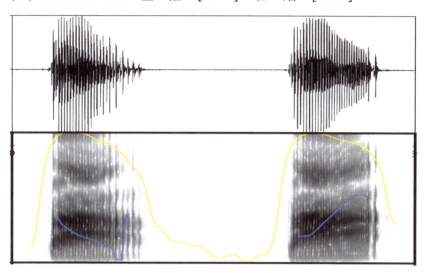

(3b) Informant ZXR: 左 "得" [tik43]，右 "直" [tik45]

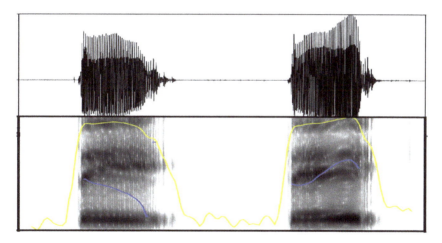

Fig. 6.14 (continued)

syllable, which lends support to the claim that non-modal phonation will influence fundamental frequency.

The situation in T4b is more complicated. Here the increase of intensity indicative of fortis voice (final-glottalization) occurs in the latter part of the syllable. The final-glottalization leads to the higher pitch of the latter portion of the syllable. However,

(4a) Informant ZJF: 左"塔" [thaʔ43]，右"叠" [thaʔ45]

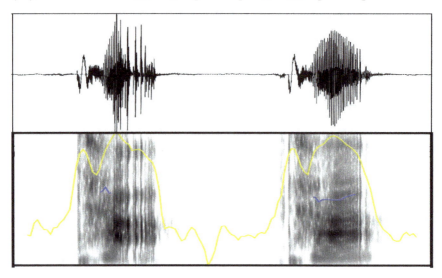

(4b) Informant ZJF: 左"漆" [tshak43]，右"贼" [tshak45]

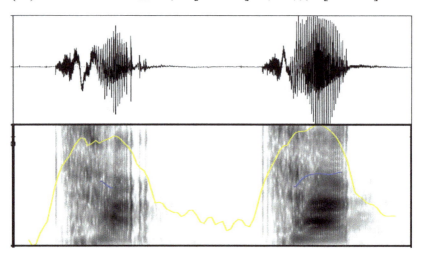

Fig. 6.14 (continued)

it usually culminates in a creaky voice which results in a sudden fall of pitch height just as the spectrogram shows.[2]

Accordingly, we are sure that there are different phonation types existing in T4a and T4b. Based on the different spectrograms, different impacts on the development

---

[2]Zhu and Hong (2009), Hong (2013) have already pointed out that besides glottal stop, there may be compound phonation, namely creaky-falsetto, occurring in T4b.

6.3 Different Phonation Types of Checked Tones

Table 6.2 Different phonation types in T4a and T4b

Tone		T4a	T4b
Coda	Stop coda	(C)V(V)–ʔk, (C)V(V)–ʔp	(C)V(V)–ʔk, (C)V(V)–ʔp
	Glottal stop	(C)V(V)–ʔ	(C)V(V)–ʔ
Phonation types		Creaky voice (Stiff phonation)	Final glottal stop (Fortis phonation)

of pitch and the distinctive auditory impression, we assert that in Yun'ao dialect, the phonation of T4a is creaky voice (stiff phonation) while that of T4b is final-glottalization (fortis phonation).

One criticism this research is bound to meet is that we treat the two checked tone syllables (glottal stop syllables and stop coda syllables) as one homogeneous entity. One justification we can offer is from the viewpoint of phonation (Table 6.2). According to previous studies, it is clear that the two types of checked tone syllables both involve certain kinds of phonations, which opens up the possibility for homogeneous treatment.

6.4 Experimental Measures of Acoustic Cues for Phonations in T4a and T4b

It has been demonstrated in Zhu and Hong (2009), Hong (2013) that the acoustic cues between unchecked tones and checked tones are significantly different in Chaozhou dialect, in which the development of the checked tone is at the final stage ("Yin-low versus Yang-high"). In this session, we will further examine the related acoustic correlates within checked tones to see which cue is the most salient one in distinguishing T4a and T4b. Furthermore, the data used is selected from Yun'ao dialect, whose checked tone development is at the intermediate stage.

There are at least three phonation types in Yun'ao dialect. They are modal voice in the unchecked tone syllables and two kinds of non-clear phonations occurring in checked tone syllables. Since the differences between unchecked and checked tones are obvious, we will pay more attention to the distinctions within checked tones.

In short, we have two aims in conducting the following experiments: first is to verify whether the acoustic cues are different between T4a and T4b in Yun'ao dialect. If the answer is yes, our second aim is to see which acoustic cue is the most salient one.

6.4.1 Acoustic Measures

Across languages with phonation contrasts, the phonation categories can be distinguished by multiple acoustic cues, but not every cue works in every language. In this experiment, seven acoustic measures are obtained automatically over the entire syllable duration with VoiceSacue (Shue et al. 2009) to measure the acoustic cues of checked tones. The syllable durations are label in Praat. The onset is set at the second glottal pulse and the end point is set at the last glottal pulse.

These seven acoustic cues are chosen by reference to Keating et al. (2011), and they are: H1(*)[3]–H2(*), H2(*)–H4(*), H1(*)–A1(*), H1(*)–A2(*), H1(*)–A3(*), Energy and Cepstral Peak Prominence (CPP). For each "input. Wav" file, Voice-Sauce produced a MATLAB file with values every millisecond, over the syllable portion delimited by the Praat Textgrid. The mean values of these acoustic measures for each syllable are obtained for further analysis.

6.4.2 Stimuli

The stop coda in Yun'ao dialect only includes [−p, −k]. Coda [−t] has merged with [−k]. Therefore, according to the different types of coda, the checked tones in Yun'ao can be divided into four categories:

(1) T4a + [−ʔ] "滴[tiʔ43]"
(2) T4a + [−p, −k] "得[tik43]"
(3) T4b + [−ʔ] "碟[tiʔ45]"
(4) T4b + [−p, −k] "直[tik45]"

The wordlist used during the recording process includes monophthongs and diphthongs with the aim to cover as many syllable types as possible. Stimuli are listed in Table 6.3.

Stimuli are divided into three recording lists, which are arranged in the following sequence as demonstrated in Table 6.3: the first part contains contrastive minimal pairs of T4a and T4b ending with coda [−ʔ]; those ending in stop coda [−p/−k] are included in the second part; and the third part consists of the minimal pairs of coda [−ʔ] and [−p/−k] in T4a and T4b respectively.

6.4.3 Informant

The recordings of ten informants (five males and five female) are chosen for measurement, including nine from Yun'ao town and one from Shen'ao town. All of them are native speakers of Yun'ao and Shen'ao dialects. Their gender, age (at the time when they were recorded), occupation and educational background are given in Table 6.4.

---

[3] Asterisks indicate that the harmonic/spectral amplitudes are reported with and without correction for formant frequencies and bandwidths as described on the Voicesauce website. https://www.seas.ucla.edu/spapl/voicesauce/.

6.4 Experimental Measures of Acoustic Cues for Phonations in T4a and T4b

Table 6.3 Stimuli for the analysis of checked tones

(1) T4a vs. T4b: Coda [-ʔ]		滴[tiʔ]-碟[tiʔ], 迹[tsiaʔ]-食[tsiaʔ], 接[tsiʔ]-舌[tsiʔ], 百[peʔ]-白[peʔ], 索[soʔ]-镯[soʔ], 借[tsioʔ]-石[tsioʔ], 约[ioʔ]-药[ioʔ], 歇[hiaʔ]-额[hiaʔ], 桌[toʔ]-择[toʔ], 尺[tsioʔ]-席[tsioʔ], 塔[tʰaʔ]-叠[tʰaʔ], 节[tsoiʔ]-截[tsoiʔ], 薛[siʔ]-蚀[siʔ];
(2) T4a vs. T4b: Coda [-p/-k]		得[tik]-直[tik], 色[sek]-熟[sek], 室[sik]-实[sik], 啄[tok]-独[tok], 漆[tsʰak]-贼[tsʰak], 北[pak]-缚[pak], 洁[kiak]-杰[kiak], 竹[tek]-笛[tek], 束[sok]-俗[sok], 发[huak]-罚[huak], 福[hok]-服[hok], 菊[kek]-局[kek], 激[kek]-极[kek], 骨[kuk]-滑[kuk], 剁[tok]-毒[tok], 湿[sip]-习[sip], 忽[huk]-核[huk], 汁[tsap]-十[tsap], 叔[tsek]-蜀[tsek], 踢[tʰak]-读[tʰak], 博[pʰak]-曝[pʰak]
(3) [-ʔ] vs [-p/k]:	T4a	割[kuaʔ]-诀[kuak], 滴[tiʔ]-得[tik], 粕[pʰoʔ]-朴[pʰok], 职[tseʔ]-叔[tsek], 雪[soʔ]-束[sok], 作[tsoʔ]-祝[tsok], 鸭[aʔ]-恶[ak], 只[tsiaʔ]-浙[tsiak], 格[keʔ]-揭[kek], 摘[tiaʔ]-哲[tiak], 塔[tʰaʔ]-踢[tʰak], 百[peʔ]-迫[pek], 客[kʰeʔ]-刻[kʰek], 拆[tʰiaʔ]-彻[tʰiak], 策[tsʰeʔ]-测[tsʰek], 甲[kaʔ]-结[kak], 拍[pʰaʔ]-博[pʰak]; 插[tsʰaʔ43]-贼[tsʰak45], 旭[hiok43]-叶[hioʔ45];
	T4b	叠[tʰaʔ]-读[tʰak], 碟[tiʔ]-直[tik], 合[haʔ]-学[hak], 绝[tsoʔ]-族[tsok], 额[hiaʔ]-协[hiap], 活[uaʔ]-获[uak], 剧[kiaʔ]-杰[kiak], 膜[moʔ]-寞[mok], 裂[liʔ]-日[dzik], 入[dzip], 粒[liap]

Table 6.4 Informants for analysis of checked tones in Yun'ao and Shen'ao dialects

Code	Speaker	Gender	Age	Occupation	Educational background
M1	DZW	Male	74	Teacher (Retired)	Technical secondary school
M2	ZZL	Male	62	Self-employed	High school
M3	XCX	Male	50	Teacher	Technical secondary school
M4	CCS	Male	20	Student	Junior College
M5	SZ	Male	13	Student	Junior Middle School
F1	ZXR	Female	51	Housewife	High school
F2	CMY	Female	41	Housewife	Middle school
F3	ZJF	Female	28	Graduated student	College
F4	ZJW	Female	25	Office Clerk	Junior College
F5	LYS	Female	24	Housewife	Technical secondary school

6.4.4 Result

The average values of each acoustic measure from ten informants are shown in Table 6.5.

The different performances of each acoustic cue are further demonstrated in bar charts. Figures 6.15, 6.16, 6.17, 6.18, 6.19, 6.20 and 6.21 are bar charts with error bars representing the standard error of the mean for each acoustic cue, namely H1-H2 (Fig. 6.15), H2-H4 (Fig. 6.16), H1-A1 (Fig. 6.17), H1-A2 (Fig. 6.18), H1-A3 (Fig. 6.19), CPP (Fig. 6.20), Energy (Fig. 6.21).

Table 6.5 The average values of each acoustic measure among ten speakers of Yun'ao type dialects

Speaker	Tones	H1−H2	H2−H4	H1−A1	H1−A2	H1−A3	CPP	Energy
M1	T4a	−2.754	4.884	12.403	12.847	9.188	21.265	4.523
	T4b	−2.367	5.925	11.523	12.081	8.661	22.230	5.569
M2	T4a	7.690	6.962	23.113	31.559	19.887	18.184	0.439
	T4b	8.113	6.223	21.409	28.949	17.398	17.967	0.431
M3	T4a	−0.047	6.707	16.358	17.211	17.245	19.333	6.302
	T4b	1.557	6.776	17.022	19.095	18.064	19.982	5.906
M4	T4a	−2.645	5.622	13.297	12.290	5.124	24.520	0.525
	T4b	−1.975	6.014	13.502	11.760	4.407	24.792	0.593
M5	T4a	6.025	3.262	19.027	17.650	13.497	20.473	0.550
	T4b	5.859	3.071	18.730	16.815	11.919	22.927	0.740
F1	T4a	5.017	5.681	21.191	22.940	20.505	23.897	0.385
	T4b	5.417	5.369	19.757	21.273	19.027	24.301	0.390
F2	T4a	0.970	2.224	11.251	7.292	3.895	22.667	0.277
	T4b	2.073	2.912	13.137	9.162	5.533	23.652	0.356
F3	T4a	6.098	4.084	20.623	17.709	13.522	22.705	0.106
	T4b	7.373	4.042	21.328	18.540	13.648	24.160	0.126
F4	T4a	4.847	3.818	19.478	15.694	15.116	22.135	0.240
	T4b	5.427	4.259	19.261	15.058	13.108	23.216	0.251
F5	T4a	4.853	4.896	20.710	17.380	14.368	21.594	0.261
	T4b	7.148	4.458	20.698	16.701	12.304	22.832	0.287

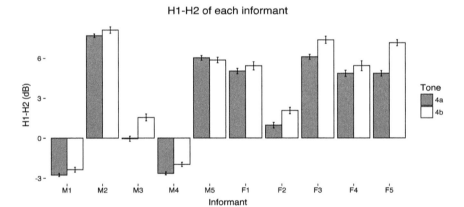

Fig. 6.15 Bar chart with error bar representing the standard error of the mean for H1−H2

6.4 Experimental Measures of Acoustic Cues for Phonations in T4a and T4b 143

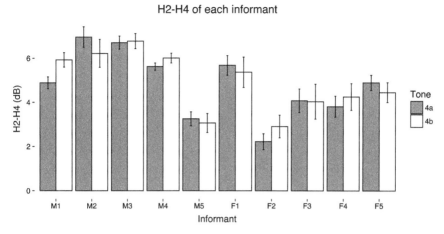

Fig. 6.16 Bar chart with error bar representing the standard error of the mean for H2−H4

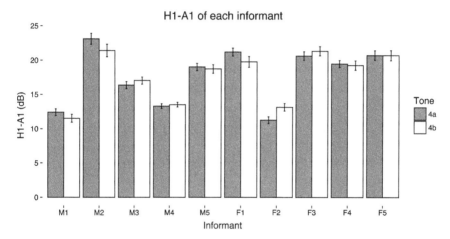

Fig. 6.17 Bar chart with error bar representing the standard error of the mean for H1−A1

Calculated in R, ANOVA is used to indicate whether the cue is significant in distinguishing T4a and T4b. And the statistical results are illustrated in Table 6.6.

In Table 6.6, NS means non-significant, while * denotes statistical significance and *** means high statistical significance just as the significance codes imply. Informants' performances in employing acoustic cues to distinguish T4a and T4b are quite different. Table 6.7 gives a summary of these differences.

All the above statistics lead to the statement that the phonations between checked tones are different. CPP (Cepstral Peak Prominence) turns out to be the most salient cue among speakers to differentiate T4a and T4b (except M2 and M4). CPP distinguishes T4a and T4b in eight out of ten speakers as shown in Table 6.7. CPP is thought

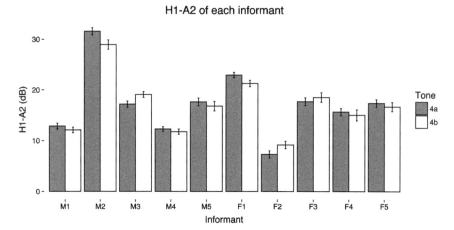

Fig. 6.18 Bar chart with error bar representing the standard error of the mean for H1−A2

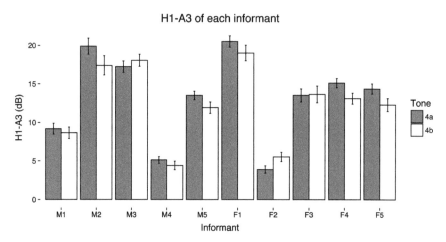

Fig. 6.19 Bar chart with error bar representing the standard error of the mean for H1−A3

to reflect the harmonics-to-noise ratio (Hillenbrand et al. 1994; Thomas 2011: 237–239). A more prominent cepstral peak indicates stronger harmonics above the floor of the spectrum. Less periodic signals such as those often produced in breathy or creaky phonation have a spectrum with a less defined harmonic, resulting in a cepstrum with a low peak. This indicates that the average value of CPP in T4a should be lower than that in T4b, which is true for most speakers (except M2) as shown in Table 6.5 and Fig. 6.20.

The second important cue is H1−H2, which has been found to be useful in distinguishing contrastive phonations in many studies (Keating et al. 2011; Kuang 2011). Hong (2009) finds that H1−H2 is partly successful at separating checked tone syllables from other syllables. Only five speakers employ H1−H2 as a significant cue

6.4 Experimental Measures of Acoustic Cues for Phonations in T4a and T4b 145

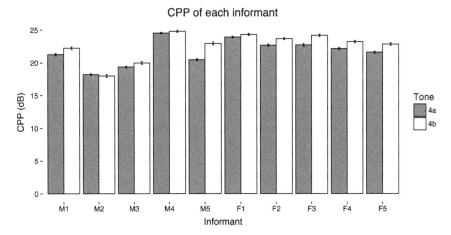

Fig. 6.20 Bar chart with error bar representing the standard error of the mean for CPP

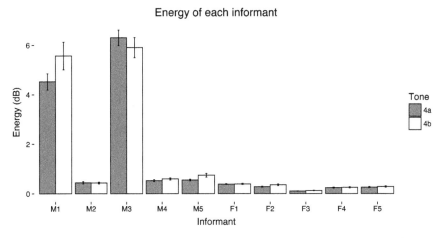

Fig. 6.21 Bar chart with error bar representing the standard error of the mean for ENERGY

to differentiate T4a and T4b as demonstrated in Table 6.7 in our experiment. In the creaky voice, the amplitude of the second harmonic (H2) is slightly greater than that of the fundamental harmonic (H1). Since T4a belongs to creaky voice and T4b belongs to fortis voice, the value of H1−H2 in T4a should be lower than that of T4b. This is true of the mean value of H1−H2 among nine out of ten speakers (except M5) as shown in Table 6.5 and Fig. 6.15.

The cues of H1−A*(A1, A2, A3) turn out to be not successful at separating T4a and T4b. Less than half of ten speakers produce statistically significant differences in the contrast of T4a and T4b. The other two cues, namely H2−H4 and Energy, behave poorly in distinguishing T4a and T4b, with only one or two speaker(s) producing statistically significant differences in T4a and T4b. There are also asymmetries among

Table 6.6 The results of ANOVA on seven acoustic cues

Speaker	H1–H2	H2–H4	H1–A1	H1–A2	H1–A3	CPP	Energy
M1	NS 0.0559	* 0.0153	NS 0.251	NS 0.369	NS 0.611	*** 0.000391	NS 0.0871
M2	NS 0.109	NS 0.336	NS 0.158	* 0.0221	NS 0.124	NS 0.404	NS 0.897
M3	*** 9.9e−07	NS 0.88	NS 0.381	* 0.0302	NS 0.454	** 0.00642	NS 0.431
M4	*** 0.000558	NS 0.149	NS 0.677	NS 0.455	NS 0.292	NS 0.168	NS 0.23
M5	NS 0.546	NS 0.716	NS 0.716	NS 0.487	NS 0.0845	*** <2e−16	** 0.00647
F1	NS 0.266	NS 0.692	NS 0.132	* 0.0446	NS 0.223	* 0.0397	NS 0.862
F2	*** 0.000587	NS 0.267	* 0.0117	NS 0.0684	* 0.0301	*** 5.2e−06	* 0.0365
F3	*** 0.000122	NS 0.964	NS 0.448	NS 0.49	NS 0.925	*** 8.26e−07	NS 0.0791
F4	NS 0.165	NS 0.571	NS 0.795	NS 0.612	* 0.0335	*** 3.43e−05	NS 0.735
F5	*** 1.16e−11	NS 0.433	NS 0.99	NS 0.558	* 0.0494	*** 2.74e−06	NS 0.447

(Significance level: 0.05; Significance codes: 0 '***' 0.001 '**' 0.01 '*' 0.05 '.' 0.1 ' ' 1)

Table 6.7 The different performances of employing acoustic cues to distinguish T4a and T4b by ten speakers

Speaker	H1–H2	H2–H4	H1–A1	H1–A2	H1–A3	CPP	Energy
M1	−	+ (*)	−	−	−	+ (***)	−
M2	−	−	−	+ (*)	−	−	−
M3	+ (***)	−	−	+ (*)	−	+ (**)	−
M4	+ (***)	−	−	−	−	−	−
M5	−	−	−	−	−	+ (***)	+ (**)
F1	−	−	−	+ (*)	−	+ (*)	−
F2	+ (***)	−	+ (*)	−	+ (*)	+ (***)	+ (*)
F3	+ (***)	−	−	−	−	+ (***)	−
F4	−	−	−	−	+ (*)	+ (***)	−
F5	+ (***)	−	−	−	+ (*)	+ (***)	−

(Significance level: 0.05; Significance codes: 0 '***' 0.001 '**' 0.01 '*' 0.05 '.' 0.1 ' ' 1)

speakers in the number of cues that are significant in differentiating T4a and T4b. For instance, only one cue is exploited significantly by M2 to signal the contrast, while F3 produces significant distinctions in most of the cues examined in this experiment.

6.4.5 Conclusion

In a nutshell, there is at least one acoustic cue that is significant in distinguishing T4a and T4b for each speaker. This suggests that there are actually different phonation types existing in T4a and T4b, and speakers vary in the number of phonetic correlates they use to signal the phonation contrast.

Acoustic cues for stiff and fortis voice vary cross-linguistically; moreover, speakers within the same language may employ different cues. Then what acoustic cues best differentiate the phonations of T4a and T4b across speakers? In our experiments, the most salient cue emphasized by most speakers is CPP, followed by H1(*)−H2(*). In addition, there is no special pattern concerning the within-sex variations in our test. The use of acoustic cues varies from speaker to speaker, indicating the existence of individual difference in phonetic implementation.

6.5 The Significance of the Yun'ao Case

Motivated by different phonation types, the evolutionary routes of T4a and T4b are distinct. T4a becomes a low tone while T4b changes to a high tone. The Yun'ao case is of great significance for it denotes the transitional stage of the above changes.

Two tentative statements with respect to Yun'ao dialect can be made at present.

First, the change of checked tone is not a sudden "flip-flop" but a gradual phonetic change motivated by different phonation types. Such a claim casts doubt on our existing understanding of phonological change. If "flip-flop" is viewed as occurring in small cumulative phonetic increments, how can a historical "flip-flop" between a high tone and low tone be brought about without the two tones merging with each other at some stage? This is exactly the question asked in Wang (1967). The contour distinctions, being the primary reason, can explain this historical mystery of "flip-flop".

Among the multiple acoustic correlates of checked tones, pitch contour serves as a primary cue in Yun'ao dialect. This leads to our second tentative statement—phonetically short tone syllables can have contour distinctions as well. The emergence of different contours of T4a and T4b can be attributed to the distinction of phonations, with creaky voice (stiff voice) in T4a and glottal stop (fortis voice) in T4b, as shown in the above discussion. Using data from ten informants (introduced in Table 6.4), we further calculate the Pearson's product-moment correlation coefficient[4] between slope and absolute duration in T4a and T4b respectively. According to Cohen's effect size benchmarks (Cohen 1988: 79–80), Pearson's product-moment correlation between slope and absolute duration for T4a is close to zero ($r = -0.0763548$, p-value $= 0.04012$), and the correlation for T4b is small ($r = 0.1696595$, p-value $= 4.135e{-}05$). It seems that absolute duration may be an indicator of T4b's contour in synchronic system, but this is not the case for T4a. The presence of T4a tokens close to the x-axis throughout the slope's entire range indicates that duration is not a factor in controlling the contour of T4a. Therefore, contours of T4a should not be viewed as a byproduct of extended duration. The positive correlation of slope and duration in T4b implies that duration will increase when slope is extended. The discrepancy of the correlation between T4a and T4b may suggest that rising contour needs more duration to realize its contour target compared with falling contour.

The covariation values of slope and CPP in T4a and T4b are not big. Pearson's product-moment correlation between slope and CPP for T4a is near zero ($r = -0.0456792$, p-value $= 0.2199$), indicating no meaningful slope-CPP pattern; and the correlation for T4b is medium ($r = -0.2711341$, p-value $= 3.381e{-}11$). However, the small values of covariation of slope and CPP do not invalidate the correlation between contour and phonation, since we use only one acoustic cue to calculate.

As is shown above, phonation may have multiple phonetic manifestations. It is safe at present to say that contour has become an independent production target for checked tones notwithstanding the fact that they are triggered by phonation. All in all, the Yun'ao case provides better support for the claim that the historical "flip-flop" is accomplished through gradual phonetic change. At the same time, two distinctions, namely different contours and different phonations, between T4a and T4b are the reason why they do not merge in the process of this "flip-flop" change.

6.6 Summary

With the aid of the different pitch relations of checked tones, an evolutionary path for the checked tones of Chaoshan dialect can be proposed. Four stages are identified for the "flip-flop" change from "Yin-high versus Yang-low" to "Yin-low versus Yang-high".

Being the transitional stages, Yun'ao type and Dahao type are characterized by distinctive pitch contours in T4a and T4b. Experimental measures of acoustic cues using data from ten Yun'ao speakers confirm that there are different phonation types in T4a and T4b. Among the multiple acoustic measures, CPP turns out to be the most salient cue in distinguishing T4a and T4b because most speakers in our sample have

---

[4]Pearson's product-moment correlation coefficient is a measure of the linear correlation between two variables X and Y, giving a value between $+1$ and -1 inclusive, where 1 is total positive correlation, 0 is no correlation, and -1 is total negative correlation. This definition is cited from Wikipedia: https://en.wikipedia.org/wiki/Pearson_product-moment_correlation_coefficient.

6.6 Summary

produced significantly differences in CPP. It is plausible that the phonation contrasts lead to contour distinctions of checked tones. After the emergence of pitch contours for checked tones, they become independent production targets to some extent.

As can be seen in the above discussion, contour is an important dimension for contrast between T4a and T4b in the first three stages. However, Chaozhou type dialects, being at the last stage of checked tone development, do not maintain the distinction of contours. By contrast, the distinction of pitch heights is more salient when distinguishing between T4a and T4b in Chaozhou type dialects.

The most important finding in this chapter is that the historical "flip-flop" is accomplished via a process of gradual phonetic change. Different tonal contours and different phonation types are the reason why this process of gradual phonetic change does not cause a tonal merger of T4a and T4b. Triggered by different phonations, contour becomes an independent production target for checked tones. In the transitional stage seen in Yun'ao dialect, pitch contours as well as phonations are significantly different between T4a and T4b in all informants investigated. Simply put, contour and phonation are two pivotal factors that shape the development of checked tones in Chaoshan dialects. Moreover, the change of the so-called "flip-flop" of checked tones in Chaoshan dialects can shed a light on the evolution of checked tones of other Chinese.

References

Chen, Limin. 2014. Glottal stop production and its interaction with tonal evolution: A case study of entering tone sound change in Puxian Min. Mphil thesis. The Hong Kong University of Science and Technology.

Cohen, J. 1988. *Statistical Power Analysis for the Behavioral Sciences*. Routledge.

Edmondson, J.A., and J.H. Esling. 2006. The valves of the throat and their functioning in tone, vocal register, and stress: Laryngoscopic case studies. *Phonology* 23: 157–191.

Esling, J.H., K.E. Fraser, and J.G. Harris. 2005. Glottal stop, glottalized resonants, and pharyngeals: A reinterpretation with evidence from a laryngoscopic study of Nuuchahnulth (Nootka). *Journal of Phonetics* 3(4): 383–410.

Garellek, Marc. 2013. "Production and Perception of Glottal Stops." Ph.D dissertation, University of California, Los Angeles.

Gordon, M., and P. Ladefoged. 2001. Phonation types: A cross-linguistic overview. *Journal of Phonetics* 4: 383–406. https://doi.org/10.1006/jpho.2001.0147.

Hillenbrand, James, Ronald Cleveland, and A and Erickson, Robert. L. 1994. Acoustic correlates of breathy vocal quality. *Journal of Speech and Hearing Research*. 37: 769–778.

Hong, Ying. 2009. Phonation Types in the entering tone syllables of Chaozhou dialect. M.Phil Thesis, Hong Kong: The Hong Kong University of Technology and Science.

Hong, Ying. 2013. A phonetic study of Chaozhou Chinese. Ph.D. Thesis, Hong Kong: The University of Hong Kong Science and Technology.

Iwata, R. 岩田礼. 1984. 南部中国语の音节末闭锁音. *Speech Studies* 言语研究 87: 21–39.

Iwata, R. 岩田礼. 1992. Hanyu fangyan Rusheng yinjie de shengli tezheng—jianlun Rusheng yunwei de lishi bianhua. 汉语方言入声音节的生理特征——兼论入声韵尾的历时变化. *Zhongguo Jingnei Yuyan Ji Yuyanxue* 中國境內語言暨語言學 1: 523–537.

Keating, P., C. Esposito, M. Garellek, S. Khan, and ud D., and Kuang, J. 2011. *Phonation contrasts across languages*. Hong Kong: Presented at the ICPhS XVII.

Kong, Jiangping. 孔江平. 2001. *Lun Yuyan Fasheng* 论语言发声. Beijing: Zhongyang Minzu Daxue Chubanshe 中央民族大学出版社.

Kuang, Jianjing. 2011. Phonation Contrast in Two Register Contrast Languages and Its Influence on Vowel Quality and Tone. In *Proceedings of the 17th International Congress of Phonetic Sciences*, 1146–1149. Hong Kong.

Ladefoged, P., and Maddieson, I. 1996. *The Sounds of the World's Languages*. Blackwell Publishers.

Laver, J. 1994. *Principles of Phonetics*. Cambridge: Cambridge University Press.

Ohala, J.J. 1987. Sound change is drawn from a pool of synchronic variation. *Presented at the Symposium on The causes of Language Change, Do We Know Them Yet?* Norway: University of Troms.

Ren, Chao Yuen, Li Fang Kuei, and Luo Changpei. 1948. *Translation, Zhongguo Yinyunxue Yanjiu* 中国音韵学研究. Beijing: Shangwu yinshuguan 商务印书馆.

Thomas, E. 2011. *Sociophonetics: An Introduction*. Palgrave Macmillan.

Wang, William S-Y. 1967. Phonological Features of Tone. *International Journal of American Linguistics* 33(2): 93–105.

Yue-Hashimoto, A.O. (1986). Tonal Flip-Flop in Chinese Dialects. *Journal of Chinese Linguistics* 14(2): 161–82.

Zhu, Xiaonong. Jiao, Lei. Yim, Chi Sing and Hong, Ying. 朱晓农 & 焦磊 & 严至诚 & 洪英. 2008. 入声演化三途. [Three ways of Rusheng sound change]. *Zhongguo Yuwen* 中国语文 4: 324–338.

Zeng, Nanyi. 曾南逸. 2013. Quanxia Fangyan Yinyun Bijiao Yanjiu. 泉厦方言音韵比较研究. Peking University (A dissertation for the degree Doctor of Philosophy). 北京大学博士学位论文.

Zhu, Xiaonong and Hong, Ying. 朱晓农 & 洪英. 2009. 潮州话入声的阴低阳高 [The Phonetic Nature of the Entering Tones in Chaozhou Dialect]. *Bulletin of Chinese Linguistics* 4 (1): 115–128.

Zhu, Xiaonong. 朱晓农. 2005. 上海声调实验录 *An Experimental Study of Shanghai Tones*. 上海教育出版社 Shanghai: Shanghai Educational Press.

Zhu, Xiaonong. 朱晓农. 2008. 音节和音节学 [Syllable and syllabics]. *Oriental Linguistics* 4: 142–164.

Zhu, Xiaonong. 朱晓农. 2010. 语音学. *Phonetics: An Introduction*. Beijing: Commercial Press.

Zhu, Xiaonong. 朱晓农. 2011. 语言语音学和音法学:理论新框架 [Linguistic phonetics and panchronic phonology: A new theoretical framework. 语言研究 31.1: 4–85.

Zhu, Xiaonong. 朱晓农. 2015. *Phonetics, Articulatory*. International Encyclopedia of the Social and Behavioral Sciences, 2nd edition,/Edited by James D. Wright. Elsevier, pp. 65–74.

Chapter 7
Conclusion

Abstract This chapter briefly highlights some major findings as well as topics that should be on the research agenda for the future. This book not only presents tonal patterns based on abundant acoustic data, but also offers theoretical considerations on the tonal changes of Chaoshan Chinese. Improving sampling method, conducting more perceptual experiments, and enlarging the stylistic range are the three main tasks that the author will take in the future.

Keywords Conclusion · Major findings · Possible improvements

Tonal patterns and evolutionary routes of tones in the Chaoshan area are the chief topics of this book. I hope by doing this research to reinforce the natural alliance of phonetics, historical linguistics, sociolinguistics and dialect geography—fields that share a common interest in observing objective data. The connections made benefit from the development of sound recording techniques, instrumental analysis methods and field survey methodology, etc.

When compared to traditional research on Chaoshan dialect, ours differs in several ways. First, it uses firsthand acoustic data to study the tonal patterns of Chaoshan Chinese. Second, the models of MRFL ("Multi-register and four-level" model) and TAS ("Tonal Acoustic Space" model) are exploited to demonstrate the tonal variations within and across speakers as well as dialectical varieties. Finally, armed with the perspective of evolution, several tonal changes have been identified to account for the existence of diversified tonal patterns.

Having demonstrated the tonal patterns and worked through certain phenomena relating to tonal changes in Chaoshan Chinese in Chaps. 3 through 6, in this final chapter, I would like to briefly highlight some major findings as well as topics that should be on the research agenda for the future.

7.1 Summary of the Major Findings

This book not only presents tonal patterns based on abundant acoustic data, but also offers theoretical considerations on the tonal changes of Chaoshan Chinese.

7.1.1 Phonetic Data Exploration

1. Enrich the "universal tonal inventories"

    Tono-types identified in Chaoshan Chinese can enrich the "universal tonal inventories" and facilitate our reconsideration of the phonetic representation of each tono-type in different dialects. For the sake of simplicity, we are now mainly concerned with the following four aspects.

    (1) Tri-length distinction

    Previously, length has been deemed a key factor in separating checked tones from unchecked tones; and its role in unchecked tones is seldom noticed. Our data show that length also plays a pivotal role in distinguishing two unchecked falling tones. The tri-length distinction of tones in Lugang (in Chaonan District) and Yun'ao (in Nan'ao County) dialects is of great typological significance.

    (2) Short tones with contour distinctions

    Yun'ao dialect suggests that phonetically short tone syllables can have contour distinctions as demonstrated in Chap. 6. Short tone syllables are usually thought to be ineligible for contour realization. Therefore, checked tones, being short tones in most dialects, are often transcribed with a single number under FPS indicating their non-contour characteristic. However, the Yun'ao case shows that short tones can maintain contour differences too, and those different contours may serve as a critical factor in the course of tonal evolution.

    (3) Two slight falling tones

    Two slight falling tones co-exist in Houzhai dialect in Nan'ao County, and they are T1b and T3b (see Sect. 3.12). Their distinction mainly relies on pitch height, as demonstrated in the tonal acoustic space in Fig. 7.1.

    (4) The phonetic manifestations of the pure low tone

    According to our field investigations, there are at least two phonetic manifestations of the pure low tone. One is without fixed contour and can be realized as the lowest level {22}, the lowest falling {32}, the lowest rising {23} and the lowest dipping {323}. The pure low tone in Jinping dialect (Shantou City) belongs to this type. The other has a fixed contour, like the

7.1 Summary of the Major Findings

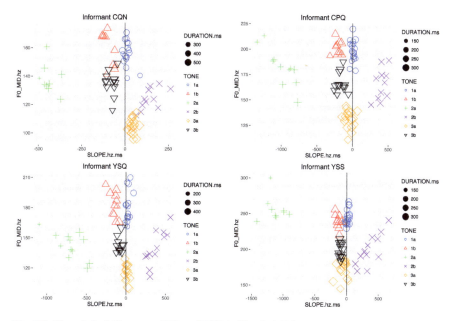

Fig. 7.1 Two slight falling tones (T1b and T3b) in Houzhai dialect

case in Liusha dialect. The pure low tone in Liusha dialect is T3a, which is always realized as the lowest falling {32}.

The pure low tone with a fixed contour may serve as an indicator of sound change in progress. T1a is the pure low tone of Lugang dialect (Chaonan District); its phonetic representation is the lowest falling contour and does not alter with other contours. This suggests that T1a may be undergoing some kind of evolution. This speculation is supported by the multiple tonal variations displayed by younger speakers, whose T1a has evolved to the low falling tone /42/. Figures 7.2 and 7.3 plot the frequency curves and

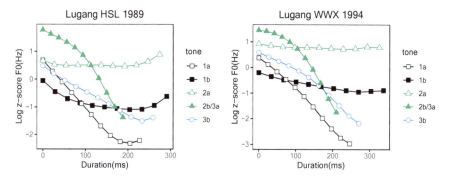

Fig. 7.2 Frequency curves of five unchecked tones produced by two younger Lugang speakers

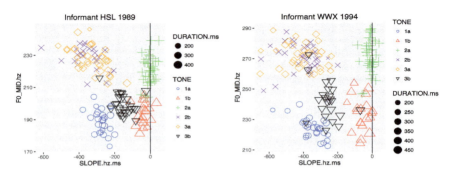

Fig. 7.3 Tonal acoustic space of five unchecked tones produced by two younger Lugang speakers

tonal acoustic space of the five unchecked tones from two younger Lugang speakers (Figs. 7.4, 7.5, 7.6 and 7.7).

2. Make a classification of Chaoshan dialects based on tonal patterns

In Chap. 3, we have demonstrated fourteen tonal patterns under the MRFL model in the Chaoshan area. If we take the typological and evolutionary approach, we can divide these eleven out of fourteen tonal patterns into three groups, namely Shaojie type, Huipu type and Chaoyang type. Each group displays diversified tonal patterns that can be explained by the process of tonal evolution. It should be noted that tone systems in the Chaoshan area evolve mainly through merger and

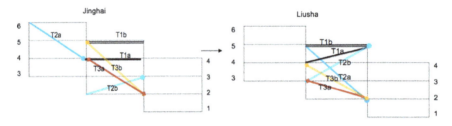

Fig. 7.4 Tonal patterns from Jinghai dialect to Liusha dialect

(2) From older speakers of Jinghai to their younger counterparts

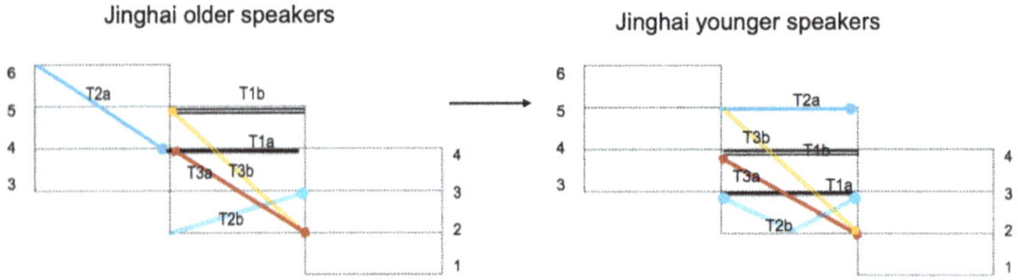

Fig. 7.5 Tonal patterns from older speakers of Jinghai to their younger counterparts

7.1 Summary of the Major Findings

(3) From suburban Chaoyang (Lugang) dialect to central Chaoyang (Miancheng) dialect

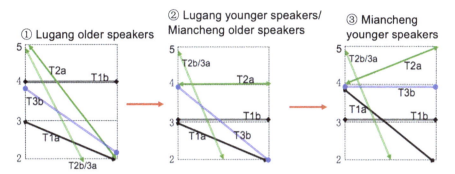

Fig. 7.6 Tonal patterns from Lugang dialect (older speaker) to Miancheng dialect (younger speaker)

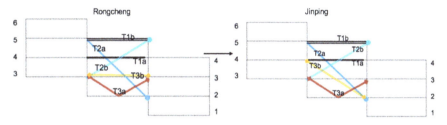

Fig. 7.7 Tonal patterns from Rongcheng dialect to Jinping dialect

phonetic changes in the phonation type or the pitch (both height and contour). Tone splitting—a way that tonal languages gain new tonal contrasts—is not spotted in this region yet.

3. Find out evolutionary routes of Chaoshan tones
   From the perspective of tonal patterns, the main evolutionary paths of unchecked tones in the Chaoshan area can be summarized as follows.

   (1) From Jinghai dialect to Liusha dialect (Fig. 7.4)
   (2) From older speakers of Jinghai to their younger counterparts (Fig. 7.5)
   (3) From suburban Chaoyang (Lugang) dialect to central Chaoyang (Miancheng) dialect (Fig. 7.6)
   (4) Tonal changes within the Shanjie type
       A. From Rongcheng (Jieyang) dialect to Jinping (Shantou) dialect (Fig. 7.7)
       B. From Rongcheng (Jieyang) dialect to Fenghuang (Chaozhou) dialect (Fig. 7.8).

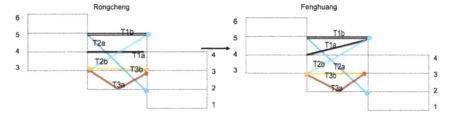

Fig. 7.8 Tonal patterns from Rongcheng dialect to Fenghuang dialect

7.1.2 Theoretical Explorations

1. The approach of variation towards tonal change

   This book confirms the effectiveness of the perspective of variations in investigating the sound change in progress. The focus on variation has offered new insights with regard to tonal changes.

   First of all, the models to quantify tonal variations make possible dramatic improvements in the observational and descriptive adequacy of our accounts of sound change. A single speaker sometimes shows multiple variations, from which sound change will emerge. For instance, tonal variations among older speakers of Jinghai dialect reveal that the fortis voice in the production of T2a is not stable; and this instability may trigger further tonal changes. Another example is the case from Miancheng dialect, and the tonal pull chain shift is determined by referring to the multiple variations presented by different speakers.

   Secondly, the direction of sound change can be inferred from age-based differences as well as geographic variations. If sound change is actually under way, we can further study the social and linguistic mechanisms underlying this change; as with the Chaoyang dialects, younger speakers are the leaders in T2a's change from a high convex falling tone to a high-level tone.

   Lastly, synchronic differences across dialects may reflect diachronically different stages of sound change. Based on the different relationships of T4a and T4b across different Southern Min dialects, four stages are identified for the "flip-flop" change from "Yin-high vs. Yang-low" to "Yin-low vs. Yang-high" of checked tones.

2. The clock explanation of tone change

   Dramatic tonal changes in the Huipu and Chaoyang areas have enabled us to elaborate an insightful "clock model" to account for those changes. The methodology to tackle the development of tones in Chaoshan Chinese is within the scope of historical linguistics.

   The basic assumption is that dialects within one specific area share a common proto-language. Differences displayed by different dialects actually reflect the distinctive stages of diachronic change from this proto-language. When faced with a single tonal pattern, we gain little knowledge about the diachronic changes of tones. However, if enough tonal patterns within one area and tonal variations from multiple speakers are noted, a rich field of possible tonal chain shifts begins to emerge.

We propose a V-shaped chain shift and a pull chain shift to account for the tonal developments in the Huipu area and the Miancheng town, respectively. By putting falling tones on the left side and rising tones on the right side, with level tones at the top and the pure low tone at the bottom, we can connect the relevant individual tone changes.

Consequently, a clock model that signals the direction of tone changes can be established. The V-shaped shift in the Huipu area progresses in an anti-clockwise direction; while the pull chain shift in Miancheng dialect takes a clockwise direction. The clock model can provide us with a plausible interpretation with regard to tonal changes in the Huipu and Chaoyang areas. How the situation plays out when tonal changes actually happen in other dialects or languages remains to be documented.

The clock model can be used to denote and explain the tonal developments in a very explicit way. However, it lacks predictability, and should not be used to infer future sound change, because the underlying motive that will probably decide the direction of tonal change varies from dialect to dialect. The theory of the clock model should further be tested using other tonal languages worldwide. We believe that the chief value of a theory is in establishing the most important matters of fact.

7.2 Future Research and Improvement

There are a number of directions in which we can extend and improve our tentative study. Three possible improvements are discussed below.

1. Improve sampling method

   One shortcoming of this book lies in the sampling method, which is far from rigorous. The number of informants interviewed varies with different age groups and geographic regions, since they are recruited merely by using the social network of the author. This method will lead to the bias of selecting the most available informant in a given area. Moreover, dialects in Shanwei City have not been covered yet. What are the tonal patterns and developments of tones in Shanwei City? In particular, are there any interactions between Shanwei dialects and the nearby Huilai dialects? This should be one of the topics I will address in the future.

   In future work, we will improve our method of sampling with respect to choosing the dialects and informants. For instance, in probing the change of T2a in the Chaoyang area, we will include more informants covering different genders, ages, occupations, educational levels, family background, etc. Only by doing this can we show the social distribution of T2a's change and establish the social motivation of this change. An adequate number of samples is a prerequisite for making statements about developments through various social factors. Simply put, the sampling requirements should be more rigid; and the statistical techniques used to assess the role of social factor in language change should be more advanced.

2. Conduct more perceptual experiments

    This book mainly studies the acoustic characteristics of tones, so the perceptual property of tones is still little known. Although the perceptual experiment conducted here is somewhat crude (Sect. 5.2.2), the results are very promising. With tentative findings from the above perceptual experiments in hand, it would be possible to gain more insight into the mechanism of sound changes through more perceptual experiments. We should refine and improve the methods used, and recruit more informants to participate in the perceptual experiments.

3. Enlarge the stylistic range

    We are only concerned with citation tones in this book, so the tonal variations presented here are far from comprehensive. If we want to obtain more details about tonal evolution, the source of our data should be substantially enlarged. For example, the method of having informants read carrying sentences or phrases will give a wider range of contexts, making the comparison between variations in different positions possible. Given the complexity of the Chaoshan citation tones, it is of great interest to see what happens to them in tone sandhi. In addition, our sample of data is recorded via reading wordlists. What will the tonal system be like in other speech styles, such as in casual speech and careful speech?

    In conclusion, the area of variation is very promising with regard to tonal change in Chinese and this book is only a beginning.

Appendix A
Wordlists for Analysis of Tonal System

(1) The first wordlist

Groups	T1a	T1b	T2a	T2b	T3a	T3b	T4a	T4b
1. taŋ	东	铜	党	重	放	洞	答	毒
2. to	刀	逃	短	在	倒水	袋	剁	独
3. ti	低	池	比	弟	帝	地	得	直
4. ku	龟	衫橱	久	舅	句	旧	骨	滑

(2) The second wordlist

Tones	Stimuli
T1a	曝干家胶龟机歌刀波猪一支笔居牙膏
T1b	鹅橱池旗茶无爬逃
T2a	嫂举饱语宝武真假比米久短稿马一把米
T2b	下矮父咬根据弟舅杂技工具币在
T3a	帝报嫁智句痣神秘架教戴帽霸记两块富
T3b	治代袋避旧帽味地箸筷子关闭作弊准备
T4a	百迫鸭恶桌剁滴得搭答砌急甲角吸骨竹索雪
T4b	踏毒碟直合学择滑缚白

Appendix B
Dialect Sites and Number of Informants

Num. of informants	Dialect sites
9	Jinping district, Shantou City 汕头市金平区
2	Longhu district, Shantou City 汕头市龙湖区
7	Chenghai district, Shantou City 汕头市澄海区
12	Haojiang district, Shantou City 汕头市濠江区
25[a]	Miancheng town, Chaoyang distrcict, Shantou City 汕头市潮阳区棉城镇
2	Jinpu town, Chaoyang distrcict, Shantou City 汕头市潮阳区金浦镇
4	Haimen town, Chaoyang distrcict, Shantou City 汕头市潮阳区海门镇
12[b]	Gurao town, Chaoyang distrcict, Shantou City 汕头市潮阳区谷饶镇
5	Tongyu town, Chaoyang distrcict, Shantou City 汕头市潮阳区铜盂镇
9	Guiyu town, Chaoyang distrcict, Shantou City 汕头市潮阳区贵屿镇
9[c]	Xilu town, Chaoyang distrcict, Shantou City 汕头市潮阳区西胪镇
2	Guanbu town, Chaoyang distrcict, Shantou City 汕头市潮阳区关埠镇
1	Jinzao town, Chaoyang distrcict, Shantou City 汕头市潮阳区金灶镇
9	Lugang town, Chaonan distrcict, Shantou City 汕头市潮南区胪岗镇
8	Liangying town, Chaonan distrcict, Shantou City 汕头市潮南区两英镇
3[d]	Xiashan town, Chaonan distrcict, Shantou City 汕头市潮南区峡山镇
2	Longtian town, Chaonan distrcict, Shantou City 汕头市潮南区陇田镇
1	Chendian town, Chaonan distrcict, Shantou City 汕头市潮南区陈店镇
1	Xiancheng town, Chaonan distrcict, Shantou City 汕头市潮南区仙城镇
1	Simapu, Chaonan distrcict, Shantou City 汕头市潮南区司马浦镇
1	Hongchang town, Chaonan distrcict, Shantou City 汕头市潮南区红场镇
15	Yun'ao town, Nanao County, Shantou City 汕头市南澳县云澳镇
5	Houzhai town, Nanao County, Shantou City 汕头市南澳县后宅镇
4	Shen'ao town, Nanao County, Shantou City 汕头市南澳县深澳镇
4	Qing'ao town, Nanao County, Shantou City 汕头市南澳县青澳镇

(continued)

(continued)

Num. of informants	Dialect sites
11	Rongcheng Distrcict, Jieyang City 揭阳市榕城区
1	Yuhu town, Rongcheng Distrcict, Jieyang City 揭阳市榕城区渔湖镇
3	Denggang town, Rongcheng Distrcict, Jieyang City 揭阳市榕城区登岗镇
1	Paotai town, Rongcheng Distrcict, Jieyang City 揭阳市榕城区炮台镇
1	Didu town, Rongcheng Distrcict, Jieyang City 揭阳市榕城区地都镇
1	Quxi town, Jiedong Distrcict, Jieyang City 揭阳市揭东区曲溪镇
1	Yuecheng town, Jiedong Distrcict, Jieyang City 揭阳市揭东区月城镇
2	Xinheng town, Jiedong Distrcict, Jieyang City 揭阳市揭东区新亨镇
1	Yunlu town, Jiedong Distrcict, Jieyang City 揭阳市揭东区云路镇
2	Mianhu town, Jiexi County, Jieyang City 揭阳市揭西县棉湖镇
1	Tatou town, Jiexi County, Jieyang City 揭阳市揭西县塔头镇
9	Liusha District, Puning county-level City, Jieyang City 揭阳市普宁市流沙区
1	Hongyang town, Puning county-level City, Jieyang City 揭阳市普宁市洪阳镇
2	Nanxi town, Puning county-level City, Jieyang City 揭阳市普宁市南溪镇
1	Meitang town, Puning county-level City, Jieyang City 揭阳市普宁市梅塘镇
1	Lihu town, Puning county-level City, Jieyang City 揭阳市普宁市里湖镇
1	Daba town, Puning county-level City, Jieyang City 揭阳市普宁市大坝镇
3	Qilin town, Puning county-level City, Jieyang City 揭阳市普宁市麒麟镇
3	Zhanlong town, Puning county-level City, Jieyang City 揭阳市普宁市占陇镇
1	Nanjing town, Puning county-level City, Jieyang City 揭阳市普宁市南径镇
2	Puqiao District, Puning county-level City, Jieyang City 揭阳市普宁市普侨区
4	Huicheng town, Huilai County, Jieyang City 揭阳市惠来县惠城镇
6	Jinghai town, Huilai County, Jieyang City 揭阳市惠来县靖海镇
1	Donglong town, Huilai County, Jieyang City 揭阳市惠来县东陇镇
1	Xian'an town, Huilai County, Jieyang City 揭阳市惠来县仙庵镇
2	Longjiang town, Huilai County, Jieyang City 揭阳市惠来县隆江镇
2	Huahu town, Huilai County, Jieyang City 揭阳市惠来县华湖镇
1	Qianzhan town, Huilai County, Jieyang City 揭阳市惠来县前詹镇
1	Shenquan town, Huilai County, Jieyang City 揭阳市惠来县神泉镇
1	Kuitan town, Huilai County, Jieyang City 揭阳市惠来县葵潭镇
6[e]	Xiangqiao District, Chaozhou City. 潮州市湘桥区
6[f]	Anbu town, Chao'an District, Chaozhou City 潮州市潮安区庵埠镇
4	Dongfeng town, Chao'an District, Chaozhou City 潮州市潮安区东凤镇

(continued)

Appendix B: Dialect Sites and Number of Informants

(continued)

Num. of informants	Dialect sites
1	Fuyang town, Chao'an District, Chaozhou City 潮州市潮安区浮洋镇
3[g]	Fenghuang town, Chao'an District, Chaozhou City 潮州市潮安区凤凰镇
6[h]	Huanggang town, Raoping County, Chaozhou City 潮州市饶平县黄冈镇
2	Haishan town, Raoping County, Chaozhou City 潮州市饶平县海山镇
2	jingzhou town, Raoping County, Chaozhou City 潮州市饶平县汫洲镇
1	Suocheng town, Raoping County, Chaozhou City 潮州市饶平县所城镇
1	Xinxu town, Raoping County, Chaozhou City 潮州市饶平县新圩镇
1	Fubin town, Raoping County, Chaozhou City 潮州市饶平县浮滨镇
Total: 255	65 Sites

[a] Lin Qing collected two Miancheng informants' data
[b] Lin Qing collected four informants' data and Prof. Zhu Xiaonong collected four informants' data, while Lin Wenfang collected three informants' data. It is very generous of them to share the data with me
[c] Lin Qing collected three Xilu informants' data
[d] Lin Qing collected two Xiashan informants' data
[e] Lin Qing collected three informants' data and Hongying collected two informants' data
[f] Data of Anbu, Dongfeng and Fuyang are collected by Hong Ying. Tonal data of Chaozhou colledted by Hongying are presented in Hong (2013). We reanalyzed the data and used them as a reference when discussing tonal system of Chaozhou City
[g] Lin Qing collected the data of Fenghuang town
[h] Lin Qing collected three informants' data and Hongying collected two informants' data

Reference

Hong, Ying. 2013. A phonetic study of Chaozhou Chinese. Ph.D. Thesis, Hong Kong: The University of Hong Kong Science and Technology.

Appendix C
Informants From the Shanjie Type

Dialect sites		Name of speakers	Gender	Year of birth	Occupation	Educational background
Rongcheng District, Jieyang City	Meiyun Street	LWR	Male	1973	Self-employed	Primary school
	Sima Street	CW	Male	1984	Bank clerk	College
	Ronghua Street	CLL	Female	1991	Graduated student	College
	Xiaoqiao Street	HMF	Female	1988	Civil servant	College
	Paotai Town	HM	Female	1985	Self-employed	Technical secondary school
	Denggang Town	ZST	Male	1979	Self-employed	Middle school
	Ditu Town	ZHD	Male	1987	Civil servant	College
	Yuhu Town	YQZ	Female	1985	Teacher	College
Jiexi County, Jieyang City	Mianhu Town	SJW	Male	1979	Self-employed	Middle school
	Tatou Town	WMC	Male	1991	Graduated student	College
Jiedong District, Jieyang City	Quxi Town	WXH	Female	1994	Student	Junior College
	Xinheng Town	CHX	Female	1992	Civil servant	College
	Yuecheng Town	ZDB	Male	1989	Civil servant	College
	Yunlu Town	LB	Male	1978	Bank clerk	College

(continued)

(continued)

Dialect sites		Name of speakers	Gender	Year of birth	Occupation	Educational background
Puning County-level City, Jieyang City	Daba Town	TGX	Male	1983	Lawyer	College
	Hongyang Town	FZZ	Male	1987	Teacher	College
	Nanxi Town	ZXR	Female	1977	Teacher	Junior College
	Lihu Town	ZXQ	Male	1991	Graduated student	College
	Meitang Town	LSZ	Female	1973	Teacher	Technical secondary school
	Puqiao District	FHL	Female	1980	Teacher	Junior College
Chao'an District, Chaozhou City	Anbu Town	CH	Female	1979	/	College
	Dongfeng Town	CSR	Male	1948	/	College
	Fuyang Town	TYM	Female	1977	/	College
Raoping County, Chaozhou City	Fubin Town	XJL	Female	1989	Nurse	Junior College
	Haishan Town	LWF	Male	1986	Fisherman	Middle school
	Huanggang Town	LH	Female	1956	/	High school
	Jingzhou Town	MWP	Male	1979	Self-employed	Primary schoole
	Suocheng Town	YZS	Male	1991	Lawyer	College
	Xinxu Town	WCJ	Male	1992	Student	Junior College
Chenghai District, Shantou City	Guangyi Street	XJ	Female	1993	Student	College
	Fengxiang Street	WSH	Male	1983	Civil servant	College
	Dongli Town	CDF	Male	1985	Civil servant	College
	Lianxia Town	LXP	Male	1986	Doctor	College
	Shanghua Town	ZGX	Female	1990	Student	College
Long hu District, Shantou City	Xinxi Town	XRE	Female	1985	Housewife	Junior College

(continued)

Appendix C: Informants From the Shanjie Type

(continued)

Dialect sites		Name of speakers	Gender	Year of birth	Occupation	Educational background
Chaoyang District, Shantou City	Jinzao Town	HJH	Male	1984	Graduated student	College
	Guanbu Town	HZP	Male	1985	Doctor	College
		XXW	Male	1987	Student	College
Shantou City	Jinping District	CQY	Female	1962	Housewife	Middle school
		ZWP	Female	1987	Research fellow	College
Chaozhou City	Xiangqiao District	YZR	Male	1994	Student	College

Appendix D
Informants From the Huipu Type

Dialect sites		Name of speakers	Gender	Year of birth	Occupation	Educational background
Puning County-level City, Jieyang City	Liusha Street	CPH	Female	1979	Housewife	Technical secondary school
		CWH	Female	1979	Teacher	Junior College
		QSN	Female	1988	Teacher	College
		HJR	Female	1989	Graduated student	College
		ZP	Male	1991	Graduated student	College
		ZZB	Male	1999	Graduated student	College
	Liaoyuan Street	LHL	Male	1994	Student	Junior College
	Chiwei Street	CGW	Male	1990	Student	College
	Zhanlong Town	HHB	Male	1979	Civil servant	Junior College
		YLY	Female	1980	Teacher	Junior College
Huilai County, Jieyang City	Huicheng Town	YLW	Male	1958	Self-employed	Middle school
		CDF	Female	1985	Bank clerk	College
		LDX	Female	1988	Teacher	College
	Shenquan Town	XYW	Male	1985	Doctor	College

(continued)

(continued)

Dialect sites		Name of speakers	Gender	Year of birth	Occupation	Educational background
	Kuitan Town	DHR	Male	1958	Teacher	Junior College
	Donglong Town	WRF	Male	1989	Civil servant	College
	Longjiang Town	CXD	Male	1988	Student	College
		WZG	Male	1994	Student	College
	Qianzhan Town	ZXY	Female	1994	Student	Junior College
	Huahu Town	FWQ	Male	1998	Worker	Primary school
	Jinghai Town	LYC	Male	1955	Fisherman	Primary school
		LHZ	Male	1967	Fisherman	Primary school
		LQJ	Male	1980	Clerk	Junior College
		SZX	Male	1988	Teacher	College
		LCR	Female	1999	Student	Middle school
	Xian'an Town	WWJ	Female	1991	Teacher	College

Appendix E
Informants From the Chaoyang Type

Dialect sites		Name of speakers	Gender	Year of birth	Occupation	Educational background
Chaonan District, Shantou City	Lugang Town	WQB	Male	1947	Self-employed	Primary school
		WHS	Male	1949	Self-employed	Primary school
		WLY	Female	1956	Housewife	Middle school
		WXS	Male	1973	Self-employed	Primary school
		WWH	Male	1985	Lawyer	College
		HSL	Female	1989	Housewife	Middle school
		WWL	Female	1990	Civil servant	College
		WWX	Female	1994	Student	College
		WZP	Male	1995	Student	Junior College
	Liangying Town	WYR	Female	1952	Civil servant	High school
		WZL	Male	1952	Civil servant	Technical Secondary School
		LGZ	Male	1955	Civil servant	High school
		CPH	Female	1981	Housewife	Primary school
		WXQ	Male	1982	Doctor	College
		HSQ	Female	1984	Housewife	Primary school

(continued)

(continued)

Dialect sites		Name of speakers	Gender	Year of birth	Occupation	Educational background
		CYZ	Female	1985	Reporter	Junior College
		LZQ	Female	1987	Teacher	College
	Simapu Town	LGZ	Male	1978	Doctor	College
	Xiancheng Town	LQC	Male	1979	Self-employed	Middle school
	Hongchang Town	LWN	Male	1991	Doctor	College
	Chendian Town	MYH	Female	1982	Teacher	College
	Longtian Town	ZZH	Male	1988	Civil servant	College
	Xiashan Street	CXY	Female	1994	Student	College
		LMN	Female	1994	Student	College
		CSJ	Female	2000	Student	High school
Chaoyang District, Shantou City	Gurao Town	ZHJ	Male	1968	Teacher	Technical Secondary School
		ZWJ	Male	1969	Civil servant	Technical Secondary School
		HSM	Male	1973	Self-employed	Middle school
		WSB	Male	1973	Teacher	College
		CPL	Male	1993	Student	College
		ZYL	Male	1977	Teacher	College
	Guiyu Town	WCR	Male	1962	Self-employed	Middle school
		CYZ	Male	1964	Self-employed	Primary school
		GHL	Male	1981	Self-employed	College
		GCR	Male	1982	Self-employed	College
		CZHB	Male	1987	Civil servant	College
		CZB	Male	1988	Self-employed	College
		CYM	Female	1990	Housewife	Middle school
		GZY	Male	1990	Student	College

(continued)

(continued)

Dialect sites		Name of speakers	Gender	Year of birth	Occupation	Educational background
		GPW	Male	1994	Self-employed	Middle school
	Tongyu Town	XRQ	Male	1955	Self-employed	Middle school
		XZP	Male	1988	Technician	College
		XZH	Male	1991	Student	Junior College
	Miancheng Town	CB	Male	1940	Retire	High school
		LZJ	Male	1952	Teacher (Retire)	Middle school
		CPH	Male	1953	Worker	Primary school
		CXX	Female	1953	Clerk (Retire)	High school
		HYZ	Female	1958	Housewife	High school
		XBJ	Female	1959	Housewife	High school
		ZGQ	Male	1959	Self-employed	High school
		YYH	Female	1959	Housewife	High school
		YYP	Male	1974	Self-employed	Middle school
		WH	Male	1984	Teacher	College
		ZDP	Male	1984	Clerk	College
		ZJH	Male	1985	Teacher	College
		ZLF	Female	1985	Clerk	College
		YDW	Male	1986	Teacher	College
		XTF	Male	1986	Graduated student	College
		HDN	Female	1987	Teacher	College
		ZDL	Male	1987	Clerk	College
		HXT	Female	1987	Teacher	College
		CL	Female	1988	Teacher	College
		ZRZ	Male	1989	Clerk	College
		ZYQ	Female	1991	Student	College
		KZH	Male	1992	Student	College
		YWB	Male	1994	Student	Junior College
		LXH	Female	1994	Student	College
		HXY	Female	1994	Student	College
		XDW	Female	1994	Student	College

(continued)

(continued)

Dialect sites		Name of speakers	Gender	Year of birth	Occupation	Educational background
		ZZX	Male	1996	Self-employed	Middle school
	Haimen Town	PWX	Male	1977	Doctor	Junior College
		LXL	Female	1991	Student	College
		XBT	Female	1995	Nurse	Technical secondary school
		LZY	Female	1998	Student	High school
Haojiang District, Shantou City	Dahao Street	LXB	Male	1984	Self-employed	Middle school
		LZ	Male	1985	Designer	Junior College
		GJQ	Female	1987	Housewife	Junior College
		XYL	Female	1989	Student	College
		CJH	Female	1992	Student	College
		CDL	Female	1993	Student	College
		DLQ	Female	1993	Clerk	Technical secondary school
		HZR	Female	1994	Student	College
		CTX	Male	1998	Student	College
		ZSY	Female	1998	Student	College
		CCX	Female	1998	Student	College
		LWJ	Female	1999	Student	College
Puning County-level City, Jieyang City	Nanjing Town	LWK	Male	1986	Teacher	College
	Zhanlong Town	CWS	Male	1961	Civil servant	College

Appendix F
Informants From Other Types

Dialect sites		Name of speakers	Gender	Year of birth	Occupation	Educational background
Chaoyang District, Shantou City	Xilu Town	LXZ	Male	1971	Teacher	Junior College
		LLP	Male	1991	Student	College
		YWZ	Male	1991	Clerk	Middle school
		HZT	Male	1992	Clerk	Middle school
		CSK	Female	1998	Student	College
		ZZX	Female	1998	Student	College
		ZCX	Female	1999	Student	College
Nan'ao County, Shantou City	Houzhai Town	CQN	Male	1952	Teacher	College
		CPQ	Female	1967	Teacher	Junior College
		YSQ	Male	1967	Teacher	Junior College
		WWH	Male	1981	Teacher	College
		YSS	Female	1982	Teacher	College
	Yun'ao Town	DQD	Male	1930	Retire	College
		DZW	Male	1942	Teacher (Retired)	Technical secondary school
		ZZL	Male	1952	Self-employed	High school
		ZXR	Female	1963	Housewife	High school
		CDT	Male	1969	Teacher	College
		SAJ	Female	1970	Self-employed	Primary school

(continued)

(continued)

Dialect sites		Name of speakers	Gender	Year of birth	Occupation	Educational background
		ZJZ	Male	1974	Teacher	College
		CMY	Female	1974	Housewife	Middle school
		HCJ	Female	1980	Teacher	College
		ZJF	Female	1986	Graduated student	College
		ZJW	Female	1988	Office Clerk	Junior College
		LYS	Female	1990	Housewife	Technical secondary school
		CCS	Male	1994	Student	Junior College
		SZ	Male	2001	Student	Middle school
		ZJL	Female	2003	Student	Primary school
	Shen'ao Town	XCX	Male	1964	Teacher	Junior College
		CXP	Male	1966	Teacher	Junior College
		SWH	Female	1975	Teacher	Junior College
		LRJ	Female	1979	Teacher	College
	Qing'ao	CLX	Male	1940	Retire	Junior College
		WCM	Male	1966	Teacher	Junior College
		ZCH	Female	1969	Teacher	Junior College
		YYK	Male	1977	Teacher	Junior College
Jinjiang City, Quanzhou	Anhai Town	ZNY	Male	1983	Teacher	College

Appendix G
Tono-Types of Each Tonal Pattern

178 Appendix G: Tono-Types of Each Tonal Pattern

Type	Pattern		T1a	T1b	T2a	T2b	T3a	T3b
One: Shanjie type	A: falling-level-level-level-low-rising (Rongcheng etc.)		Middle level /44/	High level /55/	High falling /52/	High rising /25/	Pure low tone /323/	Low level /33/
	B: falling-falling-level-level-low-rising (Jinping etc.)		Middle level /44/	High level /55/	High falling /52/	High rising /25/	Pure low tone /323/	Low falling /42/
	C: falling-level-level-low-rising-rising (Fenghuang etc.))		High slight rising /45/	High level /55/	High falling /52/	High rising /25/	Pure low tone /323/	Low level /33/
Two: Huipu type	D: falling-falling-level-low-rising-rising (Liusha etc.)		High slight rising /45/	High level /55/	High falling /52/	High rising /25/	The lowest falling /32/	Low falling /42/
	E: falling-falling-level-low-rising	E1 (Huicheng-older)	Low slight rising /34/	Middle level /44/	High falling /52/	Pure low tone /23/	Low falling /42/	= T3a
		E2 (Kuitan)	Low slight rising /34/	Middle level /44/	High falling /52/	Pure low tone /323/	Low falling /42/	= T2b
	F: falling-level-level-low-rising (Huicheng-younger)		Low slight rising /34/	Middle level /44/	High level /55/	Pure low tone /23/	Low falling /42/	= T3a
	G: falling-falling-level-level-low-high (Jinghai-older)		Middle level /44/	High level /55/	Reg Upper /64/	Pure low tone /23/	Low falling /42/	High falling /52/
	H: falling-falling-level-level-level-low (Jinghai-younger)		Low level /33/	Middle level /44/	High level /55/	Pure low tone /23/	Low falling /42/	High falling /52/
Three: Chaoyang type	I: falling-falling-falling-level-low	Lugang, Guiyu-older	The lowest falling /32/	Low level /33/	Deferred high falling /552/	= T3a	Mid-short high falling /52/	Low falling /42/

(continued)

Appendix G: Tono-Types of Each Tonal Pattern

(continued)

Type	Pattern		T1a	T1b	T2a	T2b	T3a	T3b
		Hongchang	The lowest falling /32/	Low level /33/	Deferred high falling /552/	= T3a	Mid-short low falling /42/	Low falling /42/
		Shanpu (Zhanlong)	Low level /33/	Middle level /44/	Deferred high falling /552/	= T3a	Mid-short low falling /42/	Low falling /42/
	J: falling-falling-level-level-low (Lugang-younger)		The lowest falling /32/	Low level /33/	High level /55/	= T3a	= T2b	High falling /52/
	K: falling-falling-level-level-rising	Miancheng	Low falling /42/	Low level /33/	High slight rising /45/	= T3a	High falling /52/	Middle level /44/
		Haimen	Low falling /42/	Low level /33/	High slight rising /45/	= T1a	High falling /52/	Middle level /44/
Others	L: falling-falling-falling-level-level-rising	Xilu	Low level /33/	Middle level /44/	High falling /52/	High rising /35/	Mid-short low falling /42/	Low falling /42/
	M: falling-falling-falling-level-low-rising	Houzhai	High level /55/	High slight falling /54/	High falling /52/	High rising /35/	Pure low tone /323/	Low slight falling /43/
	N: falling-level-level-level-low-rising	Yun'ao	Middle level /44/	High rising /25/	High falling /52/	= T3b	Pure low tone /323/	Low level /33/
	Guiyu-younger[a]: falling-falling-level-low-rising		The lowest falling /32/	High rising /35/	High level /55/	= T3a	High falling /52/	Low falling /42/
	Dahao: falling-falling-level-low-rising		The lowest falling /32/	Low level /33/	High rising /35/	= T3a	High falling /52/	Low falling /42/

Note that the number between the two slashes (//) denotes the tono-type regardless of the detailed phonetic manifestations.

[a] The tonal patterns of Guiyu-younger and Dahao are the same as Pattern E, but the corresponding rules are not the same. As judged by the method of tonal merger, the dialects of Guiyu-younger and Dahao certainly belong to type three (Chaoyang type)

Bibliography

Ashby, M., and Maidment, J. 2005. *Introducing Phonetic Science.* Cambridge: Cambridge University Press.
Cheng, Chin-Chuan & Wang, William S-Y. 1971/1977. Tone change in Chao-zhou Chinese: a study in lexical diffusion. in *The lexicon in phonological change.* Ed by Wang William S-Y. Walter de Gruyter. 86–100.
Chinese Academy of Social Sciences (中国社会科学院), and Academy of the Humanities in Australia (澳大利亚人文科学院). 1987. 中国语言地图集 [Language Atlas of China]. Hong Kong: Xianggang Langwen (Yuandong) Youxian Gongsi.
Chu, Man-ni 朱曼妮. 2009. Motivating the Change of Stop Codas in Chaoshan: A Perceptual Study 从语言感知探究潮汕入声韵尾的变迁. Ph.D. Thesis, National Tsing Hua University, Taibei.
Committee for Nan'ao Chorography 南澳县地方志编纂委员会(2000)《南澳县志》,中华书局, 北京.
Crystal, D. 1987/1997. The Cambridge Encyclopedia of language (2nd Edition). Cambridge: Cambridge University Press.
Cun, Xi 寸熙. 2009. A Phonetic Study on Implosives in China. Ph.D. Thesis, The University of Hong Kong Science and Technology, Hong Kong.
Guy, Gregory R. 2003. Variationist approaches to phonological change. In *The handbook of historical linguistics.* eds. Brian D. Joseph & Richard D. Janda, 369–400. Malden, Mass. and Oxford: Blackwell.
Kingston, John. 2011. Tonogenesis. In *The Blackwell Companion to Phonology*, 2304–2333.
Kuang, Jianjing. 2011/2013. *Phonation in Tonal Contrasts (A dissertation for the degree Doctor of Philosophy).* University of California Los Angeles.
Lin, Lunlun. 林伦伦. 1995. Chaoshan fangyan shengdiao yanjiu 潮汕方言声调研究. *Yuwen Yanjiu* 语文研究 1: 52–59.
Lin, Lunlun. 林伦伦. 1996.*Chenghai fangyan yanjiu* 澄海方言研究. Shantou: Shantoudaxue chubanshe 汕头大学出版社.
Norman, Jerry. 1973. Tonal Development in Min. *Journal of Chinese Linguistics* 1(2): 222–238.
Ohala, J.J. 1986. Against the direct realist view of speech perception.pdf. *Journal of Phonetics* 14: 75–82.
Ohala, J.J. 1992. What's cognitive, what's not in sound change.pdf. In *Diachrony within synchrony: Language history and cognition*, eds G. Kellermann, and Morrissey, 309–355.
Ohala, J.J. 1997. The relationship between Phonetics and Phonology. In *The Handbook of phonetic science*, 2010th ed., ed. William J. By, 653–677. Hardcastle and John: Laver. Blackwell Publishing.
Peng, G. 2006. Temporal and tonal aspects of Chinese syllables: A corpus-based comparative study of Mandarin and Cantonese. *Journal of Chinese Linguistics* 34(1): 134–154.

Shue, Y.-L., P. Keating, C. Vicenik, and K. Yu. 2010. VoiceSauce: A program for voice analysis. *Energy* 1(H2): H1-A1.

Wang, Futang 王福堂. 1999. Hanyu Fangyan Yuyin de Yanbian he Cengci 汉语方言语音的演变和层次. Yuwen Chubanshe语文出版社.

Yip, Moira. 2002. *Tone*. Cambridge: Cambridge University Press.

Yip, Moira. 1986. Tonal flip-flop in Chinese dialects. 汉语方言里的声调阴阳对转. *Journal of Chinesse Linguistics* 14.2: 161–183.

Yip, Moira. 2001. The Historic Role of the Late Professor YR Chao's 1929 Field Materials. *Language and Linguistics* 2: 197.

Zhu, Xiaonong and Cun, Xi. 朱晓农、寸熙. 2006. 清浊音变圈: 兼论吴、闽语内爆音非出于侗台底层,《民族語文》3: 3–13.

CPSIA information can be obtained
at www.ICGtesting.com
Printed in the USA
LVHW061655100121
676166LV00001B/2